Charles Fort's
NEW LANDS

This edition published by John Brown Publishing Ltd,
The Boathouse, Crabtree Lane, Fulham, London, SW6 6LU

Distributed in Canada and the United States of America by
the INFO Research Library,
Box 220, Wolfe Island, Ontario, K0H 2Y0, Canada

British Library Cataloguing in Publication Data available.
ISBN 1-870870-62-X

Printed in Great Britain by
Redwood Books, Trowbridge, Wilts.

NEW LANDS

Charles Hoy Fort

Revised by X

Introduction by Jerome Clark

John Brown Publishing
London 1996

A NOTE ON THIS EDITION

This is the first wholly new edition of *New Lands* for 73 years. It is also, as far as known, the first paperback edition since those by Ace Books (N.Y., 1972) and Sphere (London, 1974). Where those reprinted the text from the collected edition of Fort's works (Henry Holt & Co, N.Y., 1941; reprinted Dover Publications, Inc., 1974), which was edited by Tiffany Thayer for his Fortean Society and contains many of his own interventions, the text of this *Fortean Times* edition, if so it may be called, is based on the first edition, published in hardback by Boni and Liveright of New York in 1923.

Special thanks must go to the Canadian scholar of Fort's works, Mr X, whose contribution to this edition makes it a landmark in Fortean publishing. He has devoted years to the rediscovery of Fort's source material and has applied his considerable experience to the preparation of this text, restoring lines that were missing or corrupt, correcting typographical and other errors and standardising the chaotic citation of references. I have added an index.

While there has been some correction of factual errors and expansions of Fort's occasionally vague references, these have largely been left to Mr X's work in progress – a definitive and annotated edition for scholars and purists. In this project, Mr X (his legal name) deserves the admiration and thanks of all Forteans.

The cover is a detail from a collage by Max Ernst.

Fort's first book, *The Book of the Damned*, has already been published in this series (1995). The remaining two books, *Lo!* and *Wild Talents*, will be published as uniform editions in due course.

SM

INTRODUCTION

"Beware when the great God lets loose a thinker on this planet," Ralph Waldo Emerson warned. "Then all things are at risk. It is as when a conflagration has broken out in a great city, and no man knows what is safe, or where it will end."

It was, appropriately, from Emerson that Charles Fort took the title of *New Lands*, first published in 1923. In his celebrated essay *Nature* (1838) Emerson wrote in a voice that could have been Fort's own:

> *Our age is retrospective. It builds the sepulchres of the fathers. It writes biographies, histories, and criticism. The foregoing generations beheld God and nature face to face; we, through their eyes. Why should not we have a poetry and philosophy of insight and not of tradition, and a religion by revelation to us, and not the history of theirs? Embosomed for a season in nature, whose floods of life stream around and through us, and invite us by the power they supply, to action proportioned to nature, why should we grope among the dry bones of the past, or put the living generation into masquerade out of its faded wardrobe? The sun shines today also. There is more wool and flax in the fields. There are new lands, new men, new thoughts. Let us demand our own works and laws and worship.*

Except that Fort would not, could not, put it that way. Even the radical smashers of the old order could themselves be suspect in a world whose intrinsic assumptions were so fundamentally flawed. What if "all discussion and supposed progress are the conflicts of phantoms and the overthrow of old delusions by new delusions"?

> *Nevertheless I am searching for some wider expression that will rationalize all of us — conceiving that what we call irrationality is our view of parts and functions out of relation to an underlying whole; an underlying something that is working out its development in terms of planets and acids and bugs, rivers and labor unions and cyclones, politicians and islands and astronomers. Perhaps we conceive of an underlying nexus in which all things, in our experience, are different manifestations — torn by its hurricanes and quaked by the struggles of Labor against Capital — and then, for the sake of balance, requiring relaxations.*

In *New Lands*, as in his other books (*Book of the Damned* [1919], *Lo!*[1931], and *Wild Talents* [1932]), Fort is less successful at locating that "underlying whole" than in chronicling the "conflicts of phantoms" and exposing the "overthrow of old delusions by new delusions." In early autumn 1881, Fort records, residents of Delaware, Maryland and Virginia reported the passage of phantom armies through the sky. The "witnesses", sniffed *Scientific American*, "exhibited a medieval condition of intelligence scarcely less than marvellous." An old delusion, surely. Something had been seen, the august journal allowed, but it could only have been "auroral", thereby spinning, out of an impossibly fragile thread only pretending to bind occurrence to explanation, a new delusion. Meanwhile the armies of the damned — "By the damned," Fort wrote in the second sentence of his first book, "I mean the excluded" — march on.

By the damned Fort also meant unorthodox physical, not psychical, phenomena, even if only his habitual jokiness could transform a ghostly legion skipping the atmosphere's light fantastic into "space-armies" battling over aerial real estate. But what grabbed Fort's interest immediately were anomalies of a material sort: phenomena associated, if only by cheerfully outrageous assertion, with visitation from other worlds, either neighbouring planets or the sky islands (the literal "new lands") for whose existence Fort argued, presumably in the interest of advancing new delusions: phenomena such as unusual objects in air, space and sea, falls of substances organic and inorganic, disappearances, archæological enigmas and other threats to consensus and comfort.

Old delusion: The apparition of a city manifests in the late-afternoon sky over Ashland, Ohio, on 12 March 1890 and is identified by some as a "vision of the new Jerusalem". New delusion: The phantom city is identified, via dubious application of physics, as a mirage of Sandusky, some 60 miles away. "May have been a revelation of heaven," Fort remarks, "and for all I know heaven may resemble Sandusky, and those of us who have no desire to go to Sandusky may ponder that point."

* * *

In May 1926, Fort remarked to a young correspondent, science-fiction writer Edmond Hamilton, that "psychic phenomena and occult powers, and alleged communications with the dead, are in very different categories" and so outside his range of interests. Yet in *New Lands* he promised "a future expression" in which he would show that "some kinds of beings from outer space can adapt to our conditions ... and have been seen, but have been supposed to be psychic phenomena." Presumably this was the proposed work to which he alluded in *Book of the Damned*, the one in which "I expect ... to rationalize demonology." Regrettably, perhaps, the book was never written. A later generation of Forteans and ufologists would propose their own rationalizations of demonology. Fort, one presumes, would have done it better.

Nonetheless the adjective "Fortean" would soon be attached to phenomena outside the purview of psychical researchers, occultists, and church-sponsored or inspired miracle collectors. It would also define a certain attitude, a certain set of mind, which would see in the small-minded human need to explain everything in sight a hugely comic foolishness. Such need has, if anything, expanded since Fort's time. A recent instance: in October 1987 a well-regarded resident and experienced outdoorsman of Salisbury, New Hampshire, reported encountering a large, bipedal apelike creature in a field in broad daylight. According to the witness, its "hands were like yours or mine, only three times bigger, with pads on the front paws, like a dog ... Long legs, long arms. It was just like ... a gorilla, but this here wasn't a gorilla." It certainly wasn't, a local game warden agreed; the man had seen, the warden maintained with a straight face (and faces are always straight in these circumstances), a moose.

Such an hypothesis (if that is the word for it) gives, as George Orwell once wrote in a different but relevant context, "an appearance of solidity to pure wind." Worse, the game warden's is supposed to be the rational explanation. Here "rational" is not a synonym for "reasonable" or "logical" but a rhetorical device in the service of an ideological claim, bowing (and scraping) to what behavioural scientist/folklorist David J. Hufford calls "traditions of disbelief". He observes (in *New York Folklore*, Summer 1983) that "scientism, as the ideology of science has been called, has so thoroughly captured the central epistemological terrain that a word such as 'rational' has come to mean a proposition with which one would expect a hypothetical modern scientist to agree, rather than a process by which one may reach conclusions about everything from what to have for breakfast to how to build a hammered dulcimer."

Confronted with questions raised by reports of Sasquatch-like entities, or by sightings of structured flying discs with extraordinary performance characteristics, or other unwelcome presences, practically no one is willing to concede, "I have no idea what these sort of accounts or experiences mean." Human nature abhors an explanatory vacuum, and into the void fall mooses, swamp gas, and other things that didn't happen to be there at the time. So, however, do other sorts of goofy, empty ideas: such as hairy bipeds and UFOs as "transmogrifications" of etheric energy (whatever the hell that is supposed to mean). It should be noted, since it seldom is, that Fort's deliriously loopy "explanations" for anomalous manifestations poke fun at both the squinty-eyed orthophile and the pop-eyed heretic. Of course each age defines what is orthodox and what is heretical, and a new delusion may be no more than an old delusion in fresh and fashionable garb.

* * *

The bare biographical facts are these (for a fuller account, I heartily recommend Bob Rickard's splendid treatment in the introduction to the John Brown edition of *Book of the Damned*):

Charles Hoy Fort was born in Albany, New York, on 9 August 1874. Bright, consumed with curiosity, young Fort pursued interests in books and natural sciences until at 17, escaping the clutches of his father, the tyrannical Charles Nelson Fort, he went to work for newspapers in Albany, Long Island and Brooklyn. Determined to become a writer, he travelled some 30,000 miles around world. In South Africa he contracted a fever and carried it home to New York City. During his convalescence he renewed a friendship from Albany days with an English immigrant, Anna Filing, who nursed him back to health and whom he married on 26 October 1896.

That very fall, on the other side of the continent, the first great UFO wave in American history was about to jar the sensibilities of the complacent. In short order the skies of California were to be filled with majestic "airships" afloat over cities, towns, and farms, giving rise to the speculations about secret inventors — nonexistent, it would turn out — or even extraterrestrial visitors. A month and a day after the Forts' wedding, the first published UFO-abduction claim in history appeared in the *Stockton Evening Mail*. One Col. H.G. Shaw ("formerly of the *Mail* editorial staff") and a companion encountered, near Lodi, California, three nude, "warbling", human-looking entities who tried to drag them into a nearby airship but failed in the effort owing to the fact that these beings, though "possessed of a strange beauty", weighed less than an ounce and were in no position to push anybody around. Shaw, clearly of Fortean temperament, denounced other airship reports as "clumsy fakes" — competing delusions, one might say — which "should not be given credence by anyone".

Had he ever heard it, Fort would have enjoyed the good colonel's preposterous yarn, but the California chapter of the turn-of-the-century airship scare appears forever to have escaped his attention, though he was aware of its sequel, played out to the east in the spring of 1897. *New Lands* recounts, in Part 2, Chapter 16, sightings from Kansas City, Chicago, Texas and West Virginia. It also mentions the hoaxes and the scientists' conventionalizations. Fort is resigned and philosophical: "Against such an alliance as this, between the jokers and the astronomers, I see small chance for our data. The chance is in the future. If, in April, 1897, extra-mundane voyagers did visit this earth, likely enough they will visit again, and then the alliance against the data may be guarded against."

In the years ahead, Charles and Anna lived modestly at best as Fort tried to make a living as a writer. In 1905 he met the celebrated and already fiercely controversial novelist Theodore Dreiser, who published some of his short stories in a magazine Dreiser was then editing. A commercially unsuccessful novel, *The Outcast Manufacturers* (1909), followed, as did dreary periods of financial and emotional turmoil, including periodic evictions. Meanwhile Fort was spending hours every day in libraries, where he pursued a variety of obsessions having to do with oddities of nature and behaviour. He learned that such things were not isolated marvels, but "quite ordinary occurrences". These resulted in two unpublished books, neither extant, called *X* and *Y*. "Crank books", Fort's biographer Damon Knight would conclude from the limited available evidence.

After coming into small inheritances in 1916 and 1917, Fort was free to continue his "search for the unexplained" through "all scientific periodicals, at least by way of indexes, published in English and French, from the year 1800, available in the libraries of New York and London". In 1919, through Dreiser's efforts, *Book of the Damned* saw print. In his review of the book in the *Chicago Daily News*, Ben Hecht, the Hollywood screenwriter, coined the word "Fortean" to characterize the particular outlook, at once open and skeptical, that Fort brought to a certain class of rejected phenomena and experiences. His iconoclasm and good humour endeared him to some of the era's leading artists, journalists, critics, and intellectuals. By the time *New Lands* appeared four years later (with an introduction by Booth Tarkington), the Forts were living in London.

His health failing, Fort returned with Anna to New York in 1929. There were two more books, *Lo!* and *Wild Talents*, before his death on 3 May 1932. The year before, Tiffany Thayer formed the Fortean Society, which Fort, who wanted no one to follow him, refused to join. Fort did not want to be a Fortean "any more than I'd be an Elk".

* * *

New Lands is the second of three books (*Lo!* being the third) that, for all the satirical content, address a possibility Fort did take seriously: what would be called decades later in the UFO era, the extraterrestrial hypothesis. As always, Fort was as interested in the human response as he was in the actual stimulus for the cognitive dissonance. Between 1924 and 1926, in four letters published in the *New York Times*, he argued that sightings over time of odd lights and moving structures in the sky might indicate that the earth was under surveillance from elsewhere. In one particularly prescient observation, he wrote (in the last of the letters, published on 5 September 1926): "If it is not the conventional or reasonable thing upon this earth to believe in visitors from other worlds, most of us could watch them a week and declare that they were something else, and likely enough make things disagreeable for anybody who thought otherwise."

Fort, of course, would not be among them. "I think that we shall be noted in recognitions of good works for our bizarre charities", he says in *New Lands*. The uncharitable astronomer J. Allen Hynek, in 1949 the U.S. Air Force's house scientist-debunker (a role he would emphatically disavow years later), grumbled that Fort's works were "entirely reprehensible in viewpoint". In a 1981 book one prominent UFOphobe snarled: "The accusation (and such it is) that our present understanding of the universe cannot account for certain data must be established without a shadow of a doubt." In other words, the extraordinary claim Fort is making, and for which he must produce positive proof, is that science is not omniscient. Lord help us! This individual is a member of a remarkable organization, the Committee for the Scientific Investigation of Claims of the Paranormal (CSICOP), which professes to believe that sympathetic views of anomalous claims of practically any sort amount to evidence not only of unreason among the intellectually unwashed but of dangerous unreason which threatens to herd the human race back into the caves. Fort would have loved these guys.

There are, of course, more measured — dare we say rational? — ways of judging the worth of anomalous claims. In the case of *New Lands*, the evidence for extraterrestrial visitation Fort marshals is, it must be admitted, only occasionally compelling. The modern reader is well advised to supplement Fort's treatment of cosmic curiosities with William R. Corliss' survey of the same and others in his compilation *Mysterious Universe: A Hand book of Astronomical Anomalies* (1979), which places records of the passage of objects through deep space in the context of the greater astronomical knowledge of the late 20th century.

Nonetheless, Fort's suggestions that artificial structures may be out there in interplanetary space is surely not to be discounted entirely. In December 1991 astronomers at Kitt Peak Observatory observed a 10-metre object on a heliocentric orbit. In a technical paper published in the ultra-respectable journal *The Observatory* (Vol. 115, April 1995), astronomer Duncan Steel of the University of Adelaide argues that the object's "very Earth-like orbit and observations of rapid brightness fluctuations argue for it being an artificial body rather than an asteroid" — quite possibly "an alien probe observed in the vicinity of our planet". Though much more is known about "transient lunar phenomena" (their current appellation) than was known when Fort considered them in *New Lands*, "many puzzling aspects still remain", Winifred S. Cameron acknowledges at the conclusion of a long survey in the astrophysical journal *Icarus* (Vol. 16, 1972) five decades later.

The best evidence, albeit still disputed, for extraterrestrial visitation consists of reports of UFOs: craftlike objects in the atmosphere or on the ground. Where the latter are concerned, *New Lands* contains only one report that by any stretch could be rated a close encounter of the third kind (CE3); in Part 1, Chapter 10, citing as his source a Spiritualist pamphlet, Fort writes of a Warwickshire sighting, said to have been independently witnessed, of three "perfectly white" human forms sailing through the sky under a strange cloud. They were said to be emitting a moaning sound. The witnesses thought they were "angels". Hmmm. (The only other proto-CE3 to figure in Fort's work is in *Lo!* [Chapter 11], a story Fort dismisses — correctly I think — as a hoax.)

More to the point are some strikingly modern-sounding UFO sightings, including one of a Saturn-shaped device (Norwood, New York, 3 July 1884; see Part 2, Chapter 9) perhaps much like the one memorably photographed over Trindade Island, Brazil, on 6 January 1958. Another is of an oscillating "disc falling [as if] through water", moving from side to side (France, 29 August 1871; Part 2, Chapter 15); mid-century witnesses would characterize this as a "falling leaf" manoeuvre. There is also the "airship" that, in the fashion of many thousands of UFOs to come, sails casually about, then dashes off "at lightning speed" (Ipswich, 25 February 1913; Part 2, Chapter 23).

In taking note of such sightings, Fort discovered the "UFO phenomenon", the name Hynek would give it many years later. There were sightings before Fort was born, of course (the UFO phenomenon begins, as far as we can tell, in the early years of the nineteenth century), but to witnesses and chroniclers alike these were isolated occurrences, unrelated to anything but comparable sightings occurring at about the same time and in the same approximate space, as during the turn-of-the-century airship waves. Even here historical memory was nonexistent. When airships returned to the United Kingdom, the United States and New Zealand/ Australia in 1909, not a single findable contemporary reference mentions the events of 1896/97. Only Fort connected the dots. No other pre-UFO-era books but Fort's discuss the world's first UFO waves. None but Fort grasped that something interesting, possibly very interesting, had taken place on an international scale and could well take place again. When "flying saucers" were splashed in large type over newspapers everywhere in the summer of 1947, only readers of Fort knew they were nothing new. They also knew, though every consulted authority figure pronounced otherwise, that they were not going to go away.

* * *

The new delusions hover all around us, so this sorry, fading century attests. At the moment we confront the unseemly spectacle of reactionaries posing as revolutionaries, even as in the previous moment we saw revolutionaries, like the emperors they overthrew in the moment before that, build their empires on mountains of human bones, from whose peaks the millennium could be glimpsed even if only from an ever-receding distance. Pious souls preen in the guise of militant skeptics; only the truest believer could fail to detect the oxymoron in "militant skeptics". Real skepticism of our claims to final knowledge — the kind of skepticism that Fort, who doubted himself most of all, practiced — is hard. It subverts any faith to which anything like militance could ever attach itself. It tracks the aspirant as relentlessly as a hell hound on a blues singer's tail. If it offers us "revolution", it is the revolution of the constantly revolving wheel, moving us always to someplace else down some dark road in deepest night.

New Lands is a night kind of book. A good chunk of the narrative takes place in the nocturnal hours, where eerie dramas are witnessed under cover of darkness. Astronomers watch the passage of mysterious objects in space and record odd luminosities in lunar craters. They fall all over themselves chasing after explanations which for all their adequacy, Fort wisecracks, might as well be a "cloud of rubbish by day and a pillar of bosh by night". Unidentified flying objects pass through the evening sky, flashing search-lights, while "science and idealism", muttering of Venus and fire balloons, take wing like "a vampire that lulls consciousness that might otherwise foresee catastrophe ... [E]xtramundane vandals may often have swooped down upon this earth, and they may swoop again; and it may be a comfort to us, some day, to mention in our last gasp that we told about this".

Fort told us about this and much, much more, and offered up new lands, new thoughts, a way of glimpsing the world and ourselves by the reflection of flashing lights on the moon, or through thick rains of falling frogs, or in visions of vast armies of the damned forever on the march.

Let us now join the procession.

Jerome Clark
Minnesota,
August 1995

PART ONE

PART ONE

CHAPTER 1

Lands in the sky —
That they are nearby —
That they do not move.

I take for a principle that all being is the infinitely serial, and that whatever has been will, with differences of particulars, be again —

The last quarter of the fifteenth century — land to the west!

This first quarter of the twentieth century — we shall have revelations.

There will be data. There will be many. Behind this book, unpublished collectively, or held as constituting its reserve forces, there are other hundreds of data, but independently I take for a principle that all existence is a flux and a re-flux, by which periods of expansion follow periods of contraction; that few men can even think widely when times are narrow times, but that human constrictions cannot repress extensions of thoughts and lives and enterprise and dominion when times are wider times — so then that the pageantry of foreign coasts that was revealed behind blank horizons after the year 1492, can not be, in the course of development, the only astounding denial of seeming vacancy — that the spirit, or the animation, and the stimulations and the needs of the fifteenth century are all appearing again, and that requital may appear again —

Aftermath of war, as in the year 1492: demands for readjustments; crowded and restless populations, revolts against limitations, intolerable restrictions against emigrations. The young man is no longer urged, or is no longer much inclined, to go westward. He will, or must, go somewhere. If directions alone no longer invite him, he may hear invitation in dimensions. There are many persons, who have not investigated for themselves, who think that both poles of this earth have been discovered. There are too many women travelling luxuriously in "Darkest Africa." Eskimos of Disco, Greenland, are publishing a newspaper. There must be outlet, or there will be explosion —

Outlet and invitation and opportunity —

San Salvadors of the Sky — a Plymouth Rock that hangs in the heavens of Serbia — a foreign coast from which storms have brought materials to the city of Birmingham, England.

Or the mentally freezing, or dying, will tighten their prohibitions, and the chill of their censorships will contract, to extinction, our lives, which, without sin, represent matter deprived of motion. Their ideal is Death, or approximate death, warmed over occasionally only enough to fringe with uniform, decorous icicles — from which there will be no escape, if, for the living and sinful and adventurous there be not San Salvadors somewhere else, a Plymouth Rock of reversed significance, coasts of sky-continents.

But every consciousness that we have of needs, and all hosts, departments, and sub-divisions of data that indicate the possible requital of needs are opposed — not by the orthodoxy of the common Puritans, but by the Puritans of Science, and their austere, disheartening, dried or frozen orthodoxy.

Islands of space — see *Scientific American*, vol. this and p. that — accounts from the *Annual Report of the British Association for the Advancement of Science* — *Nature*, etc. — except for an occasional lapse, our sources of data will not be sneered at. As to our interpretations, I consider them, myself, more as suggestions and gropings and stimuli. Islands of space and the rivers and oceans of an extra-geography —

Stay and let salvation damn you — or straddle an auroral beam and paddle it from Rigel to Betelgeuse. If there be no accepting that there are such rivers and oceans beyond this earth, stay and travel upon steamships with schedules that can be depended upon, food so well cooked and well served, comfort looked after so carefully — or some day board the thing that was seen over the city of Marseilles, Aug. 19, 1887, and ride on that, bearing down upon the moon, giving up for lost, escaping collision by the swirl of a current that was never heard of before.

There are, or there are not, nearby cities of foreign existences. They have, or they have not, been seen, by reflection, in the skies of Sweden and Alaska. As one will. Whether acceptable, or too preposterous to be thought of, our data are of rabbles of living things that have been seen in the sky; also of processions of military beings — monsters that live in the sky and die in the sky, and spatter this earth with their red life-fluids — ships from other worlds that have been seen by millions of inhabitants of this earth, exploring, night after night, in the sky of France, England, New England, and Canada — signals from the moon, which, according to notable indications, may not be so far from this earth as New York is from London — definitely reported and, in some instances, multitudinously witnessed, events that have been disregarded by our opposition —

A scientific priestcraft —

"Thou shalt not!" is crystallised in its frozen textbooks.

I have data upon data upon data of new lands that are not far away. I hold out expectations and the materials of new hopes and new despairs and new triumphs and new tragedies. I hold out my hands and point to the sky — there is a hierarchy that utters me manacles, I think — there is a dominant force that pronounces prisons that have dogmas for walls for such thoughts. It binds its formulas around all attempting extensions.

But sounds have been heard in the sky. They have been heard, and it is not possible to destroy the records of them. They have been heard. In their repetitions and regularities of series and intervals, we shall recognise perhaps interpretable language. Columns of clouds, different-coloured by sunset, have vibrated to the artillery of other worlds like the strings of a cosmic harp, and I conceive of no buzzing of insects that can forever divert attention from such dramatic reverberations. Language has shone upon the dark parts of the moon: luminous exclamations that have fluttered in the lunar crater Copernicus; the eloquence of the starlike light in Aristarchus; hymns that have been chanted in lights and shades upon Linné; the wilder, luminous music in Plato —

But not a sound that has been heard in the sky, not a thing that has fallen from the sky, not a thing that "should not be," but that has nevertheless been seen in the sky can we, with any sense of freedom, investigate, until first we find out about the incubus that in the past has suffocated even speculation. I shall find out for myself: anybody who cares to may find out with me. A ship from a foreign world does, or does not, sail in the sky of this earth. It is in accordance with observations by hundreds of thousands of witnesses that this event has taken place, and, if the time be when aeronautics upon this earth is of small development, that is an important circumstance to consider — but there is suffocation upon the whole occurrence and every one of its circumstances. Nobody can give good attention to the data, if diverting his mind is consciousness, altogether respectful, of the scientists who say that there are no other physical worlds except planets, millions of miles away, distances that conceivable vessels could not traverse. I should like to let loose, in an opening bombardment, the data of the little black stones of Birmingham, which, time after time, in a period of eleven years, fell obviously from a fixed point in the sky, but such a release now, would be wasted. It will have to be prepared for. Now each one would say to himself that there are no such fixed points in the sky. Why not? Because astronomers say that there are not.

But there is something else that is implied. Implied is the general supposition that the science of astronomy represents all that is most accurate, most exacting, painstaking, semi-religious in human thought, and is therefore authoritative.

Anybody who has not been through what I've been through, in investigating this subject, would ask what are the bases and what is the consistency of the science of astronomy. The miserable, though at times amusing, confusions of thought that I find in this field of supposed research word my inquiry differently — what of dignity, or even of decency, is in it?

Phantom dogmas, with their tails clutching at vacancies, are coiled around our data.

Serpents of pseudo-thought are stifling history.

They are squeezing "Thou shalt not!" upon Development.

New Lands — and the horrors and lights, explosions and music of them; rabbles of hellhounds and the march of military angels. But they are Promised Lands, and first must we traverse a desert. There is ahead of us a waste of parallaxes and spectrograms and triangulations. It may be weary going through a waste of astronomic determinations, but that depends —

If out of a dreary, academic zenith shower betrayals of frailty, folly, and falsification, they will be manna to our malices —

Or sterile demonstrations be warmed by our cheerful cynicisms into delicious little lies — blossoms and fruits of unexpected oases —

Rocks to strike with our suspicions — and the gush of exposures foaming with new implications.

Tyrants, dragons, giants — and, if all be dispatched with the skill and the might and the triumph over awful odds of the hero who himself tells his story —

I hear three yells from some hitherto undiscovered, grotesque critter at the very entrance of the desert.

CHAPTER 2

"Prediction Confirmed!"

"Another Verification!"

"A Third Verification of Prediction!"

Three times, in spite of its long-established sobriety, the *Journal of the Franklin Institute* (106: 286, 353; 107, 210) reels with an astronomer's exhilarations. He might exult and indulge himself, and that would be no affair of ours, and, in fact, we'd like to see everybody happy, perhaps, but it is out of these three chanticleerities by Prof. Pliny Chase that we materialise our opinion that, so far as methods and strategies are concerned, no particular differences can be noted between astrologers and astronomers, and that both represent engulfment in Dark Ages. Lord Bacon pointed out that astrologers had squirmed into prestige and emolument by shooting at marks, disregarding their misses, and recording their hits with unseemly advertisement. When, in August 1878, Prof. Swift and Prof. Watson said that, during an eclipse of the sun, they had seen two luminous bodies that might be planets between Mercury and the Sun, Prof. Chase announced that, five years before, he had made a prediction, and that it had been confirmed by the positions of these bodies (*Proceedings of the American Philosophical Society,* 13: 237-252, 470-7). Three times, in capital letters, he screamed, or announced, according to one's sensitiveness, or prejudices, that the "new planets" were in the exact positions of his calculations. Prof. Chase wrote that, before his time, there had been two great instances of astronomic calculation confirmed: the discovery of Neptune and the discovery of "the asteroidal belt," a claim that is disingenuously worded (*Journal of the Franklin Institute,* 106, 314). If by mathematical principles, or by any other definite principles, there has ever been one great, or little, instance of astronomic discovery by means of calculations, confusion must destroy us, in the introductory position that we take, or expose our irresponsibility, and vitiate all that follows: that our data are oppressed by a tyranny of false announcements; that there never has been an astronomic discovery other than the observational or the accidental.

In *The Story of the Heavens* (rev. ed., p. 230), Sir Robert Ball's opinion of the discovery of Neptune is that it is a triumph unparalleled in the annals of science. He lavishes — the great astronomer Leverrier, buried for months in profound meditations — the dramatic moment — Leverrier rises from his calculations and points to the sky — "Lo!" there a new planet is found (p. 330).

My desire is not so much to agonize over the single fraudulencies or delusions, as to typify the means by which the science of Astronomy has established and maintained itself:

According to Leverrier, there was a planet external to Uranus; according to Hansen, there were two; according to Airy, "doubtful if there were one."

One planet was found — so calculated Leverrier, in his profound meditations. Suppose two had been found — confirmation of the brilliant computations by Hansen. None — the opinion of the great astronomer, Sir George Airy.

Leverrier calculated that the hypothetical planet was at a distance from the sun, within the limits of 35 and 37.9 times this earth's distance from the sun. The new planet was found in a position said to be 30 times this earth's distance from the sun. The discrepancy was so great that, in the United States, astronomers refused to accept that Neptune had been discovered by means of calculation: see such publications as the *American Journal of Science*, of the period. Upon August 29, 1849, Dr. Babinet read to the French Academy, a paper in which he showed that, by observations of three years, the revolution of Neptune would have to be placed at 165 years (*Amer. Jour. Sci.*, s. 2, 6, 438). Between the limits of 207 and 233 years was the period that Leverrier had calculated. Simultaneously, in England, Adams had calculated. Upon Sept. 2, 1846, after he had, for at least a month, been charting the stars in the region toward which Adams had pointed, Prof. Challis wrote to Sir George Airy that this work would occupy his time for three more months. This indicates the extent of the region toward which Adams had pointed.

The discovery of the asteroids, or in Prof. Chase's not very careful language, the discovery of the "asteroidal belt as deduced from Bode's Law":

We learn that Baron Von Zach had formed a society of twenty-four astronomers to search, in accordance with Bode's Law, for "a planet" — and not "a group," not "an asteroidal belt" — between

Jupiter and Mars. The astronomers had organised, dividing the zodiac into twenty-four zones, assigning each zone to an astronomer. They searched. They found not one asteroid. Seven or eight hundred are now known.

Philosophical Magazine (12, 69):

That Piazzi, the discoverer of the first asteroid, had not been searching for a hypothetic body, as deduced from Bode's Law, but, upon an investigation of his own, had been charting stars in the constellation Taurus, night of Jan. 1, 1801. He noticed a light that he thought had moved, and, with his mind a blank, so far as asteroids and brilliant deductions were concerned, announced that he had discovered a comet.

As an instance of the crafty way in which some astronomers now tell the story, see Sir Robert Ball's *The Story of the Heavens* (rev. ed., p. 230):

The organisation of astronomers of Lilienthal, but never a hint that Piazzi was not one of them — "the search for a small planet was soon rewarded by a success that has rendered the evening of the first day of the nineteenth century memorable in astronomy." Ball tells of Piazzi's charting of the stars, and makes it appear that Piazzi had charted stars as a means of finding asteroids deductively, rewarded soon by success, whereas Piazzi had never heard of such a search, and did not know an asteroid when he saw one. "This laborious and accomplished astronomer had organised an ingenious system of exploring the heavens, which was eminently calculated to discriminate a planet among the starry host ... at length he was rewarded by a success which amply compensated him for all his toil."

Prof. Chase — these two great instances not of mere discovery, but of discovery by means of calculation according to him — now the subject of his supposition that he, too, could calculate triumphantly — the verification depended upon the accuracy of Prof. Swift and Prof. Watson in recording the positions of the bodies that they had announced —

Sidereal Messenger (6, 84):

Prof. Colbert, Superintendent of the Dearborn Observatory, leader of the party of which Prof. Swift was a member, says that the observations by Swift and Watson agreed, because Swift had made his observations agree with Watson's. The accusation is not that Swift had falsely announced a discovery of two unknown bodies, but that his precise determining of positions had occurred after Watson's determinations had been published.

Popular Astronomy (7, 13):

Prof. A⁻aph Hall writes that, several days after the eclipse, Prof. Watson told him that he had seen "a" luminous body near the sun and that his declaration that he had seen two unknown bodies was not made until after Swift had been heard from.

Perched upon two delusions, Prof. Chase crowed his false raptures. The unknown bodies, whether they had ever been in the orbit of his calculations or not, were never seen again.

So it is our expression that hosts of astronomers calculate, and calculation-mad, calculate and calculate and calculate, and that, when one of them does point within 600,000,000 miles (by conventional measurements) of something that is found, he is the Leverrier of the text-books; that the others are the Prof. Chases not of the text-books.

As to most of us, the symbols of the infinitesimal calculus humble independent thinking into the conviction that used to be enforced by drops of blood from a statue. In the farrago and conflicts of daily lives, it is relief to feel such a *rapport* with finality, in a religious sense, or in a mathematical sense. So then, if the seeming of exactness in Astronomy be either infamously, or carelessly and laughingly, brought about by the connivances of which Swift and Watson were accused, and if the prestige of Astronomy be founded upon nothing but huge capital letters and exclamation points, or upon the disproportionality of balancing one Leverrier against hundreds of Chases, it may not be better that we should know this, if then to those of us who, in the religious sense, have nothing to depend upon, comes deprivation of even this last, lingering seeming of foundation, or seeming existence of exactness and realness, somewhere —

Except — that, if there be nearby lands in the sky and beings from foreign worlds that visit this earth, that is a great subject, and the trash that is clogging an epoch must be cleared away.

We have had a little sermon upon the insecurity of human triumphs, and, having brought it to a climax, now seems to be the time to stop; but there is still an involved "triumph" and I'd not like to have inefficiency, as well as probably everything else, charged against us —

The Discovery of Uranus.

We mention this stimulus to the text-book writers' ecstasies, because out of phenomena of the planet Uranus, the "Neptune-triumph" developed. For Richard Proctor's reasons for arguing that this discovery was not accidental, see *Old and New Astronomy* (646). *Philosophical Transactions of the Royal Society of London* (71, 492) — a paper by Herschel — an "Account of a comet" discovered on March 13, 1781. A year went by, and not an astronomer in the world knew a planet when he saw one: then Lexell did find out that the supposed comet was a planet.

Statues from which used to drip the life-blood of a parasitic cult —

Structures of parabolas from which bleed equations —

As we go along we shall develop the acceptance that astronomers might as well try to squeeze blood from images as to try to seduce symbols into conclusions, because applicable mathematics has no more to do with planetary inter-actions than have statues of saints. If this denial that calculi have place in gravitational astronomy be accepted, the astronomers lose their supposed god; they become an unfocussed priesthood; the stamina of their arrogance wilts. We begin with the next to the simplest problem in celestial mechanics: that is the formulation of the inter-actions of the sun and the moon and this earth. In the highest mathematics, final, sacred mathematics, can this next to the simplest problem in so-called mathematical astronomy be solved?

It cannot be solved.

Every now and then, somebody announces that he has solved the Problem of the Three Bodies, but it is always an incomplete, or impressionistic demonstration, compounded of abstractions, and ignoring the conditions of bodies in space. Over and over we shall find vacancy under supposed achievements; elaborate structures that are pretensions without foundation. Here we learn that astronomers can not formulate the inter-actions of three bodies in space, but calculate anyway, and publish what they call the formula of a planet that is inter-acting with a thousand other bodies. They explain. It will be one of our most lasting impressions of astronomers: they explain and explain and explain. The astronomers explain that, though in finer terms, the mutual effects of three planets can not be determined, so dominant is the power of the sun that all other effects are negligible.

Before the discovery of Uranus, there was no way by which the miracles of the astro-magicians could be tested. They said that their formulas worked out, and external inquiry was panic-stricken at the mention of a formula. But Uranus was discovered, and the magicians were called upon to calculate his path. They did calculate, and, if Uranus had moved in a regular path, I do not mean to say that astronomers or college boys have no mathematics by which to determine anything so simple.

They computed the orbit of Uranus.

He went somewhere else.

They explained. They computed some more. They went on explaining and computing, year in and year out, and the planet Uranus kept on going somewhere else. Then they conceived of a powerful perturbing force beyond Uranus — so then that at the distance of Uranus the sun is not so dominant — in which case the effects of Saturn upon Uranus and Uranus upon Saturn are not so negligible — on through complexes of inter-actions that infinitely intensify by cumulativeness into a black outlook for the whole brilliant system. The palæo-astronomers calculated, and for more than fifty years pointed variously at the sky. Finally two of them, of course agreeing upon the general background of Uranus, pointed within distances that are conventionally supposed to have been about six hundred millions of miles of Neptune, and now it is religiously, if not insolently, said that the discovery of Neptune was not accidental —

That the test of that which is not accidental is ability to do it again —

That it is within the power of anybody, who does not know a hyperbola from a cosine, to find out whether the astronomers are led by a cloud of rubbish by day and a pillar of bosh by night —

If, by the magic of his mathematics, any astronomer could have pointed to the position of Neptune, let him point to the planet past Neptune. According to the same reasoning by which a planet past Uranus was supposed to be, a Trans-Neptunian planet may be supposed to be. Neptune shows perturbations similar to those of Uranus.

According to Prof. Todd there is such a planet, and it revolves around the sun once in 375 years. There are two according to Prof. Forbes: one revolving once in 1,000 years, and the other once in 5,000 years. See MacPherson's *A Century's Progress in Astronomy*. It exists according to Dr. Eric Doolittle, and revolves once in 283 years, (*Sci. Amer.* n.s., 122, 641). According to Mr. Hind it revolves once in 1,600 years (*Bulletin of the Philosophical Society of Washington*, 3, 20; *Miscellaneous Collections of the Smithsonian Institute*, 20, 20).

So then we have found out some things, and, relatively to the oppressions that we felt from our opposition, they are reassuring. But also they are depressing. Because, if, in this existence of ours, there is no prestige higher than that of astronomic science, and, if that seeming of substantial renown has been achieved by a composition of bubbles, what of anything like soundness must there be to all lesser reputes and achievements?

Let three bodies inter-act. There is no calculus by which their inter-actions can be formulated. But there are a thousand inter-acting bodies in this solar system — or supposed solar system — and we find that the higher prestige in our existence is built upon the tangled assertions that there are magicians who can compute in a thousand quantities, though they cannot compute in three.

Then all other so-called human triumphs, or moderate successes, products of anybody's reasoning processes and labours — and what are they, if higher than them all, more academic, austere, rigorous, exact are the methods and the processes of the astronomers? What can be thought of our whole existence, its nature and its destiny?

That our existence, a thing within one solar system, or supposed solar system, is a stricken thing that is mewling through space, shocking able-minded, healthy systems with the sores on its sun, its ghastly moons, its civilisations that are all broken out with sciences; a celestial leper, holding out doddering expanses into which charitable systems drop golden comets? If it be the leprous thing that our findings seem to indicate, there is no encouragement for us to go on. We cannot discover: we can only betray new symptoms. If I be part of such a stricken thing, I know of nothing but sickness and sores and rags to reason with: my data will be pustules; my interpretations will be inflammations —

CHAPTER 3

Southern plantations and the woolly heads of negroes pounding the ground — cries in northern regions and round white faces turned to the sky — fiery globes in the sky — a study in black, white, and golden formations in one general glow. Upon the night of November 13-14, 1833, occurred the most sensational celestial spectacle of the nineteenth century: for six hours fiery meteors gushed from the heavens, and were visible along the whole Atlantic coast of the United States.

One supposes that astronomers do not pound the ground with their heads, and presumably they do not screech, but they have feelings just the same. They itched. Here was something to formulate. When he hears of something new and unquestionable in the sky, an astronomer is diseased with ill-suppressed equations. Symbols persecute him for expression. His is the frenzy of someone who would stop automobiles, railroad trains, bicycles, all things, to measure them; run, with a yardstick, after sparrows, flies, all persons passing his door. This is supposed to be scientific, but it can be monomaniac. Very likely the distress and the necessity of Prof. Olmsted were keenest. He was the first to formulate. He "demonstrated" that these meteors, known as the Leonids, revolved around the sun once in six months.

They didn't.

Then Prof. Newton "demonstrated" that the "real" period was thirty-three and a quarter years. But this was done empirically, and that is not divine, nor even aristocratic, and the thing would have to be done rationally, or mathematically, by someone, because, if there be not mathematical treatment, in gravitational terms, of such phenomena, astronomers are in reduced circumstances. It was Dr. Adams, who, emboldened with his experience in not having to point anywhere near Neptune, but nevertheless being acclaimed by all patriotic Englishmen as the real discoverer of Neptune, mathematically "confirmed" Prof. Newton's "findings." Dr. Adams predicted that the Leonids would return in November, 1866, and in November, 1899, occupying several years, upon each occasion, in passing a point in this earth's orbit.

There were meteors upon the night of Nov. 13-14, 1866. They were plentiful. They often are in the middle of November. They no more resembled the spectacle of 1833 than an ordinary shower resembles a cloudburst. But the "demonstration" required that there should be an equal display, or, according to some aspects, a greater display, upon the corresponding night of the next year. There was a display, the next year; but it was in the sky of the United States, and was not seen in England. Another occurrence nothing like that of 1833 was reported from the United States.

By conventional theory, this earth was in a vast, wide stream of meteors, the earth revolving so as to expose successive parts to bombardment. So keenly did Richard Proctor visualise the earth so immersed and so bombarded, that, when nothing was seen in England, he explained. He spend most of his life explaining. In the *Student and Intellectual Observer*, (2, 254), he wrote: "Had the morning of Nov. 14, 1867, been clear in England, we should have seen the commencement of the display, but not its more brilliant part."

We have had some experience with the "triumphs" of astronomers: we have some suspicions as to their greatly advertised accuracy. We shall find out for ourselves whether the morning of Nov. 14, 1867 was clear enough in England or not. We suspect that it was a charming morning, in England —

Monthly Notices of the Royal Astronomical Society (28, 32):

Report by E.J. Lowe, Highfield House, night of Nov. 13-14, 1867:

Clear at 1:10 A.M.; high, thin cumuli, at 2 A.M., but sky not covered until 3:10 A.M., and the moon's place visible until 3:55 A.M.; sky not overcast until 5:50 A.M.

The determination of the orbital period of thirty-three years and a quarter, but with appearances of a period of thirty-three years, was arrived at by Prof. Newton by searching old records, finding that, in an intersection-period of thirty-three years, there had been extra-ordinary meteoric displays, from the year 902 A.D. to the year 1833 A.D. He reminds me of an investigator who searched old records for appearances of Halley's comet, and found something that he identified as Halley's comet, exactly on time, every seventy-five years back to times of the Roman Empire. See the *Edinburgh Review* (61, 89). It seems that he did not know that orthodoxy does not attribute exactly a seventy-five year period to Halley's comet. He got what he went looking for, anyway. I have no disposition for us to enjoy ourselves at Prof. Newton's expense, because, surely enough, his method, if regarded as only experimental, or tentative, is legitimate enough, though one does suspect him of very loose behaviour in his picking and choosing. But Dr. Adams announced that, upon mathematical grounds, he had arrived at the same conclusion.

The test:

The next return of the Leonids was predicted for November, 1899.

Memoirs of the British Astronomical Association (9, 6):

"No meteoric event ever before aroused such an intense and widespread interest, or so grievously disappointed anticipation."

There were no Leonids in November, 1899.

It was explained. They would be seen next year.

There were no Leonids in November, 1900.

It was explained. They would be seen next year.

No Leonids.

Vaunt and inflation and parade of the symbols of the infinitesimal calculus; the pomp of vectors, and the hush that surrounds quaternions: but when an axis of co-ordinates loses its rectitude, in the service of a questionable selection, disciplined symbols become a rabble. The Most High of Mathematics — and one of his supposed prophets points to the sky. Nowhere near where he points, something is found. He points to a date — nothing happens.

Prof. Serviss, in *Astronomy in a Nutshell* (213), explains. He explains that the Leonids did not appear when they should have appeared, because Jupiter and Saturn had altered their orbits.

Back in the times of the Crusades, and nothing was disturbing the Leonids — and if you're stronger for dates than I am, think of some more dates, and nothing was altering the orbit of the Leonids — discovery of America, and the Spanish Armada, in 1588, which, by some freak, I always remember, and no effects by Jupiter and Saturn — French revolution and on to the year 1866, and still nothing the matter with the Leonids — but, once removed from "discovery" and "identification," and that's the end of their period, diverted by Jupiter and Saturn, old things that had been up in the sky at least as long as

17

they had been. If we're going to accept the calculi at all, the calculus of probabilities must have a hearing. My own opinion, based upon reading many accounts of November meteors, is that decidedly the display of 1833 did not repeat in 1866: that a false priest sinned and that an equally false highpriest gave him sanction.

The tragedy goes comically on. I feel that, to all good Neo-astronomers, I can recommend the following serenity from an astronomer who was unperturbed by what happened to his science, in November, 1899, and some more Novembers —

W.W. Bryant, *A History of Astronomy* (255):

That the meteoric display of 1899 had failed to appear — "as had been predicted" by Dr. Downing and Dr. Johnstone Stoney.

One starts to enjoy this disguisement, thinking of virtually all the astronomers of the world who had predicted the return of the Leonids, and the find, by Bryant, of two who had not, and his recording only the opinion of these two, colouring so as to look like another triumph — but we may thank our sorely stimulated suspiciousness for still richer enjoyment —

That even these two said no such saving thing —

Nature (61, 28):

Dr. Downing and Dr. Stoney, instead of predicting failure of the Leonids to appear, advise watch for them several hours later than had been calculated.

I conceive of the astronomers' fictitious paradise as malarchi-tectural with corrupted equations, and paved with rotten symbols. Seemingly pure, white fountains of formal vanities — boasts that are gushing from decomposed triumphs. We shall find their furnishings shabby with tarnished comets. We turn expectantly to the subject of comets; or we turn cynically to the subject. We turn maliciously to the subject of comets. Nevertheless, threading the insecurities of our various feelings, is a motif that is the steady essence of Neo-astronomy:

That, in celestial phenomena, as well as in all other fields of research, the irregular, or the unformulable, or the uncapturable, is present in at least equal representation with the uniform: that, given any clear, definite, seemingly unvarying thing in the heavens, co-existently is something of wantonness or irresponsibility, bizarre and incredible, according to the standards of purists — that the science of Astronomy concerns itself with only one aspect of existence, because of course there can be no science of the obverse phenomena — which is good excuse for so enormously disregarding, if we must have the idea that there are real sciences, but which shows the hopelessness of positively attempting.

The story of the comets, as not told in Mr. Chambers' book of that title, is almost unparalleled in the annals of humiliation. When a comet is predicted to return, that means faith in the Law of Gravitation. It is Newtonism that comets, as well as planets, obey the Law of Gravitation, and move in one of the conic sections. When a comet does not return when it "should," there is no refuge for an astronomer to say that planets perturbed it, because one will ask why he did not include such factors in his calculations, if these phenomena be subject to mathematical treatment. In his book, Mr. Chambers avoids, or indicates that he never heard of, a great deal that will receive cordiality from us, but he does publish a list of predicted comets that did not return. Writing, in 1909, (*Story of the Comets*, 86), he mentions others for which he had hopes:

Brooks' First Periodic Comet (1886, IV) — "We must see what the years 1909 and 1910 bring forth." This is pretty indefinite anticipation — however, nothing was brought forth, according to *Monthly Notices*, 1909 and 1910: the Brooks' comet that is recorded is Brooks', 1889. Giacobini's Second Periodical Comet (1900, III) — not seen in 1907 — "so we shall have no chance of knowing anything more about it until 1914." No more known about it in 1914. Borelly's Comet (1905, II) — "Its expected return in 1911, or 1912, will be awaited with interest." This is pretty indefinite awaiting: it is now said that this comet did return upon Sept. 19, 1911. Denning's Second Periodic Comet (1894, I) — expected, in 1909, but not seen up to Mr. Chambers' time of writing — no mention in *Monthly Notices*. Swift's Comet, of Nov. 20, 1894 — "must be regarded as lost, unless it should be found in December, 1912." No mention of it in *Monthly Notices*.

Three comets were predicted to return in 1913 — not one of them returned (*Monthly Notices*, 74, 326).

Once upon a time, armed with some of the best and latest cynicisms, I was hunting for prey in the *Magazine of Science*, and came upon an account of a comet that was expected in the year 1848. I supposed that the thing had been positively predicted, and very likely failed to appear, and, for such common game, had no interest. But I came upon the spoor of disgrace, in the word "triumph" — "If it does come, it will afford another astronomical triumph" (*Magazine of Science*, 1848, 107). The astronomers had predicted the return of the great comet in the year 1848 (*Recreative Science*, 1, 139). In *Monthly Notices* (7, 260), Mr. Hind says that the result of his calculations had satisfied him that the identification had been complete, and that, in all probability, the comet "must be very near." Accepting Prof. Mädler's determinations, he predicted that the comet would return to position nearest the sun, about the end of February, 1848 (*Monthly Notices*, 8: 16, 155).

No comet.

The astronomers explained. I don't know what the mind of an astronomer looks like, but I think of a fizzle with excuses revolving around it. A writer in the *American Journal of Science*, (s. 2, 9, 442), explains excellently. It seems that, when the comet failed to return, Mr. Barber, at Etwell, again went over the calculations. He found that, between the years 1556 and 1592, the familiar attractions of Jupiter and Saturn had diminished the comet's period by 263 days, but that something else had wrought an effect that he set down positively at 751 days, with a resulting retardation of 488 days. This is magic that would petrify, with chagrin, the arteries of the hemorrhagicalest statue that ever convinced the faithful — reaching back through three centuries of inter-actions, which, without divine insight, are unimaginable when occurring in three seconds —

But there was no comet.

The astronomers explained. They went on calculating, and ten years later were still calculating. See *Recreative Science* (1, 139). It would be heroic were it not mania. What was the matter with Mr. Barber, at Etwell, and the intellectual tentacles that he had thrust through centuries is not made clear in the most contemporaneous accounts; but, in the year 1857, Mr. Hind published a pamphlet and explained. It seems that researches by Littrow had given new verification to a path that had been computed for the comet, and that nothing had been the matter with Mr. Barber, of Etwell, except his insufficiency of data, which had been corrected. Mr. Hind predicted. He pointed to the future, but he pointed like someone closing a thumb and spreading four fingers. Mr. Hind said that, according to Halley's calculations, the comet would arrive in the summer of 1865. However, an acceleration of five years had been discovered, so that the time should be set down for the middle of August, 1860. However, according to Mr. Hind's calculated orbit, the comet might return in the summer of 1864. However, allowing for acceleration, "the comet is found to be due early in August, 1858" (John Russell Hind. *The Comet of 1556*, 22).

Then Bomme calculated. He predicted that the comet would return upon August 2, 1858.

There was no comet.

The astronomers went on calculating. They predicted that the comet would return on Aug. 22, 1860.

No comet.

But I think that a touch of mercy is a luxury that we can afford; anyway, we'll have to be merciful or monotonous. For variety we shall switch from a comet that did not appear to one that did appear. Upon the night of June 30, 1861, a magnificent humiliator appeared in the heavens. One of the most brilliant luminosities of modern times appeared as suddenly as if it were dropped through the shell of our solar system — if it be a solar system. There were letters in the newspapers: correspondents wanted to know why this extraordinary object had not been seen coming, by astronomers. Mr. Hind explained. He wrote that the comet was a small object and consequently had not been seen coming by astronomers. No one could deny the magnificence of the comet; nevertheless Mr. Hind declared that it was very small, looking so large because it was near this earth. This is not the later explanation: nowadays it is said that the comet had been in southern skies, where it had been observed. All contemporaneous astronomers agreed that the comet had come down from the north, and not one of them thought of explaining that it had been invisible because it had been in the south. A luminosity, with a mist around it, altogether the apparent size of the moon, had burst into view. In *Recreative Science* (3, 143), Webb says that nothing like it had been seen since the year 1680. Nevertheless the orthodox pronouncement was that the object was small and would fade away as quickly as it had appeared. See the *Athenaeum*, July 6, 1861 (19) — "So small an object will very soon get beyond our view" (Hind).

Popular Science Review (o.s., 1, 513):

That, in April, 1862, the thing was still visible.

Something else that was seen under circumstances that cannot be considered triumphant — upon Nov. 28, 1872, Prof. Klinkerfues, of Göttingen, looking for Biela's comet, saw meteors in the path of the expected comet. He telegraphed to Pogson, of Madras, to look near the star *Theta Centauri*, and he would see the comet. I'd not say that this was in the field of magic, but it does seem consummate. A dramatic telegram like this electrifies the faithful — an astronomer in the north telling an astronomer in the south where to look, so definitely naming one special little star in skies invisible in the north. Pogson looked where he was told to look and announced that he saw what he was told to see. But at meetings of the R.A.S., Jan. 10 and March 14, 1873, Captain Tupman pointed out that, even if Biela's comet had appeared, it would have been nowhere near this star.

Among our later emotions will be indignation against all astronomers who say that they know whether stars are approaching or receding. When we arrive at that subject it will be the preciseness of the astronomers that will perhaps inflame us beyond endurance. We note here the far smaller difficulty of determining whether a relatively nearby comet is coming or going. Upon Nov. 6, 1892, Edwin Holmes discovered a comet. In the *Journal of the British Astronomical Association* (3, 181), Holmes writes that different astronomers had calculated its distance from twenty million miles to two hundred million miles and had determined its diameter to be all the way from twenty-seven thousand miles to three hundred thousand miles. Prof. Young said that the comet was approaching; Prof. Parkhurst wrote merely that the impression was that the comet was approaching the earth; but Prof. Berberich, (*English Mechanic and World of Science*, 56, 316), announced that, upon Nov. 6, Holmes' comet had been 36,000,000 miles from this earth, and 6,000,000 miles away upon the 16th, and that the approach was so rapid that, upon the 21st the comet would touch this earth.

The comet, which had been receding, kept on receding.

CHAPTER 4

Nevertheless I sometimes doubt that astronomers represent especial incompetence. They remind me too much of uplifters and grocers, philanthropists, expert accountants, makers of treaties, characters in international conferences, psychic researchers, biologists. The astronomers seem to me about as capitalists seem to socialists, and about as socialists seem to capitalists, or about as Presbyterians seem to Baptists; as Democrats seem to Republicans, or as artists of one school seem to artists of another school. If the basic fallacies, or the absence of base, in every specialisation of thought can be seen by the units of its opposition, why then we see that all supposed foundations in our whole existence are myths, and that all discussion and supposed progress are the conflicts of phantoms and the overthrow of old delusions by new delusions. Nevertheless I am searching for some wider expression that will rationalise all of us — conceiving that what we call irrationality is our view of parts and functions out of relation to an underlying whole; an underlying something that is working out its development in terms of planets and acids and bugs, rivers and labour unions and cyclones, politicians and islands and astronomers. Perhaps we conceive of an underlying nexus in which all things, in our existence, are different manifestations — torn by its hurricanes and quaked by the struggles of Labour against Capital — and then, for the sake of balance, requiring relaxations. It has its rougher hoaxes, and some of the apes and some of the priests, and philosophers and wart hogs are nothing short of horse play; but the astronomers are the ironies of its less peasant-like moments — or the deliciousness of pretending to know whether a far-away star is approaching or receding, and at the same time exactly predicting when a nearby comet, which is receding, will complete its approach. This is cosmic playfulness; such pleasantries enable Existence to bear its catastrophes. Shattered comets and sickened nations and the hydrogenic anguishes of the sun — and there must be astronomers for the sake of relaxations.

It will be important to us that the astronomers shall not be less unfortunate in their pronouncements upon motions of the stars than they have turned out to be in other respects. Especially disagreeable to us is the doctrine that stars are variable because dark companions revolve around them; also we prefer to find that nothing fit for matured minds has been determined as to stars with light companions that encircle, or revolve with them. If silence be the only true philosophy, and if every positive assertion be a myth, we should easily find requital for our negative preferences.

Prof. Otto Struve was one of the highest of the astronomic authorities, and the faithful attribute triumphs to him. Upon March 19, 1873, Prof. Struve announced that he had discovered a companion to the star Procyon. That was an interesting observation, but the mere observation was not the triumph. Some time before, Prof. Auwers, as credulous, if not jocular, as Newton and Leverrier and Adams, had computed the orbit of a hypothetic companion of Procyon's. Upon a chart of the stars, he had drawn a circle around Procyon. This orbit was calculated in gravitational terms, and a general theme of ours is that all such calculations are only ideal, and relate no more to stars and planets or anything else than do the spotless theories of uplifters to events that occur as spots in the one wide daub of existence. Specifically we wish to discredit this "triumph" of Struve's and Auwers', but in general we continue our expression that all uses of the calculus of celestial mechanics are false applications, and that this subject is for aesthetic enjoyment only, and has no place in the science of astronomy, if anybody can think that there is such a science. So, after great labour, or after considerable enjoyment, Auwers drew a circle around Procyon, and announced that that was the orbit of a companion-star. Exactly at the point in this circle where it "should" be, upon March 19, 1873, Struve saw a point of light which, it may be accepted, sooner or later someone would see. According to Agnes Clerke (*System of the Stars*, 2nd ed., 173) over and over Struve watched the point of light, and convinced himself that it moved as it "should" move, exactly in the calculated orbit. In *Reminiscences of an Astronomer* (138), Prof. Newcomb tells the story. According to him, an American astronomer then did more than confirm Struve's observations: he not only saw but exactly measured the supposed companion.

A defect was found between the lenses of Struve's telescope: it was found that this telescope showed a similar "companion," about 10" from every large star. It was found that the more than "confirmatory" determinations by the American astronomer had been upon "a long well known star" (Newcomb, 140).

Every astronomic triumph is a bright light accompanied by an imbecility, which may for a while make it variable with diminishments and then go unnoticed. Priestcrafts are not merely tyrannies: they're necessities. There must be more reassuring ways of telling this story. The good priest J.E. Gore (*Studies in Astronomy*, 104) tells it safely — not a thing except that, in the year 1873, a companion of Procyon was, by Struve, "strongly suspected." Positive assurances of the sciences — they are islands of seeming stability in a cosmic jelly. We shall eclipse the story of Algol with some modern disclosures. In all minds not convinced that earnest and devoted falsifiers are holding back Development, the story, if remembered at all, will soon renew its fictitious lustre. We are centres of tremors in a quaking black jelly. A bright and shining delusion looks like beaconed security.

Sir Robert Ball, in the *Story of the Heavens* (rev. ed., 485), says that the period in which Algol blinks his magnitudes is 2 days, 22 hours, 48 minutes and 55 seconds. He gives the details of Prof. Vogel's calculations upon a speck of light and an invisibility. It is god-like command that out of the variations of light shall come the diameters of faint appearances and the distance and velocity of the unseeable — that the diameter of the point of light is 1,054,000 miles, and that the diameter of the imperceptibility is 825,000 miles, and that their centres are 3,220,000 miles apart: orbital velocity of Algol, 26 miles a second, and the orbital velocity of the companion, 55 miles a second — should be stated 26.3 miles and 55.4 miles a second (Proctor, *Old and New Astronomy*, 773).

We come to a classic imposition like this, and at first we feel helpless. We are told that this thing is so. It is as if we were modes of motion and must go on, but are obstructed by an absolute bar of ultimate steel, shining, in our way, with an infinite polish.

But all appearances are illusions.

No one with a microscope doubts this; no one who has gone specially from ordinary beliefs into minuter examination of any subject doubts this, as to his own specific experience — so then, broadly, that all appearances are illusions, and that, by this recognition, we shall dissipate resistances, monsters, dragons, oppressors that we shall meet in our pilgrimage. This bar-like calculation is itself a mode of motion. The static cannot absolutely resist the dynamic, because in the act of resisting it becomes itself proportionately the dynamic. We learn that modifications rusted into the steel of our opposition. The period of Algol, which Vogel carried out to a minute's 55th second, was, after all, so incompetently determined that the whole impression was nullified —

Astronomical Journal (11, 113):

That, according to Chandler, Algol and his companion do not revolve around each other merely, but revolve together around some second imperceptibility — regularly.

Bulletin de la Société Astronomique de France (24, 444):

That M. Mora has shown that in Algol's variations there were irregularities that neither Vogel nor Chandler had accounted for.

The Companion of Sirius looms up to our recognition that the story must be nonsense, or worse than nonsense — or that two light comedies will now disappear behind something darker. The story of the Companion of Sirius is that Prof. Auwers, having observed, or in his mania for a pencil and something to scribble upon, having supposed he had observed, motions of the star Sirius, had deduced the existence of a companion, and had inevitably calculated its orbit. Early in the year 1862, Alvan Clark Jr. turned his new telescope upon Sirius, and there, precisely where, according to Auwers' calculations, it should be, saw the companion. The story is told by Proctor, writing thirty years later: the finding of the companion, in the "precise position of the calculations;" Proctor's statement that, in the thirty years following, the companion had "conformed fairly well with the calculated orbit."

According to the *Annual Record of Science and Industry* (1876, 18), the companion, in half the time mentioned by Proctor, had not moved in the calculated orbit. In the *Astronomical Register* (15, 186), there are two diagrams by Flammarion: one is the orbit of the companion, as computed by Auwers; the other is the orbit, according to a mean of many observations. They do not conform fairly well. They do not conform at all.

I am now temporarily accepting that Flammarion and the other observing astronomers are right, and that the writers like Proctor, who do not say that they made observations of their own, are wrong, though I have data for thinking that there is no such companion-star. When Clark turned his telescope upon Sirius, the companion was found exactly where Auwers said it would be found. According to Flammarion and the other astronomers, had he looked earlier or later it would not have been in this position. Then, in the name of the one calculus that astronomers seem never to have heard of, by what circumstances could that star have been precisely where it should be, when looked for, Jan. 31, 1862, if upon all other occasions, it would not be where it should be?

Astronomical Register (1, 94):

A representation of Sirius — but with six small stars around him — an account, by Dr. Dawes, of observations, by Goldschmidt, upon the "companion" and five other small stars near Sirius. Dr. Dawes' accusation, or opinion, is that it scarcely seems possible that some of these other stars were not seen by Clark. If Alvan Clark saw six stars, at various distances from Sirius, and picked out the one that was at the required distance, as if that were the only one, he dignifies our serials with a touch of something other than comedy. For Goldschmidt's own announcement, see *Monthly Notices* (23: 181, 243).

CHAPTER 5

Smugness and falseness and sequences of re-adjusting fatalities — and yet so great is the hypnotic power of astronomic science that it can outlive its "mortal" blows by the simple process of forgetting them, and, in general, simply by denying that it can make mistakes. Upon page 245, *Old and New Astronomy*, Richard Proctor says — "The ideas of astronomers on these questions of distance have not changed, and in the present position of astronomy, based (in such respects) on absolute demonstration, they cannot change."

Sounds that have roared in the sky, and their vibrations have shaken down villages — if these be the voices of Development, commanding that opinions shall change, we shall learn what will become of the Proctors and their "absolute demonstrations." Lights that have appeared in the sky — that they are gleams upon the armament of Marching Organization. "There can only be one explanation of meteors" — I think it is that they are shining spearpoints of slayers of dogmas. I point to the sky over a little town in Perthshire, Scotland — there may be a new San Salvador — it may be a new Plymouth Rock. I point to the crater Aristarchus, of the moon — there, for more than a century, a lighthouse may have been signalling. Whether out of profound meditations, or farrago and bewilderment, I point, directly, or miscellaneously, and, if only a few of the multitude of data be accepted, unformulable perturbations rack an absolute sureness, and the coils of our little horizons relax their constrictions.

I indicate that, in these pages, which are banners in a cosmic procession, I do feel a sense of responsibility, but how to maintain any great seriousness I do not know, because still is our subject astronomical "triumphs."

Once upon a time there was a young man, aged eighteen, whose name was Jeremiah Horrox. He was no astronomer. He was interested in astronomic subjects, but it may be that we shall agree that a young man of eighteen, who had not been heard of by one astronomer of his time, was an outsider. There was a transit of Venus in December, 1639, but not a grown-up astronomer in the world expected it, because the not always great and infallible Kepler had predicted the next transit of

Venus for the year 1761. According to Kepler, Venus would pass below the sun in December, 1639. But there was another calculation: it was by the great, but sometimes not so great, Lansberg: that, in December, 1639, Venus would pass over the upper part of the sun. Jeremiah Horrox was an outsider. He was able to reason that, if Venus could not pass below the sun, and also over the upper part of the sun, she might take a middle course. Venus did pass over the middle part of the sun's disc; and Horrox reported the occurrence, having watched it.

I suppose this was one of the most agreeable humiliations in the annals of busted inflations. One thinks sympathetically of the joy that went out from seventeenth-century Philistines. The story is told to this day by the Proctors and Balls and Newcombs: the way they tell this story of the boy who was able to conclude that something that could not occupy two extremes might be intermediate, and thereby see something that no professional observer of the time saw, is a triumph of absorption:

That the transit of Venus, in December, 1639, was observed by Jeremiah Horrox, "the great astronomer."

We shall make some discoveries as we go along, and some of them will be worse thought of than others, but there is a discovery here that may be of interest: the secret of immortality — that there is a mortal resistance to everything; but that the thing that can keep on incorporating, or assimilating within itself, its own mortal resistances, will live forever. By its absorptions, the science of astronomy perpetuates its inflations, but there have been instances of indigestion. See the New York *Herald*, Sept. 16, 1909. Here Flammarion, who probably no longer asserts any such thing, claims Dr. Cook's "discovery of the north pole" as an "astronomical conquest." Also there are other ways. One suspects that the treatment that Dr. Lescarbault received from Flammarion illustrates other ways.

In the year 1859, it seems that Dr. Lescarbault was something of an astronomer. It seems that as far back as that he may have known a planet when he saw one, because, in an interview, he convinced Leverrier that he did know a planet when he saw one. He had at least heard of the planet Venus, because in the year 1882 he published a paper upon indications that Venus has an atmosphere (*Comptes*

Rendus, 95, 1208). Largely because of an observation, or an announcement, of his, occurred the climax of Leverrier's fiascos: prediction of an intra-Mercurial planet that did not appear when it "should" appear. My suspicion is that astronomers pardonably, but frailly, had it in for Lescarbault, and that in the year 1891 came an occurrence that one of them made an opportunity. Early in the year 1891, Dr. Lescarbault announced that, upon the night of Jan. 11, 1891, he had seen a new star (*Comptes Rendus*, 112, 152). At the next meeting of the French Academy, Flammarion rose, spoke briefly, and sat down without over-doing. He said that Lescarbault had "discovered" Saturn (*Comptes Rendus*, 112, 260; W.F. Denning, *Telescopic Work for Starlight Evenings*, 350).

If a navigator of at least thirty years' experience should announce that he had discovered an island, and if that island should turn out to be Bermuda, he would pair with Lescarbault — as Flammarion made Lescarbault appear. Even though I am a writer upon astronomical subjects, myself, I think that even I should know Saturn, if I should see him, at least in such a period as the year 1891, when the rings were visible. It is perhaps an incredible mistake. However, it will be agreeable to some of us to find that astronomers have committed just such almost incredible mistakes —

In *Cosmos: Les Mondes* (s. 4, 42, 467), is a list of astronomers who reported "unknown" dark bodies that they had seen crossing the disc of the sun:

> La Concha...........Montevideo..........Nov. 5, 1789;
> Kayser..................Amsterdam..........Nov. 9, 1802;
> Fischer..................Lisbon....................May 5, 1832;
> Houzeau..............Brussels.................May 8, 1845.

According to the *Nautical Almanac and Astronomical Ephemeris*, the planet Mercury did cross the disc of the sun upon these dates.

It is either that the Flammarions do so punish those who see the new and the undesired, or that astronomers do "discover" Saturn, and do not know Mercury when they see him — and that Henry Thomas Buckle overlooked something when he wrote that only the science of history attracts inferior minds often not fit even for clergymen.

Whatever we think of Flammarion, we admire his deftness. But we shall have an English instance of the ways in which Astronomy maintains itself and controls those who say they see that which they "should" not see, which does seem beefy. One turns the not very attractive-looking pages of the *English Mechanic*, 1893, casually, perhaps, at any rate in no expectations of sensations — glaring at one, a sketch of such a botanico-pathologic monstrosity as a musk melon with rows of bunions on it (*Eng. Mech.*, 58, 198). The reader is told, by Andrew Barclay, F.R.A.S., Kilmarnock, Scotland, that this enormity is the planet Jupiter, according to the speculum of his Gregorian telescope.

In the next issue of the *English Mechanic* (58, 221), Capt. Noble, F.R.A.S., writes, gently enough, that, if he had such a telescope, he would dispose of the optical parts for whatever they would bring, and make a chimney cowl of the tube.

English Mechanic (58, 309) — the planet Mars, by Andrew Barclay — a dark sphere, surrounded by a thick ring of lighter material; attached to it, another sphere, of half its diameter — a sketch as gross and repellent to a conventionalist as the museum-freak, in whose body the head of a dangling twin is embedded, its dwarfed body lopping out from his side. There is a description by Mr. Barclay, according to whom the main body is red and the protuberance blue.

Captain Noble — "Preposterous ... last straw that breaks the camel's back!" (*English Mechanic*, 58, 353).

Mr. Barclay comes back with some new observations upon Jupiter's lumps, and then in the rest of the volume is not heard from again. One reads on, interested in quieter matters, and gradually forgets the controversy —

English Mechanic (65, 218):

A gallery of monstrosities: Andrew Barclay, signing himself "F.R.A.S.," exhibiting:

The planet Jupiter, six times encircled with lumps; afflicted Mars, with his partly embedded twin reduced in size, but still a distress to all properly trained observers; the planet Saturn, shaped like a mushroom with a ring around it.

Captain Noble — "Mr. Barclay is not a Fellow of the Royal Astronomical Society, and, were the game worth the candle, might be restrained by injunction from so describing himself!" (*Eng. Mech.*, 65, 314). And upon page 362, of this volume of the *English Mechanic*, Captain Noble calls the whole matter "a pseudo-F.R.A.S.'s crazy hallucinations."

Lists of the Fellows of the Royal Astronomical Society, from June, 1875, to June, 1896:

"Barclay, Andrew, Kilmarnock, Scotland; elected Feb. 8, 1856."

I cannot find the list for 1897 in the libraries. List for 1898 — Andrew Barclay's name omitted. Thou shalt not see lumps on Jupiter.

Every one of Barclay's observations has something to support it. All conventional representations of Jupiter show encirclements by strings of rotundities that we are told are cloud-forms, but, in the *Jour. B.A.A.*, (21, 150), is published a paper by Dr. Downing, entitled: "Is Jupiter Humpy?" suggesting that various phenomena upon Jupiter agree with the idea that there are protuberances upon the planet. A common appearance, said to be an illusion, is Saturn as an oblong, if not mushroom-shaped; see any good index for observations upon the "square-shouldered aspect" of Saturn. In *L'Astronomie* (8, 135), is a sketch of Mars, according to Fontana, in the year 1636 — a sphere enclosed in a ring; in the centre of the sphere a great protruding body, said, by Fontana, to have looked like a vast, black cone.

But, whether this or that should amuse or enrage us, should be accepted or rejected, is not to me the crux; but Andrew Barclay's own opening words are:

That, through a conventional telescope, conventional appearances are seen, and that a telescope is tested by the conventionality of its disclosures; but that there may be new optical principles, or applications, that may be, to the eye and the present telescope, what once the conventional telescope was to the eye — in times when scientists refused to look at the preposterous, enraging, impossible moons of Jupiter.

In the *English Mechanic* (33, 327), is a letter from the astronomer, A. Stanley Williams. He had written previously upon double stars, their colours and magnitudes. Another astronomer, Herbert Sadler, had pointed out some errors. Mr. Williams acknowledges the errors, saying that some were his own, and that some were from William Henry Smyth's *A Cycle of Celestial Objects*. In the *English Mechanic* (33,

377), Sadler says that, earnestly, he would advise Williams not to use the new edition of Smyth's *Cycle*, because, with the exception of vol. 40, *Memoirs of the Royal Astronomical Society*, "a more disgracefully inaccurate" catalogue of double stars had never been published. "If Mr. Williams possesses a copy of this miserable publication, I should certainly advise him to sell it for what it will fetch for waste paper, for the book is crammed with the most stupid errors."

A new character appears. He is George F. Chambers, F.R.A.S., author of a long list of astronomical works, and a tract entitled, *Where Are You Going, Sunday?* He, too, is earnest. In this early correspondence, nothing ulterior is apparent, and we suppose that it is in the cause of Truth that he is so earnest. Says one astronomer that the other astronomer is "evidently one of those self-sufficient young men, who are nothing, if not abusive." But can Mr. Sadler have so soon forgotten what was done to him, on a former occasion, after he had slandered Admiral Smyth? Chambers challenges Sadler to publish a list of, say, fifty "stupid errors" in the book. He quotes the opinion of the Astronomer Royal: that the book was a work of "sterling merit." "Airy vs. Sadler," he says: "which is it to be?"

We began not very promisingly. Few excitements seemed to lurk in such a subject as double stars, their colours and magnitudes; but slander and abuse are livelier, and now enters curiosity: we'd like to know what was done to Herbert Sadler.

In June of 1876, Herbert Sadler was elected Fellow of the Royal Astronomical Society. In *Monthly Notices* (39, 183) appears his first paper that was read to the Society: "Notes on the late Admiral Smyth's *Cycle of Celestial Objects*, Volume the Second, commonly known as the *Bedford Catalogue*." With no especial vehemence, at least according to our own standards of repression, Sadler expresses himself upon some "extraordinary discrepancies" in this work.

At the meeting of the Society, May 9, 1879, there was an attack upon Sadler, and it was led by Chambers, or conducted by Chambers, who cried out that Sadler had slandered a great astronomer and demanded that Sadler should resign. In the report of this meeting, published in the *Observatory* (3, 33), there is not a trace of anybody's endeavours to find out whether there were errors in this book or not: Chambers ignored everything but his accusation of slander, and demanded again that Sadler should resign. In *Monthly Notices* (39, 389), the Council of the Society published regrets that it had permitted publication of Sadler's paper, which was "entirely unsupported by the citation of the instances upon which his judgment was founded."

We find that it was Mr. Chambers who had revised and published the new edition of Smyth's *Cycle.*

In the *English Mechanic*, Chambers challenged Sadler to publish, say, fifty "stupid errors." See page 451, vol. 33, *English Mechanic* — Sadler lists just fifty "stupid errors." He says that he could have listed, not 50, but 250, not trivial, but of the "grossest kind." He says that in one set of 167 observations, 117 were wrong.

The *English Mechanic* drops out of this comedy with the obvious title, but developments go on. Evidently withdrawing its "regrets," the Council permitted publication of a criticism of Chambers' edition of Smyth's *Cycle*, in *Monthly Notices* (40, 497), and the language in this criticism, by S.W. Burnham, was no less interpretable as slanderous than was Sadler's: that Smyth's data were "either roughly approximate or grossly incorrect, and so constantly recurring that it was impossible to explain that they were ordinary errors of observation." Burnham lists 30 pages of errors.

Following is a paper by E.B. Knobel (*Monthly Notices*, 40, 532), who published 17 pages of instances in which, in his opinion, Mr. Burnham had been too severe. Knowing of no objection by Burnham to this reduction, we have left 13 pages of stupid errors in one standard astronomical work, which may fairly be considered as representative of astronomical work in general, inasmuch as it was, in the opinion of the Astronomer Royal, a book of "sterling merit."

I think that now we have accomplished something. After this we should all get along more familiarly and agreeably together. Thirteen pages of errors in one standard astronomical work are reassuring; there is a likeable fallibility here that should make for better relations. If the astronomers were what they think they are, we might as well make squeaks of disapproval against Alpine summits. As to astronomers who calculate positions of planets — of whom he was one — Newcomb, in *Reminiscences of an Astronomer* (64), says — "The men who have done it are therefore in intellect the select few of the human race, — an aristocracy ranking above all others in the scale of being." We could never get along comfortably with such awful selectness as that. We are grateful to Mr. Sadler, in the cause of more comfortable relations.

Chapter 6

English Mechanic (56, 184):

That, upon April 25, 1892, Archdeacon Nouri climbed Mt. Ararat. It was his hope that he should find something of archaeologic compensation for his clambering. He found Noah's Ark.

About the same time, Dr. Holden, Director of the Lick Observatory, was watching one of the polished and mysterious-looking instruments that, in the new iconology, have replaced the images of the saints. Dr. Holden was awaiting the appointed moment of the explosion of a large quantity of dynamite in San Francisco Bay. The moment came. The polished little "saint" revealed to the faithful scientist. He wrote an account of the record, and sent copies to the San Francisco newspapers. Then he learned the dynamite had not been fired off. He sent a second messenger after the first messenger, and, because messengers sometimes have velocities proportional to urgencies — "the Observatory escaped ridicule by a narrow margin." See the *Observatory* (20, 466). This revelation came from Prof. Colton, who, though probably faithful to all the "saints," did not like Dr. Holden.

The system that Archdeacon Nouri represented lost its power because its claims exceeded all conceivableness, and because, in other respects, of its inertness to the obvious. The system that Dr. Holden represented is not different: there is the same seeing of whatever may be desirable, and the same profound meditations upon the remote, with the same inattention to fairly acceptable starting-points. The astronomers like to tell audiences of just what gases are burning in an unimaginably remote star, but have never reasonably made acceptable, for instance, that this earth is round, to start with. Of course I do not mean to say that this, or anything else, can be positively proved, but it is depressing to hear it said, so authoritatively, that the round shadow of this earth upon the moon proves that the earth is round, whereas records of angular shadows are common, and whereas, if this earth were a cube, its straight sides would cast a rounded shadow upon the convex moon. That the first part of a receding vessel to disappear should be the lower part may be only such an illusion of perspective as that by which railroad tracks seem to dip toward each other in the distance. Meteors sometimes appear over one part of the horizon and then seem to curve down behind the opposite part of the horizon, whereas they describe no such curve, because to a string of observers each observer is at the centre of the seeming curve.

Once upon a time — about the year 1870 — occurred an unusual sporting event. John Hampden, who was noted for his piety and his bad language, whose avowed purpose was to support the principles of this earth's earliest geodesist, offered to bet five hundred pounds that he could prove the flatness of this earth. Somewhere in England is the Bedford Canal, and, along a part of it, is a straight, unimpeded view, six miles in length. Orthodox doctrine — or the doctrine of the newer orthodoxy, because John Hampden considered that he was orthodox — is that the earth's curvature is expressible in the formula of 8 inches for the first mile and then the square of the distance times 8 inches. For two miles, then, the square of 2, or 4, times 8 inches. An object six miles away should be depressed 288 inches, or, allowing for refraction, according to Proctor (*Old and New Astronomy*), 216 inches. Hampden said that an object six miles away, upon this part of the Bedford Canal, was not depressed as it "should" be. Dr. Alfred Russell Wallace took up the bet. Mr. Walsh, Editor of the *Field*, was the stakeholder. A procession went to the Bedford Canal. Objects were looked at through telescopes, or looked for, and the decision was that Hampden had lost. There was rejoicing in the fold of the chosen, though Hampden, in one of his furious bombardments of verses from the *Bible*, charged conspiracy and malfeasance and confiscation, and what else I don't know, piously and intemperately declaring that he had been defrauded (Proctor, *Myths and Marvels of Astronomy*, 278; Wallace, *My Life: A Record of Events and Opinions*, 362).

In the *English Mechanic* (80, 40), some one writes to find out about the "Bedford Canal Experiment." We learn that the experiment had been made again. The correspondent writes that, if there were basis to the rumours that he had heard, there must be something wrong with the established doctrine. Upon page 138, Lady Blount answers — that, upon May 11, 1904, she had gone to the Bedford Canal, accompanied by Mr. E. Clifton, a well-known photographer, who was himself uninfluenced by her motives, which were the familiar ones of attempting to restore the old gentleman who first took up the study of geodesy. However, she seethes with neither piety nor profanity. She says that, with his telescopic camera, Mr. Clifton had photographed a sheet, six miles away, though by conventional theory the sheet should have been invisible. In a later number of the *English Mechanic* (80, 277), a reproduction of this photograph is published. According to this evidence this earth is flat, or is a sphere enormously greater than is generally supposed. But at the 1901 meeting of the British Association for the Advancement of Science, Mr. H. Yule Oldham read a paper upon his investigations at the Bedford Canal. He, too, showed photographs. In his photographs, everything that should have been invisible was invisible (*B.A. Rept.*, 1901, 725).

I accept that anybody who is convinced that still are there relics upon Mt. Ararat, has only to climb Mt. Ararat, and he must find something that can be said to be part of Noah's Ark, petrified perhaps. If someone else should be convinced that a mistake has been made, and that the mountain is really Pike's Peak, he has only to climb Pike's Peak and prove that the most virtuous of all lands was once the Holy Land. The meaning that I read in the whole subject is that, in this Dark Age that we're living in, not even such rudimentary matters as the shape of this earth have ever been investigated except now and then to support somebody's theory, because astronomers have instinctively preferred the remote and the not so easily understandable and the safe from external inquiry. In *Earth Features and Their Meaning* (12), Prof. William Herbert Hobbs says that this earth is top-shaped, quite as the sloping extremities of Africa and South America suggest. According to Prof. Hobbs, observations upon the pendulum suggest this earth is shaped like a "peg top." Some years ago, Dr. Gregory read a paper at a meeting of the Royal Geographical Society (*Geographical Journal*, 13, 225), giving data to support the theory of a top-shaped earth. In the records of the Society, one may read a report of the discussion that followed. There was no ridiculing. The President of the Society closed the discussion with virtual endorsement, recalling that it was Christopher Columbus who first said that this earth is top-shaped. For other expressions of this revolt against ancient dogmas, see *Bull. S.A.F.* (17, 315; 18, 143), *Popular Science News* (31, 234), *Eng. Mech.* (77, 159), and, *Sci. Amer.* (n.s., 100, 441).

As to the supposed motions of this earth, axial and orbital, circumstances are the same, despite the popular supposition that the existence of these motions has been established by syntheses of data and by unanswerable logic. All scientists, philosophers, religionists, are today looking back, wondering what could have been the matter with their predecessors to permit them to believe what they did believe. Granted that there will be posterity, we shall be predecessors. Then what is it that is conventionally taught today that will in the future seem as imbecilic as to all present orthodoxies seem the vapourings of preceding systems?

Well, for instance, that it is this earth that moves, though the sun seems to, by the same illusion by which to passengers on a boat, the shore seems to move, though it is the boat that is moving.

Apply this reasoning to the moon. The moon seems to move around the earth — but to passengers on a boat, the shore seems to move, whereas it is the boat that is moving — therefore the moon does not move.

As to the motions of the planets and stars that co-ordinate with the idea of a moving earth — they co-ordinate equally well with the idea of a stationary earth.

In the system that was conceived by Copernicus I find nothing that can be said to resemble foundation: nothing but the appeal of greater simplicity. An earth that rotates and revolves is simpler to conceive of than is a stationary earth with a rigid composition of stars, swinging around it, stars kept apart by some unknown substance, or inter-repulsion. But all those who think that simplification is a standard to judge by are referred to Herbert Spencer's compilations of data indicating that advancing knowledge complicates, making, then, complexity, and not simplicity, the standard by which to judge the more advanced. My own acceptance is that there are fluxes one way and then the other way: that the Ptolemaic system was complex and was simplified; that, out of what was once a clarification, new complications have arisen, and that again will come flux toward simplification or clarification — that the simplification by Copernicus has now developed into an incubus of unintelligibilities revolving around a farrago of inconsistencies, to which the complexities of Ptolemy are clear geometry: miracles, incredibilities, puerilities; tottering deductions depending upon flimsy agreements; brutalised observations that are slaves to infatuated principles —

And one clear call that is heard above the rumble of readjusting collapses — the call for a Neo-astronomy — it may not be our Neo-astronomy.

Prof. Young, for instance, in his *Manual of Astronomy* (136), says that there are no common, obvious proofs that the earth moves around the sun, but that there are three abstrusities, all of modern determination. Then, if Copernicus founded the present system, he founded upon nothing. He had nothing to base upon. He either never heard of, or could not detect one of these abstrusities. All his logic represented in his reasoning upon this earth's rotundity: that this earth is round, because of a general tendency to sphericity, manifesting, for instance, in fruits and in drops of water — showing that he must have been unaware not only of abstrusities, but of icicles and bananas and oysters. It is not that I am snobbishly deriding the humble and more than questionable ancestry of modern astronomy. I am pointing out that a doctrine came into existence with nothing for a foundation: not a datum, not one observation to found upon; no astronomical principles, no mechanical principles to justify it. Our inquiry will be as to how, in the annals of false architecture, it could ever be said that — except miraculously, of course — a foundation was subsequently slipped under this baseless structure, dug under, rammed under, or God knows how devised and fashioned.

CHAPTER 7

The three abstrusities:

The aberration of light, the annual parallax of the stars; and, the regular, annual shift of the lines of the stellar spectra.

By the aberration of light is meant a displacement of all stars, during a year's observation, by which stars near the pole of the ecliptic describe circles, stars that are nearer the ecliptic describe ellipses, and the stars of the ecliptic, only little straight lines. It is supposed that light has velocity, and that these forms represent the ratio between the velocity of light and the supposed velocity of this earth in its orbit. In the year 1725, Bradley conceived of the present orthodox explanation of the aberration-forms of the stars: that they reflect or represent the path that this earth traverses around the sun, as it would look from the stars, appearing virtually circular from stars in the pole of the ecliptic, for instance. In Bradley's day there were no definite delusions as to the traversing by this earth of another path in space, as part of a whole moving system, so Bradley felt simple and satisfied. About a century later by some of the most amusing reasoning that one could be entertained with, astronomers decided that the whole supposed solar system is moving, at a rate of about 13 miles per second from the region of Sirius to a point near Vega, all this occurring in northern skies, because southern astronomers had not very much to say at that time. Now, then, if at one time in the year, and in one part of its orbit, the earth is moving in the direction in which the whole solar system is moving, there we have this earth traversing a distance that is the sum of its own motion and the general motion; then when the earth rounds about and retraces, there we have its own velocity minus the general velocity. The first abstrusity, then, is knocked flat on its technicalities, because the aberration-forms, then, do not reflect the annual motion of this earth: if, in conventional terms, though the path of this earth is circular or elliptic relatively to the sun, when compounding with solar motion it is not so formed relatively to stars; and there will have to be another explanation for the aberration-forms.

The second supposed proof that this earth moves around the sun is in the parallax of the stars. In conventional terms, it is said that opposite points in this earth's orbit are 185,000,000 miles apart. It is said that stars, so differently viewed, are minutely displaced against their backgrounds. Again solar-motion — if, in conventional terms, this earth has been travelling, as part of the solar system, from Sirius, toward Vega, in 2,000 years this earth has travelled 819,936,000,000 miles. This distance is 4,500 times the distance that is the base line for orbital parallax. Then displacement of the stars by solar-motion parallax in 2,000 years, should be 4,500 times the displacement by orbital parallax, in one year. Give to orbital parallax as minute a quantity as is consistent with the claims made for it, and 4,500 times that would dent the Great Dipper and nick the Sickle of Leo, and perhaps make the Dragon look like a dragon. But not a star in the heavens has changed more than doubtfully since the stars were catalogued by Hipparchus, 2,000 years ago. If, then, there be minute displacements of stars that are attributed to orbital parallax, they will have to be explained in some other way, if evidently the sun does not move from Sirius toward Vega, and if then, quite as reasonably, this earth may not move.

Prof. Young's third "proof" is spectroscopic.

To what degree can spectroscopy in astronomy be relied upon? Bryant, *A History of Astronomy* (206):

That, according to Bélopolsky, Venus rotates in about 24 hours, as determined by the spectroscope; that, according to Dr. Slipher, Venus rotates in about 225 days, as determined by the spectroscope.

According to observations too numerous to make it necessary to cite any, the seeming motion of the stars, occulted by the moon, show that the moon has atmosphere. According to the spectroscope, there is no atmosphere upon the moon (*Publications of the Astronomical Society of the Pacific*, 6, no. 37, 228).

The ring of light around Venus, during the transits of 1874 and 1882, indicated that Venus has atmosphere. Most astronomers say that Venus has an atmosphere of extreme density, obscuring the features of the planet. According to spectrum analysis, by Sir William Huggins, Venus has no atmosphere (*Eng. Mech.*, 4, 23).

In the *English Mechanic* (89, 439) are published results of spectroscopic examinations of Mars, by Director Campbell, of the Lick Observatory: that there is no oxygen, and that there is no water vapour on Mars. In *Monthly Notices* (27, 178) are published results of spectroscopic examinations of Mars by Huggins: abundance of oxygen; same vapours as the vapours of this earth. These are the amusements of our Pilgrim's Progress, which has new San Salvadors for its goals, or new Plymouth Rocks for its expectations — but the experiences of pilgrims have variety —

In 1895, at the Allegheny Observatory, Prof. Keeler undertook to determine the rotation-period of Saturn's rings, by spectroscopy. It is gravitational gospel that particles upon the outside of the rings move at a rate of 10.69 miles a second; particles upon the inner edge, 13.01 miles a second. Prof. Keeler's determinations were what Sir Robert Ball calls "brilliant confirmation of the mathematical deductions" (*The Story of the Heavens*, rev. ed., 291). Prof. Keeler announced that according to the spectroscope, the outside particles of the rings of Saturn move at the rate of 10.1 miles a second, and that the inner particles move at a rate of 12.4 miles a second — "as they ought to," says Prof. Young, in his gospel, *Elements of Astronomy* (248; rev. ed., 256).

One reads of a miracle like this, the carrying out into decimals of different speeds of different particles in parts of a point of light, the parts of which cannot be seen at all without a telescope, whereby they seem to constitute a solid motionless structure, and one admires, or one worships, according to one's inexperience —

Or there comes upon one a sense of imposture and imposition that is not very bearable. Imposition or imposture or captivation — and it's as if we've been trapped and have been put into a revolving cage, some of the bars revolving at unthinkable speed, and other bars of it going around still faster, even though not conceivable. Disbelieve as we will, deride and accuse, and think of all the other false demonstrations that we have encountered, as we will — there's a buzz of the bars that encircle us. The concoction that has caged us is one of the most brilliant harlots in modern prostitution: we're imprisoned at the pleasure of a favourite in the harem of the God of Gravitation. That's some relief: language always is — but how are we to "determine" that the rings of Saturn do not move as they "ought" to, and thereby add more to the discrediting of spectroscopy in astronomy?

A gleam on a planet that's like shine on a sword to deliver us —

The White Spot of Saturn —

A bright and shining deliverer.

There's a gleam that will shatter concoctions and stop velocities. There's a shining thing on the planet Saturn, and the blow that it shines is lightning. Thus far has gone a revolution of 10.1 miles a second, but it stops by magic against magic; no farther buzzes a revolution of 12.4 miles a second — that the rings of Saturn may not move as, to flatter one little god they "ought" to, because, by the handiwork of Universality, they may be motionless.

Often has a white spot been seen upon the rings of Saturn: by Schmidt, Bond, Secchi, Schroeter, Harding, Schwabe, De Vico — a host of astronomers.

It is stationary.

In the *English Mechanic* (49, 195), Thomas Gwyn Elger publishes a sketch of it as he saw it upon the nights of April 18 and 20, 1889. It occupied a position partly upon one ring and partly upon the other, showing no distortion. Let Prof. Keeler straddle two concentric merry-go-rounds, whirling at different velocities: there will be distortion. See vol. 49, *English Mechanic*, for observation after observation by astronomers upon this appearance, when seen for several months in the year 1889, the observers agreeing that, no matter what are the demands of theory, this fixed spot did indicate that the rings of Saturn do not move.

The White Spot on Saturn has blasted minor magic. He has little, black retainers who now function in the cause of completeness — the little, black spots of Saturn —

Nature (53, 109):

That, in July and August, 1895, Prof. A. Mascari, of the Catania Observatory, had seen dark spots upon the crepe ring of Saturn. The writer in *Nature* says that such duration is not easy to explain, if the rings of Saturn be formations of moving particles, because different parts of the discoloured areas would have different velocities, so that soon would they distort and diffuse.

Certainly enough, relatively to my purpose, which is to find out for myself, and to find out with anybody else who may be equally impressed with a necessity, a brilliant, criminal thing has been slain by a gleam of higher intensity. Certainly enough, then, with the execution of one of its foremost exponents, the whole subject of spectroscopy in astronomy has been cast into rout and disgrace, of course only to ourselves, and not in view of manufacturers of spectroscopes, for instance; but a phantom thing dies a phantom death, and must be slain over and over again.

I should say that just what is called the spectrum of a star is not commonly understood. It is one of the great uncertainties in science. The spectrum of a star is a ghost in the first place, but this ghost has to be further attenuated by a secondary process, and the whole appearance trembles so with the twinkling of a star that the stories told by spectra are gasps of palsied phantoms. So it is that, in one of the greatest indefinitenesses in science, an astronomer reads in a bewilderment that can be made to correspond with any desideratum. So it is our acceptance that when any faint, tremulous story told by a spectrum becomes standardised, the conventional astronomer is told, by the spectroscope, what he should be told, but that when anything new appears, for which there is no convention, the bewilderment of the astronomers is made apparent, and the worthlessness of spectroscopy in astronomy is shown to all except those who do not want to be shown. At the end of January, 1892, Dr. Thomas D. Anderson, of Edinburgh, discovered a new star that became known as Nova Aurigae (*Nature*, 45, 365). Here was something as to which there was no dogmatic "determination." Each astronomer had to see, not what he should, but what he could. We shall see that the astronomers might as well have gone, for information, to some of Mrs. Piper's "controls" as to think of depending upon their own ghosts.

In *Monthly Notices* (53, 272), it is said that probably for seven weeks, up to the time of calculation, one part of this new star had been receding at a rate of 230 miles a second, and another part approaching at a rate of 320 miles a second, giving to these components a distance apart of 550 miles x 60 x 60 x 24 x 49, whatever that may be.

But there was another séance. This time Dr. Vogel was the medium. The ghosts told Dr. Vogel that the new star had three parts: one approaching this earth at a rate of about 420 miles a second, another approaching at a rate of 22 miles a second, a third part receding at a rate of 300 miles a second. See *Jour. B.A.A.* (2, 258).

After that, the "controls" became hysterical. They flickered that there were six parts of this new star, according to Dr. Lowell's *Evolution of Worlds* (9). The faithful will be sorry to read that Lowell revolted. He says: "There is not room for so many on the stage of the cosmic drama." For other reasons for repudiating spectroscopy, or spiritualism, in astronomy, read what else Lowell says upon this subject.

Nova Aurigae became fainter. Accordingly, Prof. Klinkerfues "found" that two bodies had passed, and had inflamed each other, and that the light of their mutual disturbances would soon disappear (*Jour. B.A.A.*, 2, 365).

Nova Aurigae became brighter. Accordingly, Dr. Campbell "determined" that it was approaching this earth at a rate of 128 miles a second (*Jour. B.A.A.*, 2, 504).

Then Dr. Espin went into a trance. It was revealed to him that the object was a nebula (*Eng. Mech.*, 56, 61). Communication from Dr. and Mrs. Huggins, to the Royal Society — not a nebula, but a star (*Eng. Mech.*, 57, 397). See *Nature* (47: 352, 425) — that, according to M. Eugen Gothard the spectrum of N.A. agreed "perfectly" with the spectrum of a nebula: that, according to Dr. Huggins, no contrast could be more striking than the difference between the spectrum of N.A., and the spectrum of a nebula.

For an account of the revelations at Stonyhurst Observatory, see *Memoirs of the Royal Astronomical Society* (51, 29) — that there never had been a composition of bodies moving at the rates that were so definitely announced, because N.A. was a single star.

Though I have read some of the communications from "Rector" and "Dr. Phinuit" to Mrs. Piper, I cannot think that they ever mouthed sillier babble than was flickered by the star-ghosts to the astronomers in the year 1892. We noted Prof. Klinkerfues' "finding" that two stars had passed each other and that the illumination from their mutual perturbations would soon subside. There was no such disappearance. For observations upon N.A., ten years later, see *Monthly Notices* (62, 65). For Prof. Barnard's observations twenty years later, see *Scientific American Supplement* (76, 154).

The spectroscope is useful in a laboratory. Spoons are useful in a kitchen. If any other pilgrim should come across a group of engineers trying to dig a canal with spoons, his experience and his temptation to linger would be like ours as to the astronomers and their attempted application of the spectroscope. I don't know what of remotest acceptability may survive in the third supposed proof that this earth moves around the sun, though we have not found it necessary to go into the technicalities of the supposed proof. I think we have killed the phantom thing, but I hope we have not quite succeeded, because we are moved more by the aesthetics of slaughter than by plain murderousness: we shall find unity in disposing of the third "proof" by the means by which the two others were disposed of —

Regular Annual Shift of Spectral Lines versus Solar Motion —

That, if this earth moves around the sun, the shift might be found by scientific Mrs. Pipers so to indicate —

But that if part of the time this earth, as a part of one travelling system, moves at a rate of 19 plus 13 miles a second and then part of the time at a rate of 19 minus 13 miles a second, compounding with great complexities at transverse times, that is the end of the regular annual shift that is supposed to apply to orbital motion.

We need not have admitted in the first place that the three abstrusities are resistances: however, we have a liking for revelations ourselves. Aberration and Parallax and Spectral Lines do not indicate that this earth moves relatively to the stars: quite as convincingly they indicate that the stars in one composition gyrate relatively to a central and stationary earth, all of them in one concavity around this earth, some of them showing faintest of parallax, if this earth be not quite central to the revolving whole.

Something that I did not mention before, though I referred to Lowell's statements, is that astronomers now admit, or state, that the shift of spectral lines, which they say indicates that this earth moves around the sun, also indicates any one of three other circumstances, or sets of circumstances. Some persons will ask why I didn't say so at first and quit the meaningless subject. May be it was a weakness of mine — something of a sporting instinct, I fear me, I have at times. I lingered, perhaps slightly intoxicated, with the deliciousness of Prof. Keeler and his decimals — like someone at a race track, determining that a horse is running at a rate of 2653 feet and 4 inches a minute, by a method that means no more than it means that the horse is brown, is making clattering sounds, or has a refreshing odour. For a study of a state of mind like that of many clergymen who try to believe in Moses, and in Darwin, too, see the works of Prof. Young, for instance. This astronomer teaches the conventional spectroscopic doctrine, and also mentions the other circumstances that make the doctrine meaningless. Such inconsistencies are phenomena of all transitions from the old to the new.

Three giants have appeared against us. Their hearts are bubbles. Their bones wilt. They are weak Caryatides that uphold the phantom structure of Paleo-astronomy. By what miracle, we asked, could foundation be built subsequently under a baseless thing. But three ghosts can fit in anywhere.

Sometimes astronomers cite the Foucault pendulum-experiment as "proof" of the motions of this earth. The circumstances of this demonstration are not easily made clear: consequently one of normal suspiciousness is likely to let it impose upon him. But my practical and commonplace treatment is to disregard what the experiment and its complexities are, and to enquire whether it works out or not. It does not. See *Amer. Jour. Sci.* (s. 2, 12, 402), *Eng. Mech.* (93: 293, 306, 335), *Astronomical Register* (2, 265), and *Popular Astronomy* (12, 71). Also we are told that experiments upon falling bodies have proved this earth's rotation. I get so tired of demonstrating that there never has been any Evolution mentally, except as to ourselves, that, if I could, I'd be glad to say that these experiments work out beautifully. Maybe they do. See Proctor's *Old and New Astronomy* (229).

CHAPTER 8

It is supposed that astronomic subjects and principles and methods can not be understood by the layman. I think this, myself. We shall take up some of the principles of astronomy, with the idea of expressing that of course they can not be understood by the unhypnotized any more than the stories of Noah's Ark and Jonah and the Whale be understood, but that our understanding, if we have any, will have some material for its exercises, just the same. The velocity of light is one of these principles. A great deal in the astronomic system depends on the supposed velocity: determinations of distance, and the amount of aberration depend. It will be our expression that these are ratios of impositions to mummeries, with such clownish products that formulas turn into antics, and we shall have scruples against taking up the subject at all, because we have much hard work to do, and we have qualms against stopping so often to amuse ourselves. But, then, sometimes in a more sentimental mood, I think that the pretty story of the velocity of light, and its "determination," will some day be of legitimate service; be rhymed some day, and told to children, in future kindergartens, replacing the story of Little Bo-peep, with the tale of a planet that lost its satellites and sometimes didn't know where to find them, but that good magicians came along and formulated the indeterminable.

It was found by Roemer, a seventeenth-century astronomer, that, at times, the moons of Jupiter did not disappear behind him, and did not emerge from behind him, when they "should." He found that as distance between this earth and Jupiter increased, the delays increased. He concluded that these delays represented times consumed by the light of the moons in travelling greater distances. He found, or supposed he found, that when this earth is farthest from Jupiter, light from a satellite is seen 22 minutes later than when nearest Jupiter. Given measurement of the distance between opposite points in the earth's supposed orbit, and times consumed in travelling this distance — there you have the velocity of light.

I still say that it is a pretty story and should be rhymed; but we shall find that astronomers might as well try to formulate the gambols of the sheep of Little Bo-peep, as to try to formulate anything depending upon the satellites of Jupiter.

In the *Annals of Philosophy* (n.s., 7, 29), Col. Beaufoy writes that, upon Dec. 7, 1823, he looked for the emergence of Jupiter's third satellite, at the time set down in the *Nautical Almanac and Astronomical Ephemeris*: for two hours he looked, and did not see the satellite emerge. In *Monthly Notices* (44, 8), an astronomer writes that, upon the night of Oct. 15, 1883, one of the satellites of Jupiter was forty-six minutes late. A paper was read at the meeting of the British Astronomical Association, Feb. 8, 1907, upon a satellite that was twenty minutes late. In *Telescopic Work for Starlight Evenings* (1st ed., 191), W.F. Denning writes that, upon the night of Sept. 12, 1889, he and two other astronomers could not see satellite IV at all. See the *Observatory* (9, 237) — satellite IV disappeared 15 minutes before calculated time; about a minute later it re-appeared; disappeared again; re-appeared nine minutes later. For Todd's observations, see the *Observatory* (2, 226) — four times, between June 9 and July 21, 1878, a satellite was visible when, according to prediction, it should have been invisible. For some more instances of extreme vagaries of these satellites, see *Monthly Notices* (43, 427) and *Jour. B.A.A.* (14, 25): observations by Noble, Turner, White, Holmes, Freeman, Goodacre, Ellis, and Molesworth. In periodical astronomical publications, there is no more easily findable material for heresy than such observations. We shall have other instances. They abound in *English Mechanic*, for instance. But, in spite of a host of such observations, Prof. Young (*The Sun*, rev. ed., 35) says that the time occupied by light coming from these satellites is doubtful by "fractions of a second." It is of course another instance of the astronomers who know very little of astronomy.

It would be undignified, if the astronomers had taken the sheep of Little Bo-peep for their determinations. They took the satellites of Jupiter. They said that the velocity of light is about 190,000 miles a second.

So did the physicists.

Our own notion is that there is no velocity of light: that one sees a thing, or doesn't; that if the satellites of Jupiter behave differently according to proximity to this earth, that may be because this earth affects them, so affecting them, because the planets may not, as we may find, be at a thousandth part of the "demonstrated" distances. The notion of velocity of light finds support, we are told in the text-books, in the velocity of sound. If it does, it doesn't find support in gravitational effects, because, according to the same text-books, gravitational effects have no velocity.

The physicists agreed with the astronomers. A beam of light is sent through, and is reflected back through, a revolving shutter — but it's complex, and we're simple: we shall find that there is no need to go into the details of this mechanism. It is not that a machine is supposed to register a velocity of 186,000 miles a second, or we'd have to be technical: it is that the eye is supposed to perceive —

And there is not a physicist in the world who can perceive when a parlour magician palms off playing-cards. Hearing, or feeling, or if one could smell light, some kind of a claim might be made — but the well-known limitations of seeing; common knowledge of little boys that a brand waved about in the dark cannot be followed by the eyes. The limit of the perceptible is said to be ten changes a second.

I think of the astronomers as occupying a little vortex of their own in the cosmic swoon in which wave all things, at least in this one supposed solar system. Call it swoon, or call it hypnosis — but that it is never absolute, and that all of us sometimes have awareness of our condition, and moments of wondering what it's all about and why we do and think the things that sometimes we wake up and find ourselves doing and thinking. Upon page 281, *Old and New Astronomy*, Richard Proctor wakens momentarily, and says: "The agreement between these results seems close enough, but those who know the actual difficulty of precise time-observations of the phenomena of Jupiter's satellites, to say nothing of the present condition of the theory of their motions, can place very little reliance on the velocity of light deduced from such observations." Upon pages 603-607, Proctor reviews some observations other than those that I have listed — satellites that have disappeared, come back, disappeared, returned again so bewilder-ingly that he wrote what we have quoted — observations by Gorton, Wray, Gambart, Secchi, Main, Grover, Smyth-Maclean-Pearson, Hodgson, Carlisle, Siminton. And that is the last of his awareness: Proctor then swoons back into his hypnosis. He then takes up the determination of the velocity of light by the physicists, as if they can be relied upon, accepting every word, writing his gospel, glorying in this miracle of science. I call it a tainted agreement between the physicists and astronomers. I prefer mild language. If by a method by which nothing can be found out, the astronomers determined that the velocity of light is about 190,000 miles a second, and if the physicists by another method found about the same result, what kind of harmony can that be other than the reekings of two consistent stenches? Proctor wrote that very little reliance could be placed upon anything depending upon Jupiter's satellites. It never occurred to him to wonder by what miracle the physicists agreed with these unreliable calculations. It is the situation that repeats in the annals of astronomy — a baseless thing that is supposed to have a foundation slipped under it, wedged in, or God knows how introduced or foisted. I prefer not to bother much with asking how the physicists could determine anything of a higher number of changes than ten per second. If it be accepted that the physicists are right, the question is — by what miracle were the astronomers right, if they had "very little" to rely upon?

Determinations of planetary distances and determinations of the velocity of light have squirmed together: they represent either an agreeable picture of co-operation, or a study in mutual support by writhing infamies. With most emphasis I have taken the position that the vagaries of the Jovian satellites are so great that extremely little reliance can be placed upon them, but now it seems to me that the emphasis should be upon the admission that, in addition to these factors of indeterminateness, it was, up to Proctor's day, not known with anything like accuracy when the satellites should appear and disappear. In that case one wonders as to the state of the theory in Roemer's day. It was in the mind of Roemer that the two "determinations" we are now considering first most notably satisfied affinity: mutual support by velocity of light and distances in this supposed solar system. Upon his Third Law, which, as we shall see later, he constructed upon at least three absences of anything to build upon, Kepler had, upon observations of Mars, deduced 13,000,000 miles as this earth's distance from the sun. By the same method, which is the now discredited method of simultaneous observations, Roemer determined this distance to be 82,000,000 miles. I am not concerned with this great discrepancy so much as with the astronomers' reasons for starting off distances in millions instead of hundreds or thousands of miles.

In Kepler's day the strongest objection urged against the Copernican system was that, if this earth moves around the sun, the stars should show annual displacements — and it is only under modern "refinements" that the stars do so minutely vary, perhaps. The answer to this objection was that the stars are vastly farther away than was commonly supposed. Entailed by this answer was the necessity of enlarging upon common suppositions generally. Kepler determined or guessed, just as one pleases, and then Roemer outdid him. Roemer was followed by Huygens, with continued outdoing: 100,000,000 according to Huygens. Huygens took for his basis his belief that this earth is intermediate in size to Mars and Venus. Astronomers, to-day, say that this earth is not so intermediate. We see that, in the secondary phase of development, the early astronomers, with no means of knowing whether the sun is a thousand or a million miles away, guessed or determined such distances as 82,000,000 miles and 100,000,000 miles, to account for the changelessness of the stars. If the mean of the extremes is about the distance of present dogmas, we'd like to know by what miracle a true distance so averages two products of wild methods. Our expression is that these developments had their origin in conspiracy and prostitution, if one has a fancy for such accusations; or, if everybody else has been so agreeable, we think more amiably, ourselves, that it was all a matter of comfortably adjusting and being obliging all around. Our expression is that ever since the astronomers have seen and have calculated as they should see and should calculate. For instance, when this earth's distance from the sun was supposed to be 95,000,000 miles, all astronomers taking positions of Mars calculated a distance of 95,000,000 miles; but then, when the distance was cut down to about 92,000,000 miles, all astronomers, taking positions of Mars, calculated about a distance of 92,000,000 miles. It may sound like a cynicism of mine, but in saying this I am quoting Richard Proctor, in one of his lucid suspicions (*Old and New Astronomy*, 280).

With nothing but monotony, and with nothing that looks like relief for us, the data of conspiracy, or of co-operation, continue. Upon worthless observations upon the transits of Venus, 1761 and 1769, this earth's orbit was found by Encke to be about 190,000,000 miles across (distance of the sun about 95,000,000 miles). Altogether progress had been made toward the wild calculations of Huygens than toward the undomesticated calculations of Roemer. So, to agree with this change, if not progress, Delambre, taking worthless observations upon the satellites of Jupiter, cut down Roemer's worthless determinations, and announced that light crosses the plane of this earth's orbit in 16 minutes and 32 seconds — as it ought to, Prof. Young would say. It was then that the agreeably tainted physicists started spinning and squinting, calculating "independently," we are told, that Delambre was right. Everything settled — everybody comfortable — see Chambers' *Handbook of Astronomy*, published at this time — that the sun's distance had been ascertained, "with great accuracy," to be 95,298,260 miles —

But then occurred something that is badly, but protectively, explained, in most astronomical works. Foucault interfered with the deliciousness of those 95,298,260 miles. One may read many books that mention this subject, and one will always read that Foucault, the physicist, by an "independent" method, or by an "absolutely independent" method, disagreed somewhat. The "disagreement" is paraded so that one has the impression of painstaking, independent scientists not utterly slavishly supporting one another, but at the same time keeping well over the 90,000,000 mark, and so essentially agreeing, after all. But we find that there was no independence in Foucault's "experiments." We come across the same old disgusting connivance, or the same amiable complaisance, perhaps. See Clerke's *History of Astronomy* (4th ed., 230). We learn that astronomers, to explain oscillations of the sun, had decided that the sun must be, not 95,298,260 miles away, but about 91,000,000. To oblige them, perhaps, or innocently, never having heard of them, perhaps, though for ten years they had been announcing that a new determination was needed, Foucault "found" that the velocity of light is less than had been necessary to suppose, when the sun was supposed to be about 95,000,000 miles away, and he "found" the velocity to be exactly what it should be, supposing the sun to be 91,000,000 miles away. Then it was that the astronomers announced, not that they had cut down the distance of the sun because of observations upon solar oscillations, but because they had been very much impressed by the "independent" observations upon the velocity of light, by Foucault, the physicist. This squirm occurred at the meeting of the Royal Astronomical Society, February, 1864. There would have to be more squirms. If, then, the distance across this earth's orbit was "found" to be less than Delambre had supposed, somebody would have to find that light comes from the satellites of Jupiter a little slower than Delambre had "proved." Whereupon Glasenapp "found" that the time is 16 minutes and 40 seconds, which is what he should, or "ought to," find. Whereupon, there would have to be re-adjustment of Encke's calculations of distance of sun, upon worthless observations upon transits of Venus. And whereupon again, Newcomb went over the very same observations by which Encke had compelled agreement with the dogmas of his day, and Newcomb calculated, as was required, that the distance agreed with Foucault's reduction. Whether, in the first place, Encke ever did calculate, as he said he did, or not, his determination was mere agreement with Laplace's in the seventh book of *Traité de Mécanique Céleste*. Of course he said that he had calculated independently, because his method was by triangulation, and Laplace's was the gravitational.

That the word "worthless" does apply to observations upon transits of Venus:

In *Old and New Astronomy*, Proctor says that the observations upon the transits of 1761 and 1769 were "altogether unsatisfactory." One supposes that anything that is altogether unsatisfactory can't be worth much. In the next transit, of 1874, various nations co-operated. The observations were so disappointing that the Russian, Italian, and Austrian governments refused to participate in the expeditions of 1882. In *Reminiscences of an Astronomer* (178), Newcomb says that the United States Commission, of which he was Secretary, had, up to 1902 never published its observations, and probably never would, because by that time all other members were either dead or upon the retired list.

Method of Mars — more monotony — because of criticisms of the taking of parallax by simultaneous observations, Dr. David Gill went to the Island of Ascension, during the opposition of Mars of 1877, to determine alone, by the diurnal method, the distance of this earth from the sun, from positions of Mars. For particulars of Gill's method, see, for instance, Poor's *Solar System* (85). Here Prof. Poor says that, of course, the orbital motion of Mars had to be allowed for, in Gill's calculations. If so, then of course this earth's orbital motion had to be allowed for. If Dr. Gill knew the space traversed by this earth in its orbit, and the curvature of its path, he knew the size and shape of the orbit, and consequently the distance from the sun. Then he took for the basis of his allowance that this earth is about 93,000,000 miles from the sun, and calculated that this earth is about 93,000,000 miles from the sun. For this classic deduction from the known to the same known, he received a gold medal.

In our earlier surveys, we were concerned with the false claim that there can be application of celestial mechanics to celestial phenomena; but, as to later subjects, the method is different. The method of all these calculations is triangulation.

One simple question:

To what degree can triangulation be relied upon?

To great degree in measuring the height of a building, or in little distances of a surveyor's problems. It is clear enough that astronomers did not invent the telescope. They adopted the spectroscope from another science. Their primary mathematical principle of triangulation they have taken from the surveyors, to whom it is serviceable. The triangle is another emblem of the sterility of the science of astronomy. Upon the coat of arms of this great mule of the sciences, I would draw a prism within a triangle.

CHAPTER 9

According to Prof. Newcomb, for instance, the distance of the sun is about 380 times the distance of the moon — as determined by triangulation. But upon page 22, *Popular Astronomy*, Newcomb tells of another demonstration, with strikingly different results — as determined by triangulation.

A split god.

The god Triangulation is not one undivided deity.

The other method with strikingly different results is the method of Aristarchus. It cuts down the distance of the sun, from 380 to 20 times the distance of the moon. When an observer upon this earth sees the moon half-illuminated, the angle at the moon, between observer and sun, is a right angle; a third line between observer and sun completes a triangle. According to Aristarchus, the tilt of the third line includes an angle of 87 degrees, making the sun-earth line 20 times longer than the moon-earth line.

"In principle," says Newcomb, "the method is quite correct, and very ingenious, but cannot be applied in practice." He says that Aristarchus measured wrong; that the angle between the moon-earth line and the earth-sun line is almost 90 degrees and not 87 degrees. Then he says that the method can not be applied because no one can determine this angle that he said is of almost 90 degrees. He says a something that is so incongruous with the inflations of astronomers that they'd sizzle if their hypnotised readers could read and think at the same time. Newcomb says that the method of Aristarchus can not be applied because no astronomer can determine when the moon is half-illumined.

We have had some experience.

Does anybody who has been through what we've been through suppose that there is a Prof. Keeler in the world who would not declare that trigonometrically and spectroscopically and micrometrically he had determined the exact moment and exasperating, or delightful, decimal of a moment of semi-illumination of the moon, were it not that, according to at least as good a mathematician as he, determination based upon that demonstration does show that the sun is only 20 times as far away as the moon? But suppose we agree that this simple thing can not be done.

Then instantly we think of some of the extravagant claims with which astronomers have stuffed supine credulities. Crawling in their unsightly confusion that sickens for simplification, is this offense to harmony:

That astronomers can tell under which Crusade, or its decimalated moment, a shine left a star, but cannot tell when a shine reaches a line on the moon —

Glory and triumph and selectness and inflation — or that we shall have renown as evangelists, spreading the homely and whole-some doctrine of humility. Hollis, in *Chats on Astronomy* (199), tells us that the diameter of this earth, at the equator, is 41,851,160 feet. But blessed be the meek, we tell him. In the *Observatory* (19, 116) is published the determination, by the astronomer Brenner, of the time of rotation of Venus, as to which other astronomers differ by hundreds of days. According to Brenner, the time is 23 hours, 57 minutes, and 7.5459 seconds. I do note that this especial refinement is a little too ethereal for the Editor of the *Observatory*: he hopes Brenner will pardon him, but is it necessary to carry out the finding to the fourth decimal place of a second? However, I do not mean to say that all astronomers are as refined as Brenner, for instance. In the *Jour. B.A.A.* (1, 382), Edwin Holmes, perhaps coarsely, expresses some views. He says that such "extreme accuracy" as Captain Noble's in writing that the diameter of Neptune is 38,133 miles and that of Uranus is 33,836 miles is bringing science into contempt, because very little is known of these planets; that according to Neison, these diameters are 27,000 miles and 28,500 miles. MacPherson, in *A Century's Progress in Science*, quotes Prof. Serviss: that the average parallax of a star, which is an ordinary astronomic quantity, is "about equal to the apparent distance between two pins, place one inch apart, and viewed from a distance of one hundred and eighty miles." Stick pins in a cushion, in New York — go to Saratoga and look at them — be overwhelmed with the more than human powers of the scientifically anointed — or ask them when shines half the moon.

The moon's surface is irregular. I do not say that anybody with brains enough to know when he had half a shoe polished should know when the sun had half the moon shined. I do say that if this simple thing can not be known, the crowings of astronomers as to enormously more difficult determination are mere barnyard disturbances.

Triangulation that, according to his little priests, straddles orbits and on his apex wears a star — that he's a false Colossus; shrinking, at the touch of data, back from the stars, deflating below the sun and moon; stubbing down below the clouds of this earth, so that the different stories that he told to Aristarchus and to Newcomb are the conflicting vainglories of an earth-tied squatter —

The blow that crumples a god:

That, by triangulation, there is not an astronomer in the world who can tell the distance of a thing only five miles away.

Humboldt, *Cosmos* (v. 5, 138):

Height of Mauna Loa: 18,410 feet, according to Cook; 16,611, according to Marchand; 13,761, according to Wilkes — according to triangulation.

In the *Scientific American* (n.s., 119, 31), a mountain climber calls the Editor to account for having written that Mt. Everest is 29,002 feet high. He says that, in his experience, there is always an error of at least ten per cent, in calculating the height of a mountain, so that all that can be said is that Mt. Everest is between 26,100 and 31,900 feet high. In the *Scientific American* (n.s., 102: 183, 319), Miss Annie Peck cites two measurements of a mountain in India: they differ by 4,000 feet.

The most effective way of treating this subject is to find a list of measurements of a mountain's height before the mountain was climbed, and compare with the barometric determination, when the mountain was climbed. For a list of seven measurements, by triangulation, of the height of Mt. St. Elias, see the *Alpine Journal* (22, 150): they vary from 12,672 to 19,500 feet. D'Abruzzi climbed Mt. St. Elias, July 31, 1897. See a paper in the *Alpine Journal* (19, 125). D'Abruzzi barometric determination — 18,092 feet.

Suppose that, in measuring, by triangulation, the distance of anything five miles away, the error is, say, ten per cent. But, as to anything ten miles away, there is no knowing what the error would be. By triangulation, the moon has been "found" to be 240,000 miles away. It may be 240 miles or 240,000,000 miles away.

CHAPTER 10

Pseudo heart of a phantom thing — it is Keplerism, pulsating with Sir Isaac Newton's regularisations.

If triangulation can not be depended upon accurately to measure distance greater than a mile or two between objects and observers, the aspects of Keplerism that depend upon triangulation should be of no more concern to us than two pins in a cushion 180 miles away: nevertheless so affected by something like seasickness are we by the wobbling deductions of the conventionalists that we shall have direct treatment, or independent expressions, whenever we can have, or seem to have, them. Kepler saw a planetary system, and he felt that, if that system could be formulated in terms of proportionality, by discovering one of the relations quantitatively, all of its measurements could be deduced. I take from Newcomb, in *Popular Astronomy* (1st ed., 79; 2nd ed., 80), that, in Kepler's view, there was a system in the arrangement and motions of the four little traitors that sneak around Jupiter; that Kepler, with no suspicions of these little betrayers, reasoned that this central body and its accompaniments were a representation, upon a small scale, of the solar system, as a whole. Kepler found that the cubes of mean distances of neighbouring satellites of Jupiter, divided by the squares of their times, gave the same quotients. He reasoned that the same relations subsisted among planets, if the solar system be only an enlargement of the Jovian system.

Observatory (43, 431): "The discordances between theory and observation (as to the motions of Jupiter's satellites) are of such magnitude that continued observations of the precise moments of eclipses are much to be desired." In the Report of the Jupiter Section of the British Astronomical Society (*Memoirs of the British Astronomical Association*, 8, 83) is a comparison between observed times and calculated times of these satellites. Sixty-six observations, in the year 1899, are listed. In one instance prediction and observation agree. Many differences of three or four minutes are noted, and there are differences of five or six minutes.

Kepler formulated his law of proportionality between times and distances of Jupiter's satellites without knowing what the times are. It should be noted that the observations in the year 1899 took into consideration fluctuations that were discovered by Roemer, long after Kepler's time.

Just for the sake of having something that looks like opposition, let us try to think that Kepler was miraculously right anyway. Then, if something that may resemble Kepler's Third Law does subsist in the Jovian satellites that were known to Kepler, by what resemblance to logicality can that proportionality extend to the whole solar system, if a solar system can be supposed?

In the year 1892, a fifth satellite of Jupiter was discovered. Maybe it would conform to Kepler's law, if anybody could find out accurately in what time the faint speck does revolve. The sixth and seventh satellites of Jupiter revolve so eccentrically that, in line of sight, their orbits intersect. Their distances are subject to very great variations; but, inasmuch as it might be said that their mean distances do conform to Kepler's Third Law, or would, if anybody could find out what their mean distances are, we go on to the others. The eighth and ninth conform to nothing that can be asserted. If one of them goes around in one orbit at one time, the next time around it goes in some other orbit and in some other plane. Inasmuch then as Kepler's Third Law, deduced from the system of Jupiter's satellites, can not be thought to extend even within that minor system, one's thoughts stray into wondering what two pins in a cushion in Louisville, Ky., look like from somewhere up in the Bronx, rather than to dwell any more upon extension of any such pseudo-proportionality to the supposed solar system, as a whole.

It seems that in many of Kepler's demonstrations was this failure to have grounds for a starting-point, before extending his reasoning. He taught the doctrine of the music of the spheres, and assigned bass voices to Saturn and Jupiter, then tenor to Mars, contralto to the female planet, and soprano, or falsetto, rather, to little Mercury. And that is all very well and consistently worked out in detail, and it does seem reasonable that, if ponderous, if not lumpy, Jupiter does sing bass, the other planets join in, according to sex and huskiness — however, one does feel dissatisfied.

We have dealt with Newcomb's account. But other convention-alists say that Kepler worked out his Third Law by triangulation upon

Venus and Mercury, when at greatest elongation, "finding" that the relation between Mercury and Venus is the same as the relation between Venus and this earth. If, according to conventionalists, there was no "proof" that this earth moves, in Kepler's time, Kepler started by assuming that this earth moves between Venus and Mars; he assumed that the distance of Venus from the sun, at greatest elongation, represents mean distance; he assumed that observations upon Mercury indicated Mercury's orbit, an orbit that to this day defies analysis. However, for the sake of seeming to have opposition, we shall try to think that Kepler's data did give him material for the formulation of his law. His data were chiefly the observations of Tycho Brahé. But, by the very same data, Tycho had demonstrated that this earth does not move between Venus and Mars; that this earth is stationary. That stoutest of conventionalists, but at the same time seeming colleague of ours, Richard Proctor, says that Tycho Brahé's system was consistent with all data. I have never heard of an astronomer who denies this. Then the heart of modern astronomy is not Keplerism, but is one diversion of data that beat for such a monstrosity as something like Siamese Twins, serving both Keplerism and the Tychonic system. I fear that some of our attempts to find opposition are not very successful.

So far, this medieval doctrine, restricting to times and distances, though for all I know the planets sing proportionately as well as move proportionately, has data to interpret or to misinterpret. But, when it comes to extending Kepler's Third Law to the exterior planets, I have never read of any means that Kepler had of determining their proportional distances. He simply said that Mars and Jupiter and Saturn were at distances that proportionalised with their times. He argued, reasonably enough, perhaps, that the slower-moving planets are the remoter, but that has nothing to do with proportional remoteness.

This is the pseudo heart of phantom astronomy.

To it Sir Isaac Newton gave a seeming of coherence.

I suspect that it was not by chance that the story of an apple should so importantly appear in two mythologies. The story of Newton and the apple was first told by Voltaire. One has suspicions of Voltaire's meanings. Suppose Newton did see an apple fall to the ground, and was so inspired, or victimized, into conceiving in terms of universal attraction. But had he tried to take a bone away from a dog, he would have had another impression and would have been quite as well justified in explaining in terms of universal repulsion. If, as to all inter-acting things, electric, biologic, psychologic, economic, socio-logic, magnetic, chemic, as well as canine, repulsion is as much of a determinant as is attraction, the Law of Gravitation, which is an attempt to explain in terms of attraction only, is as false as would be dogmas upon all other subjects if couched in terms of attraction only. So it is that the law of gravitation has been a rule of chagrin and fiasco. So, perhaps accepting, or passionately believing in every symbol of it, a Dr. Adams calculates that the Leonids will appear in November, 1899 — but chagrin and fiasco — the Leonids do not appear. The planet Neptune was not discovered mathematically, because, though it was in the year 1846, somewhere near the position of the formula, in the year 1836 or 1856, it would have been nowhere near the orbit calculated by Leverrier and Adams. Some time ago, against the clamour that a Trans-Uranian planet had been discovered mathema-tically, it was our suggestion that, if this be not a myth, let the astronomer now discover the Trans-Neptunian planet mathematically. That there is no such mathematics, in the face of any number of learned treatises, is far more strikingly betrayed by those shining little misfortunes, the satellites of Jupiter. Satellite after satellite of Jupiter was discovered, but by accident or by observation, and not once by calculation: never were the perturbations of the earlier known satellites made the material for deducing the positions of other satellites. Astronomers have pointed to the sky, and there has been nothing; one of them pointed in four directions at once, and four times over, there was nothing; and many times when they have not pointed at all, there has been something.

Apples fall to the ground, and dogs growl, if their bones are taken away: also flowers bloom in the spring, and a trodden worm turns.

Nevertheless strong is the delusion that there is gravitational astronomy, and the great power of the Law of Gravitation, in popular respectfulness, is that it is mathematically expressed. According to my view, one might as well say that it is fetishly expressed. Descartes was as great a mathematician as Newton: veritably enough it may be said that he invented, or discovered, analytic geometry; only patriotically do Englishmen say that Newton invented, or discovered, the infinitesimal calculus. Descartes, too, formulated a law of the planets and not by a symbol was he less bewildering and convincing to the faithful, but his law was not in terms of gravitation, but in terms of vorticose motion. In the year 1732, the French Academy awarded a prize to John Bernoulli, for his magnificent mathematical demonstration, which was as unintelligible as anybody's. Bernoulli, too, formulated, or said he formulated, planetary inter-actions, as mathematically as any of his hypnotised admirers could have desired: it, too, was not gravitational (Newcomb, *Popular Astronomy*, 2nd ed., 80).

The fault that I find with a great deal of mathematics in astronomy is the fault that I should find in architecture, if a temple, or a skyscraper, were supposed to prove something. Pure mathematics is architecture: it has no more place in astronomy than has the Parthenon. It is the arbitrary: it will not spoil a line nor dent a surface for a datum. There is a faint uniformity in every chaos: in discolourations on an old wall, anybody can see recognisable appearances; in such a mixture a mathematician will see squares and circles and triangles. If he would merely elaborate triangles and not apply his diagrams to theories upon the old wall itself, his constructions would be as harmless as poetry. In our metaphysics, unity can not, of course, be the related. A mathematical expression of unity can not, except approximately, apply to a planet, which is not final, but is part of something.

Sir Isaac Newton lived long ago. Every thought in his mind was a reflection of his era. To appraise his mind at all comprehensively, consider his works in general. For some other instances of his love of numbers, see, in his book upon the Prophecies of Daniel, his determinations upon the eleventh horn of Daniel's fourth animal (*Observations upon the Prophecies of Daniel, and the Apocalypse of St. John*, ch. 7 and 8). If that demonstration be not very acceptable nowadays, some of his other works may now be archaic. For all I know Jupiter may sing bass, either smoothly or lumpily, and for all I know there may be some formulable ratio between an eleventh horn of a fourth animal and some other quantity: I complain against the dogmas that have solidified out of the vapourings of such minds, but I suppose I am not very substantial, myself. Upon general principles, I say that we take no ships of the time of Newton for models for the ships of today, and build and transport in ways that are magnificently, or perhaps disastrously, different, but that, at any rate, are not the same; and that the principles of biology and chemistry and all the other sciences, except astronomy, are not what they were in Newton's time, whether every one of them is a delusion or not. My complaint is that the still medieval science of astronomy holds back alone in a general appearance of advancement, even though there probably never has been real advancement.

There is something else to be said upon Keplerism and Newtonism. It is a squirm. I fear me that our experiences have sophisticated us. We have noted the division in Keplerism, by which, like everything else that we have examined, it is as truly interpretable one way as it is another way.

The squirm:

To lose all sense of decency and value of data, but to be agreeable; but to be like everybody else, and intend to turn our agreeableness to profit;

To agree with the astronomers that Kepler's three laws are, not absolutely true, of course, but are approximations, and that the planets do move, as in Keplerian doctrine they are said to move — but then to require only one demonstration that this earth is one of the planets;

To admire Newton's *Principia* from the beginning to the end of it, having, like almost all other admirers, never even seen a copy of it; to accept every theorem in it, without having the slightest notion what any one of them means; to accept that moving bodies do obey the laws of motion, and must move in one of the conic sections — but then to require only one demonstration that this earth is a moving body.

Kepler's three laws are popularly supposed to demonstrate that this earth moves around the sun. This is a mistake. There is something wrong with everything that is popular. As was said, by us, before, accept that this earth is stationary, and Kepler's doctrines apply equally well to a sun around which proportionately interspaced planets move in ellipses, the whole system moving around a central and stationary earth. All observations upon the motions of heavenly bodies are in accord with this interpretation of Kepler's laws. Then as to nothing but a quandary, which means that this earth is stationary, or which means that this earth is not stationary, just as one pleases, Sir Isaac Newton selected, or pleased himself and others. Without one datum, without one little indication more convincing one way than the other, he preferred to think that this earth is one of the moving planets. To this degree had he the "profundity" that we read about. He wrote no books upon the first and second horns of his dilemma: he simply disregarded the dilemma.

To anybody who may be controversially inclined, I offer simplification. He may feel at a disadvantage against batteries of integrals and bombardments of quaternions, transcendental functions, conics, and all the other stores of an astronomer's munitions —

Admire them. Accept that they do apply to the bodies that move around the sun. Require one demonstration that this earth is one of those bodies. For treatment of any such "demonstration," see our disquisition, or our ratiocinations upon the Three Abstrusities, or our intolerably painful attempts to write seriously upon the Three Abstrusities.

We began with three screams from an exhilarated mathematician. We have had some doubtful adventures, trying hard to pretend that monsters, or little difficulties, did really oppose us. We have reached, not the heart of the system, but the crotch of quandary.

CHAPTER 11

We have seen that some of the most brilliant inspirations of god-like intellects, or some of the most pestilential emanations from infected minds, have been attempts to account for the virtual changelessness of the stars. Above all other data of astronomy, that virtual changelessness of positions stands out as a crucial circumstance in my own mind. To account for constellations that have not changed in 2,000 years, astronomers say that they conceive of inconceivable distances. We shall have expressions of our own upon the virtual changeless positions of the stars; but there will be difficulties for us if the astronomers ever have found that some stars move around or with other stars. I shall take up the story of Prof. Struve and the "Companion of Procyon," with more detail, for the sake of some more light upon refinement, exactness, accuracy in astronomy, and for the sake of belittling, or for the sake of sneering, or anything else that anybody may choose to call it.

Prof. Struve's announcement of his discovery of the "Companion of Procyon" is published in the *Monthly Notices* (33, 430) — that, upon the 19th of March, 1873, Struve had discovered the companion of Procyon, having compared it micrometrically, having tested his observations with three determinations of position-angle, three measures of distance, and three additional determinations of position-angle, finding all in "excellent agreement." No optical illusion could be possible, it is said, because another astronomer, Lindemann, had seen the object. Technically, Struve publishes a table of his observations: sidereal times, distances, position-angles; from March 19 to April 2, 1873, after which his observations had to be discontinued until the following year. In *Monthly Notices* (34, 355) are published the resumed observations. Struve says that Auwers would not accept the discovery, unless, in the year that had elapsed, the "companion" had shown increase in position, consistent with theory. Struve writes — "This increase has really shown itself in the most remarkable manner." Therefore, he considers it "decisively established" that the object of his observations was the object of Auwers' calculations. He says that Ceraski, of Moscow, had seen the "companion," "without being warned of the place where it was to be looked for."

However — see back some chapters (ch. 4, page 24, herein).

It may be said that, nevertheless, other stars have companions that do move as they should move. Later we shall consider this subject, thinking that it may be that lights have been seen to change position near some stars, but that never has a star revolved around another star, as to fit palæo-astronomic theory it should. I take for a basis of analogy that never has one sat in a park and watched a tree revolve around one, but that given the affliction, or the endowment, of an astronomer, illusion of such a revolution one may have. We sit in a park. We notice a tree. Wherever we get the notion, we do have the notion that the tree has moved. Then, farther along, we notice another tree, and, as an indication of our vivid imagination or something else, we think it is the same tree, farther along. After that we pick out tree after tree, farther along, and, convinced that it is the same tree, of course conclude that the thing is revolving around us. Exactness and refinement develop: we compute the elements of its orbit. We close our eyes and predict where the tree will be when next we look; and there, by the same process of selection and identification, it is where it "should" be. And if we have something of almost everybody's mania for speed, we make that damn thing spin around with such velocity that we, too, reel in a chaos of very much unsettled botanic conventions. There is nothing far-fetched in this analogy, except the factor of velocity. Goldschmidt did announce that there were a half a dozen faint points of light around Sirius, and it was Dawes' suspicion that Clark had arbitrarily picked out one of them. It is our expression that all around Sirius, at various distances from Sirius, faint points of light were seen, and that at first, even for the first sixteen years, astronomers were not thoroughly hypnotised, and would not pick out the especial point of light that they should have picked out, so that there was nothing like agreement between the calculated and the observed orbit. Besides the irreconcilable observations noted by Flammarion, see the *Intellectual Observer* (1, 482) for others. Then came standardised seeing. So, in the *Observatory* (20, 73) is published a set of observations, in the year 1896, upon the "Companion of Sirius," placing it exactly where it should be. Nevertheless, under this set of observations is published another set, so different that the Editor asks

— "Does this mean that there are two companions?"

Dark Companions require a little more eliminative treatment. So the variable nebulae, then — and do dark nebulae revolve around light nebulae? For instances of variable nebulae, see *Memoirs of the Royal Astronomical Society* (49, 214), *Comptes Rendus* (56, 637), *Monthly Notices* (38, 104). It may be said that they are not of the Algol-type. Neither is Algol, we have shown.

According to the compulsions of data, our idea is that the stars that seem to be fixed in position are fixed in position, so now "proper motion" is as irreconcilable to us as relative motions.

As to "proper motion," the situation is this:

The stars that were catalogued 2,000 years ago have virtually not changed, or, if there be refinement in modern astronomy, have changed no more than a little more nearly exact charting would account for; but, in astronomic theory, the stars are said to be thought of as flying apart at unthinkable velocity; so then evidence of changed positions of stars is welcome to astronomers. As to well-known constellations, it can not be said that there has been change; so, with several exceptions, "proper motion" is attributed to stars that are not well-known.

The result is an amusing trap. Great proper motion is said to indicate relative nearness to this earth. Of the twenty-five stars of supposed greatest proper motion, all but two are faintest of stars; so these twenty-three are said to be nearest this earth. But when astronomers take the relative parallax of a star, by reference to a fainter star, they agree that the fainter star, because fainter, is farther away. So one time faintness associates with nearness, and then conveniences change, and faintness associates with farness, and the whole subject so associates with humourousness, that if we're going to be serious at all in these expressions of ours we had better pass on.

* * *

Observatory (March, 1914):

A group of three stars that disappeared.

If three stars disappeared at once, they were acted upon by something that affected all in common. Try to think of some one force that would not tear the seeable into visible rags, that could blot out three stars, if they were trillions of miles apart. If they were close together that ends the explanation that only because stars are trillions of miles apart have they, for at least 2,000 years, seemed to hold the same relative positions.

In Agnes Clerke's *System of the Stars* are cited many instances of stars that seem to be so closely related that it seems impossible to think that they are trillions, or billions, or millions of miles apart: such formations as "seven aligned stars appearing to be strung on a silvery filament." There are loops of stars in a cluster in Auriga; lines and arches in Ophiuchus; zig-zag figures in Sagittarius. As to stars that not only seem close together but that are coloured alike, Miss Clerke expresses her feeling that they are close together — "If these colours be inherent, it is difficult to believe that the stars distinguished by them are simply thrown together by perspective." As to figures in Sagittarius, Alfred Henry Fison (*Recent Advances in Astronomy*, 67) cites an instance of 30 small stars in the form of a forked twig, with dark rifts parallel. According to Fison, probability is overwhelmingly against the three uncommon stars in the belt of Orion falling into a straight line, by chance distribution, considering also that below this line is another of five faint stars parallel. There are dark lanes or rifts in the Milky Way that are like branches from main lines or rifts, and the rifts sometimes have well-defined edges. In many regions where there are dark rifts there are lines of stars that are roughly parallel —

That it is not distances apart that have held the stars from changing relatively to one another, because there are hosts of indications that some stars are close together, and are, or have been, affected, in common, by local formative forces.

* * *

For a detailed comparison, by J.E. Gore, of stars of today with stars catalogued by Al-Sufi about 1,000 years ago, see the *Observatory* (23: 370, 398, 449). The stars have not changed in position, but it does seem that there have been many changes in magnitude.

Other changes — *Publications of the Astronomical Society of the Pacific* (32, n. 185, 63) — discovery of the seventeenth new star in one nebula (Andromeda). For lists of stars that have disappeared, see *Monthly Notices* (8, 16; 10, 18; 11, 47), *Sidereal Messenger* (6, 319), *Jour. B.A.A.* (14, 259). Nebulae that have disappeared — see *Amer. Jour. Sci.* (s. 2, 33, 436), Clerke's *System of the Stars* (2nd ed., 293), *Nature* (30, 201).

In the *Sidereal Messenger* (5, 269), Prof. Colbert writes that, upon August 20, 1886, an astronomer, in Chicago, saw, for about half an hour, a small comet-like projection from the star *Zeta*, in Cassiopeia.

So, then, changes have been seen at the distance of the stars.

When the new star in Perseus appeared, in February, 1901, it was a point of light. Something went out from it, giving it in six months a diameter equal to half the apparent diameter of the moon. The appearances looked structural. To say loosely that they were light-effects, something like a halo, perhaps, is to ignore their complexity and duration and differences. According to Newcomb, who is occasionally quotable in our favour, these radiations were not merely light-rays, because they did not go out uniformly from the star, but moved out variously and knotted and curved.

It was visible motion, at the distance of Nova Persei.

In *Monthly Notices* (58, 334), Dr. Espin writes that, upon the night of Jan. 16, 1898, he saw something that looked like a cloud in Perseus. It could have been nothing in the atmosphere of this earth, nor anything far from the constellation, because he saw it again in Perseus, upon Jan. 24. He writes that, upon Feb. 17, Mr. Heath and Dr. Halm saw it, like a cloud, dimming and discolouring stars shining through it. At the meeting the British Astronomical Association, Feb. 23, 1898, (*Jour. B.A.A.*, 8, 216), Dr. Espin described this appearance and answered questions. "It was not a nebula, nor was it like one." "Whatever it was it had the peculiar property of dimming or blotting out stars."

This thing moved into Perseus and then moved away.

Clerke, *System of the Stars* (2nd ed., 290) — a nebula that changed position abruptly, between the years 1833 and 1835, and then changed no more. According to Sir John Herschel, a star was central in this nebula, when observed in 1827, and in 1833, but, in August, 1835, the star was upon the eastern side of the nebula.

That it is not distance from this earth that has kept changes of positions of the stars from being seen, for 2,000 years, because occasional, abrupt changes of position have been seen at the distance of the stars.

* * *

That, whether there be a shell-like, revolving composition, holding the stars in position, and in which the stars are openings, admitting light from an existence external to the shell, or not, all stars are at about the same distance from this earth, as they would be if this earth were stationary and central to such a shell, revolving around it —

According to the aberration-forms of the stars.

All stars, at the pole of the ecliptic, describe circles annually; stars lower down describe ellipses that reduce more and more the farther down they are, until at the ecliptic they describe straight lines yearly.

Suppose all the stars to be openings, fixed in position relatively to one another, in some inter-spacing substance. Conceive of a gyration to the whole aggregation, and relatively to a central and stationary earth: then, as seen from this earth, all would describe circles, near the axis, ellipses lower down, and straight lines at the limit of transformation. If all were at the same distance from this earth, or if all were points in one gyrating concave formation, equi-distant to all points from the central earth, all would have the same amplitude. All aberration-forms of the stars, whether of brilliant or faint stars, whether circles of ellipses or straight lines, have the same amplitude: about 41 seconds of arc.

* * *

If all stars are points of light admitted from externality, held fixed and apart in one shell-like composition that is opaque in some parts and translucent in some parts and perforated generally —

The Gegenschein —

That we have indication that there is such a shell around our existence.

The Gegenschein is a round patch of light in the sky. It seems to be reflected sunlight, at night, because it keeps position about opposite the sun's.

The crux:

Reflected sunlight — but reflecting from what?

That the sky is a matrix, in which the stars are openings, and that, upon the inner, concave surface of this celestial shell, the sun casts its light, even if the earth is between, no more blotted out in the middle by the intervening earth than often to considerable degree is its light blotted out upon the moon during an eclipse of the moon, occupying no time in travelling the distance of the stars and back to this earth, because the stars are near, or because there is no velocity of light.

Suppose the Gegenschein could be a reflection of sunlight from anything at a distance less than the distance of the stars. It would have parallax against its background of stars.

Observatory (17, 46):

"The Gegenschein has no parallax."

* * *

At the meeting of the Royal Astronomical Society, Jan. 11, 1878, was read a paper by W.F. Denning. It was, by its implications, one of the most exciting documents in history. The subject was: "Repetitions in Radiant-points of Shooting-Stars" (*Monthly Notices*, 38, 111; *Observatory*, 1, 366). Mr. Denning listed twenty-two radiants that lasted from three to four months each. In the year 1799, Humboldt noticed that the paths of meteors, when parts of one display, led back to one point of common origin, or one point from which all the meteors radiated. This is the radiant-point, or the radiant. When a radiant occurs under a constellation, the meteors are named relatively. In the extraordinary meteoric display of November 13-14, 1833, there was a circumstance that was as extraordinary as the display itself: that, though this earth is supposed to rotate upon its axis, giving to the stars the appearance of revolving nightly, and supposed to revolve around the sun, so affecting the seeming motions of the stars, these meteors of November, 1833, began under the constellation Leo, and six hours later, though Leo had changed position in the sky, had changed with, and seemed still coming from, Leo.

There was no parallax along the great base line from Canada

to Florida.

Then these meteors did come from Leo, or parallax, or absence of parallax, is meaningless.

The circumstance of precise position maintained under a moving constellation upon the night of Nov. 13-14, 1833, becomes insignificant relatively to Denning's data of such synchronisation with a duration of months. When a radiant-point remains under Leo or Lyra, night after night, month after month, it is either that something is shifting it, without parallax, in exact coincidence with a doubly shifting constellation, which is so unthinkable that Denning says, "that is incredible and unaccountable from existing theories" or that the constellation is the radiant-point, in which case maintenance of precise position under it is unthinkable if it be far away —

That the stars are near.

Think of a ship, slowly sailing past a seacoast town, firing with smokeless powder, say. Shells from it burst before quite reaching the town, and all explosion-points are in line between the city and the ship, or are traceable to one such radiant. The bombardment continues. The ship moves slowly. Still all points of exploding shells are traceable to one point between the ship and the town. The bombardment goes on and goes on and goes on, and the ship is far from its first position. The point of exploding shells is still between the ship and the town. Wise men in the town say that the shells are not coming from the ship. They say this because formerly they had said that shells could not come from a ship. They reason: therefore shells are not coming from this ship. They are asked how, then, the point of explosion could so shift exactly in line with the moving ship. If there be a W.F. Denning among them, he will say, "I cannot explain." But the other wise men will be like Prof. Moulton, for instance. In his books, Prof. Moulton writes a great deal upon the subject of meteors, but he does not mention the meteors that, for months at a time, appear between observers and a shifting constellation.

There are other considerations. The shells are heard to explode. So then they explode near the town. But there is something the matter with that smokeless powder aboard ship: very feeble projectile-force, because also must the shells be exploding near the ship, or the radiant-point would not have the same background, as seen from different parts of the town. Then, in this town, inhabitants, provided they be not wise men, will conclude that, if the explosion-point is near the town, and is also near the ship, the ship is near the town —

Leo and Lyra and Andromeda — argosies that sail the sky and that bombard this earth — and that they are not far away.

And some of us there may be who, instead of trying to speculate upon an unthinkable remoteness, will suffer a sensitiveness to proximity instead; enter a new revolt against a black encompassment that glitters with a light beyond, and wonder what exists in a brilliant environment not far away — and a new anguish for hyperaesthesia upon this earth: a suffocating consciousness of the pressure of the stars.

The Sickle of Leo, from which come the Leonids, gleams like a great question-mark in the sky.

The answer —

But God knows what the answer to anything is.

Perhaps it is that the stars are very close indeed.

CHAPTER 12

We try to have independent expressions. Accept that it is not distance that has held the stars in unchanging position, if occasional, abrupt change of position has been seen at the distance of the stars, and it is implied that the not enormously distant stars are all about equally far away from this earth, or some would be greatly particularised, and that this earth does not move in an orbit, or stars would be seasonally particularised, but would not be, if the stars, in one composition revolve; also if this earth be relatively close to all stars, if many changes of magnitude and of appearance and disappearance have been seen at the distance of the stars, and, if, in the revolutions of the stars, they do not swirl in displacements as bewildering as a blizzard of luminous snowflakes, and if no state of inter-repulsion can be thought of, especially as many stars merge into others, this composition is a substantial, concave formation, or shell-like enclosure in which stars are points. So many of the expressions in the preceding chapter imply others, or all others. However, we have tried to have independent expressions. Of course we realise that the supposed difference between inductive and deductive reasoning is a false demarcation; nevertheless we feel that deductions piled upon other deductions are only architecture, and a great deal in this book expresses the notion that architecture should be kept in its own place. Our general expression is not that there should be no architecture and no mathematics in astronomy, or neo-astronomy; not that there should be no poetry in biology; no chemistry in physiology — but that "pure" architecture or "pure" mathematics, biology, chemistry, has its own field, even though each is inextricably bound up with all the other aspects of being. So of course the very thing that we object to in its extreme manifestations is essential to us in some degree, and the deductive is findable somewhere in every one of our inductions, and we are not insensible to what we think is the gracefulness of some of the converging lines of our own constructions. We are not revolting against aspects, but against emphases and intrusions.

The first part of our work is what we consider neo-astronomic; and now to show that we have no rabidity against the mathematical except when over-emphasized, or misapplied, our language is that all expressions so far developed are to us of about 50% acceptability. A far greater attempted independence is coming, a second part of this work, considering phenomena so different that, if we term the first part of our explorations "neo-astronomic," even some other term, by which to designate the field of the second part will have to be thought of, and the word "extra-geographic" seems best for it. If in these two fields, our at least temporary conclusions be the same, we shall be impressed, in spite of all our cynicisms as to "agreements."

Neo-astronomy:

This supposed solar system — an egg-like organism that is shelled away from external light and life — this central and stationary earth its nucleus — around it a revolving shell, in which the stars are pores, or functioning channels, through some of which spray irradiating fountains said to be "meteoric," but perhaps electric — in which the nebulae are translucent patches, and in which the many dark parts are areas of opaque, structural substance — and that the stars are not trillions nor even millions of miles away — with proportional reductions of all internal distances, so that the planets are not millions, nor even hundreds of thousands of miles away.

We conceive of the variability of the stars and the nebulae in terms of the incidence of external light upon a revolving shell and fluctuating passage through light-admitting points and parts. We conceive of all things being rhythmic, so, if stars be pores in a substance, that matrix must be subject to some changes, which may be of different periodicities in different regions. There may be local vortices in the most rigid substance, and so stars, or pores, might revolve around one another, but our tendency is to think that if light companions there be to some stars, they are reflections of light, passing through channels, upon surrounding substance, flickering from one position to another in the small undulations of this environment. So there may be other displacements, differences of magnitude, new openings and closings in a substance that is not absolutely rigid. So "proper motion" might be accounted for, but my own preference is to think, as to such stars as *1830 Groombridge* and Barnard's "run-away" star, that they are planets — also that some of the comets, especially the tailless comets, some of which have been seen to obscure stars, so that evidently they are not wisps of highly attenuated matter, are planets, all of them not conventionally recognized as planets, because of eccentricity and remoteness from the ecliptic, two departures, however, that many of the minor planets make to great degree. If some of these bodies be planets, the irregularities of some of them are consistent with the irregularities of Jupiter's satellites.

I suggest that a combination of the Ptolemaic and the Tychonic doctrines is in good accord with all the phenomena that we have considered, and with all planetary motions that we have had no occasion to pay much attention to — that the sun, carrying Mercury and Venus with him, revolves at a distance of a few thousand miles, or a few tens of thousands of miles, in a rising and falling spiral around this virtually, but not absolutely, stationary earth, which, according to modern investigations is more top-shaped than spherical; moon, a few thousand miles away, revolving around this nucleus; and the exterior planets not only revolving around this whole central arrangement, but approaching and receding, in loops, also, quite as they seem to the remotest of them preposterously near, according to conventional "determinations."

So all the phenomena of the skies may be explained. But all were explained in another way by Copernicus, in another way by Ptolemy, and in still another way by Tycho Brahé. One supposes that there are other ways. If there be a distant object, and, if one school of wise men can by their reasoning processes excellently demonstrate that it is a tree, another school positively determine that it is a house, and other investigators of the highest authoritativeness variously find and prove that it is a cloud or a buffalo or a geranium, why then, their reasoning processes may be admired but not trusted. Right at the heart of our opposition, and right at the heart of our own expressions, is the fatality that there is no reasoning, no logic, no explanation resembling the illusions in the vainglories of common suppositions. There is only the process of correlating to, or organising or systematising around, something that is arbitrarily taken for a base, or a dominant doctrine, or a major premise — the process of assimilating with something else, making agreement with something else, or interpreting in terms of something else, which supposed base is never itself final, but was originally an assimilation with still something else.

I typify the result of all examinations of all principles or laws or dominant thoughts, scientific, philosophic, or theologic, in what we find in examining the pronouncement that motion follows the least resistance:

That motion follows least resistance.

How do we identify least resistance?

If motion follows it.

Then motion goes where motion goes.

If nothing can be positively distinguished from anything else there can be no positive logic, which is attempted positive distinguishment. Consider the popular "base" that Capital is tyranny, and almost utmost wickedness, and that Labour is pure and idealistic. But one's labour is one's capital, and capital that is not working is in no sense implicated in this conflict.

Nevertheless we now give up our early suspicion that our whole existence is a leper of the skies, quaking and cringing through space, having the isolation that astronomers suppose, because other celestial forms of being fly from infection —

That, if shelled away from external light and life, it is so surrounded and so protected in the same cause and functioning as that of similarly encompassed forms subsidiary to it — that our existence is super-embryonic.

Darkness of night and of lives and of thoughts — super-uterine entombment. Blackness of the unborn, quasi-illumined periodically by the little sun, which is not light, but less dark.

Then we think of an organism that needs no base, and needs nothing of finality, nor of special guidance to any local part to it, because all parts partake of the pre-determined development of the whole. Consequently our spleens subside, and our frequently unmannerly derisions are hushed by recognitions — that all organisations of thought must be baseless in themselves, and of course be not final, or they could not change, and must bear within themselves those elements that will, in time, destroy them — that seeming solidities that pass away, in phantom successions, are functionaries relatively to their periods, and express the passage from phase to phase of all things embryonic.

So it is that one who searches for fundamentals comes to

bifurcations; never to a base; only to a quandary. In our own field, let there be any acceptable finding. It indicates that the earth moves around the sun. Just as truly it indicates that the sun moves around the earth. What is it that determines which will be accepted, hypnotically blinding the faithful to the other aspect? Our own expression is upon Development as serial reactions to successive Dominants. Let the dominant spirit of an era require that this earth be remote and isolated; Keplerism will support it: let the dominant change to a spirit of expansion, which would be impossible under such remoteness and isolation; Keplerism will support, or will not especially oppose, the new dominant. This is the essential process of embryonic growth, by which the same protoplasmic substance responds differently in different phases.

But I do not think that all data are so plastic. There are some that will not assimilate with a prevailing doctrine. They can have no effect upon an arbitrary system of thought, or a system sub-consciously induced, in its time of dominance: they will simply be disregarded.

We have reached our catalogue of the sights and the sounds to which all that we have so far considered is merely introductory. For them there are either no conventional explanations or poor insufficiencies half-heartedly offered. Our data are glimpses of an epoch that is approaching with far-away explosions. It is vibrating on its edges with the tread of distant space-armies. Already it has pictured in the sky visions that signify new excitements, even now lapping over into the affairs of a self-disgusted, played-out hermitage.

We assemble the data. Unhappily, we shall be unable to resist the temptation to reason and theorise. May Super-embryology have mercy upon our own syllogisms. We consider that we are entitled to at least 13 pages of gross and stupid errors. After that we shall have to explain.

PART TWO

CHAPTER 1

June, 1801 — a mirage of an unknown city. It was seen, for more than an hour, at Youghal, Co. Cork, Ireland — a representation of mansions, surrounded by shrubbery and white palings — forests behind. In October, 1796, a mirage of a walled town had been seen distinctly for half an hour at Youghal. Upon March 9, 1797, had been seen a mirage of a walled town (David Purdie Thomson, *Introduction to Meteorology*, 258).

Feb. 7, 1802 — an unknown body that was seen, by Fritsch, of Magdeburg, to cross the sun (*Observatory*, 3, 136).

Oct. 10, 1802 — an unknown dark body was seen, by Fritsch, rapidly crossing the sun (*Comptes Rendus*, 83, 587).

Between 10 and 11 o'clock, morning of Oct. 8, 1803, a stone fell from the sky, at the town of Apt, France. About eight hours later, "some persons believed they felt an earthquake" (*B.A. Rept.*, 1854, 53).

Upon August 11, 1805, an explosive sound was heard at East Haddam, Connecticut. There are records of six prior sounds, as if of explosions, that were heard at East Haddam, beginning with the year 1791, but, unrecorded, the sounds had attracted attention for a century, and had been called the "Moodus" sounds, by the Indians. For the best account of the "Moodus" sounds, see the *Amer. Jour. Sci.* (s. 1, 39, 338). Here a writer tries to show the phenomena were subterranean, but says that there was no satisfactory explanation.

Upon the 2nd of April, 1808, over the town of Pignerol, Piedmont, Italy, a loud sound was heard: in many places in Piedmont an earthquake was felt. In the *B.A. Rept.* (1854, 68), it is said that aerial phenomena did occur; that, during the explosion, luminous objects had been seen in the sky over Pignerol, and that in several of the communes in the Alps aerial sounds, as if of innumerable stones colliding, had been heard, and that quakes had been felt. From April 2 to April 8, forty shocks were recorded at Pignerol; sounds like cannonading were heard at Barga. Upon the 18th of April, two detonations were heard at La Tour, and a luminous object was seen in the sky. The supposition, or almost absolute belief of most persons is that from the 2nd to the 18th of April this earth moved far in its orbit and was rotating so that, if one should explain that probably meteors had exploded here, it could not very well be thought that more meteors were continuing to pick out this one point upon a doubly moving planet. But something was specially related to this one local sky. Upon the 19th of April, a stone fell from the sky near Borgo San Donnino, about 40 miles east of Piedmont (*B.A. Rept.*, 1860, 63). Sounds like cannonading were heard almost every day in this small region. Upon the 16th of May, a red cloud such as marks the place of a meteoric explosion was seen in the sky. Throughout the rest of the year, phenomena that are now listed as "earthquakes" occurred in Piedmont. The last occurrence of which I have record was upon Jan. 22, 1810.

Feb. 9, 1812 — two explosive sounds at East Haddam (*Amer. Jour. Sci.*, s. 1, 39, 338).

July 5, 1812 — one explosive sound at East Haddam (*Amer. Jour. Sci.*, s. 1, 39, 338).

Oct. 28, 1812 — "phantom soldiers" at Havarah Park, near Ripley, England (*Edinburgh Annual Register*, 1812, pt. 2, 124). When such appearances are explained by meteorologists, they are said to be displays of the aurora borealis. Psychic research explains variously. The physicists say that they are mirages of troops marching somewhere at a distance.

Night of July 31, 1813 — flashes of light in the sky of Tottenham, near London (Timb's *Year-Book of Facts in Science and Art*, 1853, 309). The sky was clear. The flashes were attributed to a storm at Hastings, 65 miles away. We note not only that the planet Mars was in opposition at this time (July 30), but in one of the nearest of its oppositions in the 19th century.

Dec. 28, 1813 — an explosive sound at East Haddam (*Amer. Jour. Sci.* (s. 1, 39, 338).

Feb. 2, 1816 — a quake at Lisbon. There was something in the sky. Extraordinary sounds were heard, but were attributed to "flocks of birds." But immediately after the first shock, something was seen in the sky: it is said to have been a meteor (*B.A. Rept.*, 1854, 106).

Since the year 1788, many earthquakes, or concussions that were listed as earthquakes, had occurred at the town of Comrie, Perthshire, Scotland. Seventeen instances were recorded in the year 1795. Almost all records of the phenomena of Comrie start with the year 1788, but, in Macara's *Guide to Crieff*, it is said that the disturbances were recorded as far back as the year 1597. They were slight shocks, and until the occurrence upon August 13, 1816, conventional explanations, excluding all thought of relations with anything in the sky, seemed adequate enough. But, in an account in the London *Times* (Aug. 21, 1816), it is said that, at the time of the quake of Aug. 13, a luminous object, or a "small meteor," had been seen at Dunkeld, near Comrie; and, according to David Milne (*Edinburgh New Philosophical Journal*, 31, 117), a resident of Comrie had reported "a large luminous body, bent like a crescent, which stretched itself over the heavens."

There was another quake in Scotland ("Inverness and neighbourhood"), June 30, 1817. It is said that hot rain fell from the sky (*B.A. Rept.*, 1854, 112).

Jan. 6, 1818 — an unknown body that crossed the sun, according to Capel Lofft, of Ipswich; observed for more than three-hours-and-a-half (*Quarterly Journal of the Royal Institute of Great Britain*, 5, 117; *Monthly Magazine*, 45, 102).

Three unknown bodies that were seen, upon June 26, 1819, crossing the sun, according to Gruithuisen (*Annual of Scientific Discovery*, 1860, 411). Also, upon this day, Pastorff saw something that he thought was a comet, which was then somewhere near the sun, but which, according to Olbers, could not have been the comet (Webb, *Celestial Objects*, 40).

Upon Aug. 28, 1819, there was a violent quake at Irkutsk, Siberia. There had been two shocks upon Aug. 22, 1813 (*B.A. Rept.*, 1854, 101). Upon April 6, 1805, or March 25, according to the Russian calendar, two stones had fallen from the sky at Irkutsk (*B.A. Rept.*, 1860, 62). One of these stones is now in the South Kensington Museum, London (Lazarus A. Fletcher, *Introduction to the Study of Meteorites*, 10th ed., 98). Another violent shock at Irkutsk, May 7, 1820 (*B.A. Rept.*, 1854, 128).

Unknown bodies seen in the sky, Feb. 12, 1820 (*Comptes Rendus*, 83: 589, 621).

Things that marched in the sky — see Arago's *Oeuvres Complètes de François Arago* (v. 11, 576) or *Annales de Chimie et de Physique* (s. 2, 30, 416) — objects that were seen by many persons, in the streets of Embrun, during the eclipse of Sept. 7, 1820, moving in straight lines, turning and retracing in the same straight lines, all of them separated by uniform spaces.

Early in the year 1821 — and a light shone out on the moon — a bright point of light in the lunar crater Aristarchus, which was in the dark at the time. It was seen, upon the 4th and the 7th of February, by Capt. Kater (*Annual Register*, 1821, 687; *Phil. Trans.*, 111, 130); and upon the 5th by Dr. Olbers (*Memoirs of the Royal Astronomical Society* (1, 156). It was a light like a star, and was seen again, May 4th and 6th, by the Rev. M. Ward and by Francis Bailey (*Memoirs of the Royal Astronomical Society*, 1, 156). At Cape Town, nights of Nov. 28th and 29th, 1821, again a star-like light was seen upon the moon (*Phil. Trans.*, 112, 237).

Quarterly Journal of the Royal Institute of Great Britain (20, 417):

That, early in the morning of March 20, 1822, detonations were heard at Melida, an island in the Adriatic. All day, at intervals, the sounds were heard. They were like cannonading, and it was supposed that they came from a vessel, or from Turkish artillery, practising in some frontier village. For thirty days the detonations continued, sometimes thirty or forty, sometimes several hundred, a day.

Upon April 13, 1822, it seems, according to description, that clearly enough was there an explosion in the sky of Comrie, and a concussion of the ground — "two loud reports, one apparently above our heads, and the other which followed immediately under our feet" (*Edin. N. Phil. Jour.*, 31, 119).

July 15, 1822 — a fall of perhaps unknown seeds from perhaps an unknown world — a great quantity of little round seeds that fell from the sky at Marienwerder, Germany. They were unknown to the inhabitants, who tried to cook them, but found that boiling seemed to have no effect upon them. Wherever they came from, they were brought down by a storm, and two days later, more of them fell, in a storm, in Silesia. It is said that these corpuscles were identified by some scientists as seeds of *Galium spurium*, but that other scientists disagreed. Later more of them fell at Posen, Mecklenburg. See *Bulletin (Universal) des Sciences, Mathematiques, Astronomique, Physiques et Chimiques*, (s. 1, 1, 298).

Aug. 20, 1822 — a tremendous detonation at Melida — others continuing several days.

Oct. 23, 1822 — two unknown dark bodies crossing the sun;

observed by Pastorff (*Ann. Sci. Disc.*, 1860, 411).

An unknown, shining thing — it was seen, by Webb, May 22, 1823; near the planet Venus (*Nature*, 14, 195).

More unknowns, in the year 1823 — see *Comptes Rendus* (49, 810) and Webb's *Celestial Objects* (43).

Feb., 1824 — the sounds of Melida.

Upon Feb. 11, 1824, a slight shock was felt at Irkutsk, Siberia (*B.A. Rept.*, 1854, 158). Upon Feb. 18, or, according to other accounts, upon May 14, a stone that weighed five pounds, fell from the sky at Irkutsk (*B.A. Rept.*, 1860, 70). Three severe shocks at Irkutsk, March 8, 1824 (*B.A. Rept.*, 1854, 158).

Sept., 1824 — the sounds of Melida.

At five o'clock, morning of Oct. 20, 1824, a light was seen upon the dark part of the moon, by Gruithuisen. It disappeared. Six minutes later it appeared again, disappeared again, and then flashed intermittently, from 5:30 A.M., until sunrise ended the observations (*Sci. Amer. Sup.*, 7, 2712). And, upon Jan. 22, 1825, again shone out the star-like light of Aristarchus, reported by the Rev. J.B. Emmett (*Annals of Philosophy*, n.s., 12, 338).

The last sounds of Melida of which I have record, were heard in March, 1825. If these detonations did come from the sky, there was something that, for at least three years, was situated over, or was in some other way specially related to, this one small part of this earth's surface, subversively to all supposed principles of astronomy and geodesy. It is said that, to find out whether the sounds did come from the sky, or not, the Prêteur of Melida went into underground caverns to listen. It is said that there the sounds could not be heard (*Annales de Chimie*, s. 2, 30, 432).

CHAPTER 2

And our own underground investigations — and whether there is something in the sky or not. We are in a hole in time. Cavern of Conventional Science — walls that are dogmas, from which drips ancient wisdom in a patter of slimy opinions — but we have heard a storm of data outside —

Of beings that march in the sky, and of a beacon on the moon — another dark body crosses the sun. Somewhere near Melida there is cannonading, and another stone falls from the sky at Irkutsk, Siberia; and unknown grain falls from an unknown world, and there are flashes in the sky when the planet Mars is near.

In a farrago of lights and sounds and forms, I feel the presence of possible classifications that may thread a pattern of attempt to find out something. My attention is attracted by a streak of events that is beaded with little star-like points of light. First we shall find out what we can, as to the moon.

In one of the numbers of the *Observatory* (24, 254), an eminent authority, in some fields of research, is quoted as to the probable distance of the moon. According to his determinations, the moon is 37 miles away. He explains most reasonably: he is Mr. George Bernard Shaw (*Humane Review*, 1, 12). But by conventional doctrine, the moon is 240,000 miles away. My own idea is that somewhere between determinations by a Shaw and determinations by a Newcomb, we could find many acceptances.

I prefer questionable determinations, myself, or at any rate examinations that end up with questions or considerable latitude. It may be that as to the volcanoes of the moon we can find material for at least a seemingly intelligent question, if no statements are possible as to the size and the distance of the moon. The larger volcanoes of this earth are about three miles in diameter, though the craters of Haleakla, Hawaii, and Aso San, Japan, are seven miles across. But the larger volcanoes of the relatively little moon are said to be sixty miles across, though several are said to be twice that size. And I start off with just about the impression of disproportionality that I should have, if someone should tell me of a pygmy with ears five feet long.

Is there any somewhat good reason for thinking that the volcanic craters of the little moon are larger than, or particularly different in any way from, the craters of this earth?

If not, we have a direct unit of measurement, according to which the moon is not 2160, but about 100, miles in diameter.

How far away does one suppose to be an object with something like that diameter, and of the seeming size of the moon?

The astronomers explain. They argue that gravitation must be less powerful upon the moon than upon this earth, and that therefore larger volcanic formations could have been cast up on the moon. We explain. We argue that volcanic force must be less powerful upon the moon than upon this earth, and that therefore larger volcanic formations could not have been cast up on the moon.

The disproportionality that has impressed me has offended more conventional aesthetics than mine. Prof. See, for instance, has tried to explain that the lunar formations are not craters but are effects of bombardment by vast meteors, which spared this earth, for some reason not made clear (W.L. Webb, *Brief Biography and Popular Account of the Unparalleled Discoveries of T.J.J. See*, 181). Viscid moon — meteor pops in — up splash walls and a central cone. If Prof. See will jump in swimming some day, and then go back some weeks later to see how big a splash he made, he will have other ideas upon such supposed persistences. The moon would have to have been virtually liquid to fit his theory, because there are no partly embedded, vast, round meteors protruding anywhere.

There have been lights like signals upon the moon. There are two conventional explanations: reflected sunlight and volcanic action. Of course, ultra-conventionalists do not admit that in our own times there has been even volcanic action upon the moon. Our instances will be of light upon the dark part of the moon, and there are good reasons for thinking that our data do not relate to volcanic action. In volcanic eruptions upon this earth the glow is so accompanied by great volumes of smoke that a clear, definite point of light would seem not to be the appearance from a distance.

For Webb's account of a brilliant display of minute dots and streaks of light, in the Mare Crisium, July 4, 1832, see *Astro. Reg.* (20, 165). I have records of half a dozen similar illuminations here, in about 120 years, all of them when the Mare Crisium was in darkness. There can be no commonplace explanation for such spectacles, or they would have occurred oftener; nevertheless the Mare Crisium is a wide, open region, and at times there may have been uncommon percolations of sunlight, and I shall list no more of these interesting events that seem to me to have been like carnivals upon the moon.

Dec. 22, 1835 — the star-like light in Aristarchus — reported by Francis Bailey — see Proctor's *Myths and Marvels of Astronomy* (329).

Feb. 13, 1826 — in the western crater of Messier — according to Gruithuisen (*Sci. Amer. Supp.*, 7, 2696) — two straight lines of light; between them a dark band that was covered with luminous points.

Upon the nights of March 18 and 19, 1847, large luminous spots were seen upon the dark part of the moon, and a general glow upon the upper limb, by the Rev. T. Rankin and Prof. Chevalllier (*B.A. Rept.*, 1847, Trans., 18). The whole shaded part of the disc seemed to be a mixture of lights and shades. Upon the night of the 19th, there was a similar appearance upon this earth, an aurora, according to the London newspapers. It looks as if both the moon and this earth were affected by the same illumination, said to have been auroral. I offer this occurrence as indication that the moon is nearby, if moon and earth could be so affected in common.

But by signalling, I mean something like the appearance that was seen, by Hodgson, upon the dark part of the moon, night of Dec. 11, 1847 — a bright light that flashed intermittently. Upon the next night it was seen again (*Monthly Notices*, 8, 55).

* * *

The oppositions of Mars occur once in about two years and two months. In conventional terms, the eccentricity of the orbit of Mars is greater than the eccentricity of the orbit of this earth, and the part of its orbit that is traversed by this earth in August is nearest the orbit of Mars. When this earth is between Mars and the sun, Mars is said to be in opposition, and this is the position of nearest approach: when opposition occurs in August, that is the most favourable opposition. After that, every two years and about two months, the oppositions are less favourable, until the least favourable of all, in February, after which favourableness increases up to the climacteric opposition in

August again. This is a cycle of changing proximities within a period of about fifteen years.

In October, 1862, Lockyer saw a spot like a long train of clouds on Mars, and several days later Secchi saw a spot on Mars. And if that were signalling, it is very meagre material upon which to suppose anything. And May 8-22, 1873 — white spots on Mars. But, upon June 17, 1873, two months after nearest approach, but still in the period of opposition of Mars, there was either an extraordinary occurrence, or the extraordinariness is in our interpretation. See *B.A. Rept.* (1874, 270). A luminous object came to this earth, and was seen and heard upon the night of June 17, 1873, to explode in the sky of Hungary, Austria, and Bohemia. In the words of various writers, termed according to their knowledge, the object was seen seemingly coming from Mars, or from "the red star in the south," where Mars was at the time. Our data were collected by Dr. Galle. The towns of Rybnik and Ratibor, Upper Silesia, are 15 miles apart. Without parallax, this luminous thing was seen from these points "to emerge and separate itself from the disk of the planet Mars." It so happens that we have a definite observation from one of these towns. At Rybnik, Dr. Sage was looking at Mars, at the time. He saw the luminous object "apparently issue from it (the planet)." There is another circumstance, and for its reception our credulity, or our enlightenment, has been prepared. If this thing did come from Mars, it came from the planet to the point where it exploded in about fifteen seconds: from the point of the explosion, the sound travelled in several minutes. We have a description from Dr. Sage that indicates that a bolt of some kind, perhaps electric, did shoot from Mars, and that the planet quaked with the shock — Dr. Sage "was looking attentively at the planet Mars when he thus saw the meteor apparently issue from it, and the planet appear as if it was breaking up and dividing into two parts."

Some of the greatest surprises in commonplace experience are discoveries of the nearness of that which was supposed to be the inaccessibly remote.

* * *

It seems that the moon is close to this earth, because of the phenomenon of "earthshine." The same appearance has been seen upon the planet Venus. If upon the moon, it is light reflecting from this earth and back to this earth, what is it upon Venus? It is "some unexplained optical illusion," says Newcomb, (*Popular Astronomy*, 1st ed., 295; 2nd ed., 303). For a list of more than twenty observations upon this illumination of Venus, see *B.A. Rept.* (1873, 404). It is our expression that the phenomenon is "unexplained" because it does indicate that Venus is millions of miles closer to this earth than Venus "should" be.

Unknown objects have been seen near Venus. There were more than thirty such observations in the eighteenth century, not relating to so many different periods, however. Our own earliest datum is Webb's observation, of May 22, 1823. I know of only one astronomer who has supposed that these observations could relate to a Venusian satellite, pronouncedly visible sometimes, and then for many years being invisible: something else will have to be thought of. If these observations and others that we shall have, be accepted, they relate to unknown bulks that have, from outer space, gone to Venus, and have been in temporary suspension near the planet, even though the shade of Sir Isaac Newton would curdle at the suggestion. If, acceptably, from outer space, something could go to the planet Venus, one is not especially startled with the idea that something could sail out from the planet Venus — visit this earth, conceivably.

In the *B.A. Rept.* (1852: 8, 35), it is said that, early in the morning of Sept. 11, 1852, several persons at Four Oaks, Staffordshire, had seen, in the eastern sky, a luminous object. It was first seen at 4:15 A.M. It appeared and disappeared several times, until 4:45 A.M., when it became finally invisible. Then, at almost the same place in the sky, Venus was seen, having risen above the eastern horizon. These persons sent the records of their observations to Lord Wrottesley, an astronomer whose observatory was at Wolverhampton. There is published a letter from Lord Wrottesley, who says that at first he had thought that the supposititiously unknown object was Venus, with perhaps an extraordinary halo, but that he had received from one of the observers a diagram giving such a position relatively to the moon that he hesitated so to identify. It was in the period of nearest approach to this earth by Venus, and, since inferior conjunction (July

20, 1852), Venus had been a "morning star." If this thing in the sky was not Venus, the circumstances are that an object came close to this earth, perhaps, and for a while was stationary, as if waiting for the planet Venus to appear above the eastern horizon, then disappearing, whether to sail to Venus or not. We think that perhaps this thing did come close to this earth, because it was, it seems, seen only in the local sky of Four Oaks. However, if, according to many of our data, professional astronomers have missed extraordinary appearances at reasonable hours, we can't conclude much from what was not reported by them, after four o'clock in the morning. I do not know whether this is the origin of the convention or not, but this is the first note I have upon the now standardised explanation that, when a luminous object is seen in the sky at the time of the nearest approach by Venus, it is Venus, attracting attention by her great brilliance, exciting persons, unversed in astronomic matters, into thinking that a strange object had visited this earth. When reports are definite as to motions of a seemingly sailing or exploring, luminous thing, astronomers say that it was a fire-balloon.

In the *B.A. Rept.* (1856, 54), it is said that, according to "Mrs. Ayling and friends," in a letter to Lord Wrottesley, a bright object had been seen in the sky of Tillington, near Petworth, Sussex, night of August 11, 1855. According to the description, it rose from behind hills, in the distance, at half past eleven o'clock. It was a red body, or it was a red-appearing construction, because from it were projections like spokes of a wheel; or, they were "stationary" rays, in the words of the description. "Like a red moon, it rose slowly, and diminished slowly, remaining visible one hour and a half." Upon August 11, 1855, Venus was two weeks from primary greatest brilliance, inferior conjunction occurring upon Sept. 30. The thing could not have been Venus, ascending in the sky, at this time of night. An astonishing thing, like a red moon, perhaps with spokes like a wheel's, might, if reported from nowhere else, be considered something that came from outer space so close to this earth that it was visible only in a local sky, except that it might have been visible in other places, and even half past eleven at night may be an unheard-of hour for astronomers, who specialise upon sunspots for a reason that is clearing up to us. Of course an ordinary fire-balloon could be extraordinarily described.

·

June 8, 1868 — I have not the exact time, but one does suspect that it was early in the evening — an object that was reported from Radcliffe Observatory, Oxford. It looked like a comet, but inasmuch as it was reported only from Radcliffe, it may have been in the local sky of Oxford. It seemed to sail in the sky: it moved and changed its course. At first it was stationary; then it moved westward, then southward, then turning north, visible four minutes. See *Eng. Mech.* (7, 351). According to a correspondent to the Birmingham *Gazette*, May 28, 1868, there had been an extraordinary illumination upon Venus, some nights before: a red spot, visible for a few seconds, night of May 27. In the issue of the *Gazette*, of June 1st, someone else writes that he saw this light appearing and disappearing upon Venus. Upon March 15, Browning had seen something that looked like a little shaft of light from Venus (*Eng. Mech.*, 40, 129); and upon April 6, With had seen a similar appearance (*Celestial Objects*, 57). At the time of the appearance at Oxford, Venus was in the period of nearest approach (inferior conjunction July 16, 1868).

I think, myself, that there was one approximately great, wise astronomer. He was Tycho Brahé. For many years, he would not describe what he saw in the sky, because he considered it beneath his dignity to write a book. The undignified, or more or less literary, or sometimes altogether literary, astronomers, who do write books, uncompromisingly say that when a luminous object is said to have moved to greater degree than could be considered illusory, in a local sky of this earth, it is a fire-balloon. It is not possible to find in the writings of astronomers who so explain, mention of the object that was seen by Coggia, night of August 1, 1871. It seems that this thing was not far away, and did appear only in a local sky of this earth, and if it did come from outer space, how it could have "boarded" this earth, if this earth moves at a rate of 19 miles a second, or 1 mile a second, is so hard to explain that why Proctor and Hind, with their passionate itch for explaining, never took the matter up, I don't know. Upon Aug. 1, 1871, an unknown luminous object was seen in the sky of Marseilles, by Coggia (*Comptes Rendus*, 73, 397). According to description, it was a magnificent red object. It appeared at 10:43 P.M., and moved eastward, slowly, until 10:52:30. It stopped — moved northward, and again, at 10:59:30, was stationary. It turned eastward again, and, at

11:03:20, disappeared, or fell behind the horizon. Upon this night Venus was within three weeks of primary greatest brilliance, inferior conjunction occurring upon Sept. 25, 1871.

CHAPTER 3

One repeating mystery — the mystery of the local sky.

How, if this earth be a moving earth, could anything sail to, fall to, or in any other way reach this earth, without being smashed into fine particles by the impact?

This earth is supposed to rip space at a rate of about 19 miles a second.

Concepts smash when one tries to visualise such an accomplishment.

Now, three times over, we shall have other aspects of this one mystery of the local sky. First we shall take up data upon seeming relation between a region of this earth that is subject to earthquakes, or so-called earthquakes, and appearances in the sky of this especial region, and the repeating falls of objects and substances from the local sky and nowhere else at the times.

We have records of quakes that occurred at Irkutsk, Siberia, and of stones that fell from the sky to Irkutsk. Upon March 8, 1829, a severe quake, preceded by clattering sounds, was felt at Irkutsk. There was something in the sky. Dr. Erman, the geologist, was in Irkutsk, at the time. In the *B.A. Rept.* (1854, 201), it is said that, in Dr. Erman's opinion, the sounds that preceded the quake were in the sky.

The situation at Comrie, Perthshire, is similar. A stone fell, May 17, 1830, in the "earthquake region" around Comrie. It fell at Perth, 22 miles from Comrie. See Fletcher's List (Lazarus Fletcher, *An Introduction to the Study of Meteorites*, 100). Upon Feb. 8, 1837, a black powder fell upon the Comrie region (*Edin. N. Phil. Jour.*, 31, 293). Oct. 12, 1839 — a quake at Comrie. According to the Rev. M. Walker, of Comrie, the sky, at the time, was "peculiarly strange and alarming. The heavens, more especially towards the N. and N.W., appeared as if hung with sackcloth" (*Edin. N. Phil. Jour.*, 32, 111). In Mallet's Catalog (*B.A. Rept.*, 1854, 290), it is said that, throughout the month of October, shocks were felt at Comrie, sometimes slight and sometimes severe — "like distant thunder, reports of artillery" — "The noise sometimes seemed to be in the air, and was often heard without any sensible shock at the time." Upon the 23rd of October, occurred the most violent quake in the whole series of phenomena at Comrie. See the *Edin. New Phil. Jour.* (32: 111, 119, 362). All data in this publication were collected by David Milne. According to the Rev. M. Maxton, of Foulis Manse, ten miles from Comrie, rattling sounds were heard in the sky, preceding the shock that was felt. In vol. 33, page 373, of the *Journal*, someone who lived seven miles from Comrie is quoted: "In every case, I am inclined to say that the sound proceeded from the atmosphere, and not from underground. The sound seemed to be high in the air." Someone who lived at Gowrie, forty miles from Comrie, is quoted: "The most general opinion seems to be that the noise accompanying the concussion proceeded from above." See vol. 34, p. 87: another impression of explosion overhead and concussion underneath: "A noise preceded it as of a rushing wind ... The rushing noise seemed to be in the air ... But besides these, and following them, there was a rumbling noise as if of carts on a pavement, but more hollow in the sound; and this latter sound was in the earth." Milne's own conclusion — "It is plain that there are, connected with the earthquake shocks, sounds both in the earth and in the air, which are distinct and separate." If, upon the 23rd of October, 1839, there was a tremendous shock, not of subterranean origin, but from a great explosion in the sky of Comrie, and if this be accepted, there will be concussions somewhere else. The "faults" of dogmas will open; there will be seismic phenomena in science. I have a feeling of a conventional survey of this Scottish sky: vista of a fair, blue, vacant expanse—our suspicions daub the impression with black alarms — but also do we project detonating stimulations into the fair and blue, but unoccupied and meaningless. One can not pass this single occurrence by, considering it only in itself: it is one of a long series of quakes of the earth at Comrie and phenomena in the sky at Comrie. We have stronger evidence than the mere supposition of many persons, in and near Comrie, that, upon Oct. 23, 1839, something had occurred in the sky, because sounds seemed to come from the sky. Milne says that clothes, bleaching on the grass, were entirely covered with black particles which presumably had fallen from the sky. The shocks were felt in November: in November, according to Milne, a powder like soot fell from the sky, upon Comrie and surrounding regions. In his report to the British Association, 1840, Milne, reviewing the phenomena from the year 1788, says: "Occasionally there was a fall of fine, black powder."

Jan. 8, 1840 — sounds like cannonading, at Comrie, and a crackling sound in the air, according to some of the residents. Whether they were sounds of quakes or concussions that followed explosions,

256 occurrences, between Oct. 3, 1839, and Feb. 14, 1841, are listed in the *Edin. New Phil. Jour.* (32, 106). It looks like bombardment, and like most persistent bombardment — from somewhere — and the frequent fall from the sky of the debris of explosions. Feb. 18, 1841 — a shock and a fall of discoloured rain at Genoa, Italy (*Edin. N. Phil. Jour.*, 35, 144). See William Roper's *A List of Remarkable Earthquakes in Great Britain and Ireland During the Christian Era* — year after year, and the continuance of this seeming bombardment in one small part of the sky of this earth, though I can find records only of dates and no details. However, I think I have found record of a fall from the sky of debris of an explosion, more substantial than finely powdered soot, at Crieff, which is several miles from Comrie. In the *Amer. Jour. Sci.* (s. 2, 28, 275), Prof. Shepard tells a circumstantial story of an object that looked like a lump of slag, or cinders, reported to have fallen at Crieff. Scientists had refused to accept the story, upon the grounds that the substance was not of "true meteoric material." Prof. Shepard went to Crieff and investigated. He gave his opinion that possibly the object did fall from the sky. The story he tells is that, upon the night of April 23, 1855, a young woman, in the home of Sir William Murray, Ochtertyre House, Crieff, saw, or thought she saw, a luminous object falling, and picked it up, dropping it, because it was hot, or because she thought it was hot.

For a description, in a letter, presumably from Sir William Murray, or some member of his family, see *Year-Book of Facts* (1856, 273). It is said that about 12 fragments of scorious matter, hot and emitting a sulphurous odour, had fallen.

In Mungo Ponton's *Earthquakes and Volcanoes* (1st ed., 73; 2nd ed., 118), it is said that, upon the 8th of October, 1857, there had been, in Illinois, an earthquake, preceded by "a luminous appearance, described by some as a meteor and by others as vivid flashes of lightning." Though felt in Illinois, the centre of the disturbance was at St. Louis, Mo. One notes the misleading and the obscuring of such wording: in all contemporaneous accounts there is no such indefiniteness as one description by "some" and another notion by "others." Something exploded terrifically in the sky, at St. Louis, and shook the ground "severely" or "violently," at 4:20 A.M., Oct. 8, 1857. According to Timb's *Year-Book of Facts* (1858, 271), "a blinding meteoric ball from the heavens" was seen. "A large and brilliant meteor shot across the heavens" (St. Louis *Intelligencer*, Oct. 8). Of course the supposed earthquake was concussion from an explosion in the sky, but our own interest is in a series that is similar to others that we have recorded. According to the *New York Times* (Oct 12, 1857) a slight shock was said to have been felt four hours before the great concussion, and another three days before. But see Milne's "Catalogue of Destructive Earthquakes" (*B.A. Rept.*, 1911, 649) — not a mention of anything that would lead one away from safe and standardised suppositions. See *Bulletin of the Seismological Society of America* (3, 68) — here the "meteor" is mentioned, but there is no mention of the preceding concussions. Time after time, in a period of about three days, concussions were felt in and around St. Louis. One of these concussions, with its "sound like thunder or the roar of artillery" (New York *Times*, Oct. 8), was from an explosion in the sky. If the others were of the same origin — how could detonating meteors so repeat in one small local sky, and nowhere else, if this earth be a moving body? If it be said that only by coincidence did a meteor explode over a region where there had been other quakes, here is the question:

How many times can we accept that explanation as to similar series?

* * *

In the *Proceedings of the Society for Psychical Research*, (19, 144), a correspondent writes that, in Herefordshire, Sept. 24, 1854, upon a day that was "perfectly still, the sky cloudless," he had heard sounds like the discharges of heavy artillery, at intervals of about two minutes, continuing several hours. Again the "mystery of the local sky" — if these sounds did come from the sky. We have no data for thinking that they did.

In the London *Times*, Nov. 9, 1858, a correspondent writes that, in Cardiganshire, Wales, he had, in the autumn of 1855, often heard sounds like the discharges of heavy artillery, two or three reports rapidly, and then an interval of perhaps 20 minutes, also with long intervals, sometimes of days and sometimes of weeks, continuing throughout the winter of 1855-56. Upon the 5th of November, 1858, he had heard the sounds again, repeatedly, and louder than they had been three years before. In the *Times*, Nov. 12, someone else says that, at Dolgelly, he, too, had heard the "mysterious phenomenon," on the 3rd of November. Someone else — that, upon Oct. 13, he had heard the sounds at Swansea. "The reports, as if of heavy artillery, came from the west, succeeding each other at apparently regular intervals, during the greater part of the afternoon of that day. My impression was that the sounds might have proceeded from practising at Milford, but I ascertained, the following day, that there had been no firing of any kind there." Correspondent to the *Times*, November 20 — that, with little doubt, the sounds were from artillery practice at Milford. He does not mention the investigation as to the sounds of Oct. 13, but says that there had been cannon-firing, upon Nov. 3rd, at Milford. *Times*, Dec. 1 — that most of the sounds could be accounted for as sounds of blasting in quarries. *Daily News*, Nov. 16 — that similar sounds had been heard, in 1848, in New Zealand, and were results of volcanic action. *Standard*, Nov. 16 — that the "mysterious noise" must have been from Devonport, where a sunken rock had been blown up. So, with at least variety these sounds were explained. But we learn that the series began before October 13. Upon the evening of Sept. 28, in the Dartmoor District, at Crediton, a rumbling sound was heard. It was not supposed to be an earthquake, because no vibration of the ground was felt. It was thought that there had been an explosion of gunpowder. But there had been no such terrestrial explosion. About an hour later another explosive sound was heard. It was like all the other sounds, and in one place was thought to be distant cannonading — terrestrial cannonading. See *Quarterly Journal of the Geological Society of London* (15, 188).

Somewhere near Barisal, Bengal, were occurring just such sounds as the sounds of Cardiganshire, which were like the sounds of Melida. In the *Proceedings of the Royal Asiatic Society of Bengal* (1870, 289) are published letters upon the Barisal Guns. One writer says that the sounds were probably booming of the surf. Someone else points out that the sounds, usually described as "explosive," were heard too far inland to be traced to such origin. A clear, calm day, in December, 1871 — in *Nature* (53, 197), Mr. G.B. Scott writes that, in Bengal, he had heard "The dull, muffled booms as of distant cannon" — single detonations, and then two or three in quicker succession.

In the London *Times*, Jan. 20, 1860, several correspondents write as to a sound "resembling the discharge of a gun high up in the air" that was heard near Reading, Berkshire, England, Jan. 17, 1860. See the *Times*, Jan. 24th. To say that a meteor had exploded would, at present, well enough account for this phenomenon.

Sounds like those that were heard in Herefordshire, Sept. 24, 1854, were heard later. In the *English Mechanic* (100, 279), it is said that, upon Nov. 9, 1862, the Rev. T. Webb, the astronomer, of Hardwicke, fifteen miles west of Hereford, heard sounds that he attributed to gunfire at Milford Haven, about 85 miles from Hardwicke. Upon Aug. 1, 1865, Mr. Webb saw flashes upon the horizon, at Hardwick, and attributed them to gunfire at Tenby, upon occasion of a visit by Prince Arthur. Tenby, too, is about 85 miles from Hardwick. There were other phenomena in a region centring around Hereford and Worcester. Upon Oct. 6, 1863, there was a disturbance that is now listed as an earthquake; but in the London newspapers so many reports upon this occurrence state that a great explosion had been thought to occur, and that the quake was supposed to be an earthquake of subterranean origin only after no terrestrial explosion could be heard of, that the phenomenon is of questionable origin. There was a similar concussion in about the same region, Oct. 30, 1868. Again the shock was widely attributed to a great explosion, perhaps in London, and again was supposed to have been an earthquake when no terrestrial explosion could be heard of.

* * *

Arcana of Science (1829, 196):

That, near Mhow, India, Feb. 27, 1827, fell a stone "perfectly similar" to the stone that fell near Allahabad, in 1802, and a stone that fell near Mooradabad, in 1808. These towns are in the Northwestern Provinces of India.

I have looked at specimens of these stones, and in my view they are similar. They are of brownish rock, streaked and spotted with a darker brown. A stone that fell at Chandakopur, in the same general region, June 6, 1838, is like them. All are as much alike as "erratics" that, because they are alike, geologists ascribe to the same derivation, stationary relatively to the places in which they are found.

It seems acceptable that, upon July 15 and 17, 1822, and then upon a later date, unknown seeds fell from the sky to this earth (*Bulletin des Sciences, Mathematiques, Astronomique, Physiques et Chimiques*, 1, 298). If these seeds did come from some other world, there is another mystery as well as that of repetition in a local sky of this earth. How could a volume of seeds remain in one aggregation; how could the seeds be otherwise than scattered from Norway to Patagonia, if they met in space this earth, and if this earth be rushing through space at a rate of 19 miles a second? It may be that the seeds of 1822 fell again. According to L.F. Kaemetz (*A Complete Course of Meteorology*, 466), yellowish brown corpuscles, some round, a few cylindrical, were found upon the ground, June, 1830, near Griesau, Silesia. Kaemetz says that they were tubercules from roots of a well-known Silesian plant — stalk of the plant dries up; heavy rain raises these tubercules to the ground — persons of a low order of mentality think that the things had fallen from the sky. Upon the night of March 24-25, 1852, a great quantity of seeds did fall from the sky, in Prussia, in Heinsberg, Erkelenz, and Juliers, according to M. Schwann, of the University of Liége, in a communication to the Belgian Academy of Science (*La Belgique Horticole*, 2, 319).

In *Comptes Rendus* (5, 549) is Dr. Wartmann's account of water that fell from the sky, at Geneva. At nine o'clock, evening of Aug. 9, 1837, there were clouds upon the horizon, but the zenith was clear. It is not remarkable that a little rain should fall now and then from a clear sky: we shall see wherein this account is remarkable. Large drops of warm water fell in such abundance that people were driven to shelter. The fall continued several minutes and then stopped. But then, several times during an hour, more of this warm water fell from the sky. *Year-Book of Facts* (1839, 262) — that upon May 31, 1838, lukewarm water in large drops fell from the sky, at Geneva. *Comptes Rendus* (15, 290) — no wind and not a cloud in the sky — at 10 o'clock, morning of May 11, 1842, warm water fell from the sky at Geneva, for about six minutes; five hours later, still no wind and no clouds, again fell warm water, in large drops; falling intermittently for several minutes.

In *Comptes Rendus* (85, 681) is noted a succession of falls of stones in Russia: June 12, 1863, at Buschof, Courland; Aug. 8, 1863, at Pillitsfer, Livonia; April 12, 1864, at Nerft, Courland. Also — see Fletcher's List (*An Introduction to the Study of Meteorites*, 11th ed., 103) — a stone that fell at Dolgovoli, Volhynia, Russia, June 26, 1864. I have looked at specimens of all four of these stones, and have found them all very much alike, but not of uncommon meteoric material: all grey stones, but Pillitsfer is darker than the others, and in a polished specimen of Nerft, brownish specks are visible.

In the Birmingham *Daily Post*, June 14, 1858, Dr. C. Mansfield Ingleby, a meteorologist, writes: "During the storm on Saturday (12th) morning, Birmingham was visited by a shower of aerolites. Many hundreds of thousands must have fallen, some of the streets being strewed with them." Someone else writes that many pounds of the stones had been gathered from awnings, and that they had damaged greenhouses, in the suburbs. In the *Post*, of the 15th, someone else writes that, according to his microscopic examinations, the supposed aerolites were only bits of the Rowley ragstone, with which Birmingham was paved, which had been washed loose by the rain. It is not often that sentiment is brought into meteorology, but in the *B.A. Rept.* (1864, Trans., 37), Dr. Phipson explains the occurrence meteorologically, and with an unconscious tenderness. He says that the stones did fall from the sky, but that they had been carried in a "waterspout" from Rowley, some miles from Birmingham. So we are to sentimentalise over the stones in Rowley that had been torn, by unfeeling paviers, from their companions of geologic ages, and exiled to the pavements of Birmingham, and then some of these little bereft companions, rising in a whirlwind and travelling, unerringly, if not miraculously, to rejoin the exiles. More dark companions. It is said that they were little black stones.

They fell again from the sky, two years later, on June 20 1860. In *La Science Pour Tous* (5, 264), it is said that, according to the *Wolverhampton Advertiser and Spirit of the Times* (June 23, 1860), a great number of little black stones had fallen, in a violent storm, at Wolverhampton. According to all records findable by me no such stones have ever fallen anywhere in Great Britain, except at Birmingham and Wolverhampton, which is 13 miles from Birmingham.

Eight years after the second occurrence, they fell again. *English Mechanic* (7, 321) — that stones "similar to, if not identical with, the well-known Rowley ragstones" had fallen in Birmingham, having probably been carried from Rowley, in a whirlwind.

We were pleased with Dr. Phipson's story, but to tell of more of the little dark companions rising in a whirlwind and going unerringly from Rowley to rejoin exiles in Birmingham is overdoing. That's not sentiment: that's mawkishness.

In the *Birmingham Daily Post*, May 30, 1868, is published a letter from Thomas Plant, a writer and lecturer upon meteorological subjects. Mr. Plant says, I think, that for one hour, morning of May 29, 1868, stones fell, in Birmingham, from the sky. His words may be interpretable in some other way, but it does not matter: the repeating falls are indication enough of what we're trying to find out — "From nine to ten, meteoric stones fell in immense quantities in various parts of town." "They resembled, in shape, broken pieces of Rowley ragstone ... in every respect they were like the stones that fell in 1858." In the *Post*, June 1, Mr. Plant says that the stones of 1858 did fall from the sky, and were not fragments washed out of the pavement by rain, because many pounds of them had been gathered from a platform that was 20 feet above the ground.

It may be that for days before and after May 29, 1868, occasional stones fell from some unknown region stationary above Birmingham. In the *Post*, June 2, a correspondent writes that, upon the first of June, his niece, while walking in a field, was struck by a stone that injured her hand severely. He thinks that the stone had been thrown by some unknown person. In the *Post*, June 4, someone else writes that his wife, while walking down a lane, upon May 24th, had been cut on the head by a stone. He attributes this injury to stone-throwing by boys, but does not say that anyone had been seen to throw the stone.

Symons' *Meteorological Magazine* (4, 137):

That, according to the Birmingham *Gazette*, (May 27, 1869), a great number of small, black stones had been found in the streets of Wolverhampton, May 25, 1869, after a severe storm. It is said that the stones were precisely like those that had fallen in Birmingham, the year before, and resembled Rowley ragstone outwardly, but had a different appearance when broken.

CHAPTER 4

Upon page 287, *Popular Astronomy* (1st ed.; 2nd ed., 295), Newcomb says that it is beyond all "moral probability" that unknown worlds should exist in such numbers as have been reported, and should be seen crossing the solar disc only by amateur observers and not by skilled astronomers.

Most of our instances are reports by some of the best-known astronomers.

Newcomb says that for fifty years prior to his time of writing (edition of 1878) the sun had been studied by such men as Schwabe, Carrington, Secchi, and Spörer, and that they had never seen unknown bodies cross the sun —

Aug. 30, 1863 — an unknown body was seen by Spörer to cross the sun (Webb, *Celestial Objects*, 45).

Sept. 1, 1859 — two star-like objects that were seen by Carrington to cross the sun (*Monthly Notices*, 20: 13, 15, 88).

Things that have crossed the sun, July 31, 1826, and May 26, 1828 — see *Comptes Rendus* (83, 621) and Webb's *Celestial Objects* (40). From Sept. 6 to Nov. 1, 1831, an unknown luminous object was seen every cloudless night, at Geneva, by Dr. Wartmann and his assistant (*C.R.*, 2, 307). It was reported from nowhere else. What all the other astronomers were doing, Sept.-Oct., 1831, is one of the mysteries that we shall not solve. An unknown, luminous object that was seen, from May 11 to May 14, 1835, by Cacciatore, the Sicilian astronomer (*Amer. Jour. Sci.*, s. 1, 31, 158). Two unknowns that according to Pastorff, crossed the sun, Nov. 1, 1836, and Feb. 16, 1837 (*Ann. Sci. Disc.*, 1860, 410) — De Vico's unknown, July 12, 1837 (*Observatory*, 2, 424) — observation by De Cuppis, Oct. 2, 1839 (*C.R.*, 83, 622) — by Scott and Wray, last of June, 1847; by Schmidt, Oct. 11, 1847 (*C.R.*, 83, 622) — two dark bodies that were seen, Feb. 5, 1849, by Brown, of Deal (*Recreative Science*, 1, 130) — object watched by Sidebotham, half an hour, March 12, 1849, crossing the sun, (*C.R.*, 83, 622) — Schmidt's unknown, Oct. 14, 1849 (*Observatory*, 3, 135) — and an object that was watched, four nights in October, 1850, by James Ferguson, of the Washington Observatory. Mr. Hind believed this object to be a Trans-Neptunian planet, and calculated for it a period of 1,600 years. Mr. Hind was a great astronomer, and he miscalculated magnificently: this floating island of space was not seen again (*Bulletin of the Philosophical Society of Washington,* 3, 20; *Smithsonian Miscellaneous Collections,* 20, 20).

About August 30, 1853 — a black point that was seen against the sun, by Jaennicke (*Cosmos: Revue Encyclopédique,* 20, 64).

A procession — in the *B.A. Rept.* (1855, 94), R.P. Greg says that, upon May 22, 1854, a friend of his saw, near Mercury, an object equal in size to the planet itself, and behind it an elongated object, and behind that something else, smaller and round.

June 11, 1855 — a dark body of such size that it was seen, without telescopes, by Ritter and Schmidt, crossing the sun (*Observatory,* 3, 135). Sept. 12, 1857 — Ohrt's unknown world; seemed to be about the size of Mercury (*C.R.,* 83, 623) — Aug. 1, 1858 — unknown world reported by Wilson, of Manchester (*Astro. Reg.,* 9, 287).

I am not listing all the unknowns of a period; perhaps the object reported by John H. Tice, of St. Louis, Mo., Sept. 15, 1859, should not be included; Mr. Tice was said not to be trustworthy (Proctor, *Old and New Astronomy,* 425) — but who has any way of knowing? However, I am listing enough of these observations to make me feel like a translated European of some centuries ago, relatively to a wider existence — lands that may be the San Salvadors, Greenlands, Madagascars, Cubas, Australias of extra-geography, all of them said to have crossed the sun, whereas the sun may have moved behind some of them —

Jan. 29, 1860 — unknown object, of planetary size, reported from London, by Russell and three other observers (*Nature,* 14, 505). Summer of 1860 — see *Sci. Amer.* (n.s., 35, 340) for an account, by Richard Covington, of an object, that without a telescope, he saw crossing the sun. An unknown world, reported by Loomis, of Manchester, March 20, 1862 (*Monthly Notices,* 22, 232) — a newspaper account of an object that was seen crossing the sun, Feb. 12, 1864, by Samuel Beswick, of New York (*Astro. Reg.,* 2, 161) — unknown that was seen March 8, 1865, at Constantinople (*Année Scientifique et Industrielle,* 10, 16) — unknown "cometic objects" that were seen, November 4, 9, and 18, 1865 (*Monthly Notices,* 26: 242, 271).

Most of these unknowns were seen in the daytime. Several reflections arise. How can there be stationary regions over Irkutsk,

Comrie, and Birmingham, and never obscure the stars — or never be seen to obscure the stars? A heresy that seems too radical for me is that they may be beyond nearby stars. A more reasonable idea is that if nightwatchmen and policemen and other persons who do stay awake nights, should be given telescopes, something might be found out. Something else that one thinks of is that, if so many unknowns have been seen crossing the sun, or crossed by the sun, others not so revealed must exist in great numbers, and that instead of being virtually blank, space must be archipelagic.

Something that was seen at night; observer not an astronomer —

Nov. 6, 1866 — an account, in the London *Times*, Jan. 2, 1867, by Senor De Fonblanque, of the British Consulate, at Cartagena, U.S. Colombia, of a luminous object that moved in the sky. "It was of the magnitude, colour, and brilliancy of a ship's red light, as seen at a distance of 200 yards." The object was visible three minutes, and then disappeared behind buildings. De Fonblanque went to an open space to look for it, but did not see it again.

CHAPTER 5

If we could stop to sing, instead of everlastingly noting vol. this and p. that, we could have the material of sagas — of the bathers in the sun, which may be neither intolerably hot nor too uncomfortably cold; and of the hermit who floats across the moon; of heroes and the hairy monsters of the sky. I should stand in public places and sing our data — sagas of parades and explorations and massacres in the sky — having a busy band of accompanists, who set off fireworks, and send up balloons, and fire off explosives at regular intervals — extra-geographic songs of boiling lakes and floating islands — extra-sociologic metres that express the tramp of space-armies upon interplanetary paths covered with little black pebbles — biologic epics of the clouds of mammoths and horses and antelopes that once upon a time fell from the sky upon the northern coast of Siberia —

Song that interprets the perpendicular white streaks in the repeating mirages at Youghal — the rhythmic walruses of space that hang on by their tusks to the edges of space-islands, sometimes making stars variable as they swing in cosmic undulations — so a round space-island with its border of gleaming tusks, and we frighten children with the song of an ogre's head, with wide-open mouth all around it — fairy lands of the little moon, and the tiny civilizations in rocky cups that are sometimes drained to their slums by the wide-mouthed ogres. The Maelstrom of Everlasting Catastrophe that overhangs Genoa, Italy — and twines its currents around a living island. The ground underneath quakes with the struggle — then the fall of blood — and the fall of blood — three days the fall of blood from the broken red brooks of a living island whose mutilations are scenery —

But after all, it may be better that we go back to *B.A. Rept.* — see the vol. for 1849, p. 46 — a stream of black objects, crossing the sun, watched, at Naples, May 11, 1845, by Capocci and other astronomers — things that may have been seeds.

A great number of red points in the sky of Urrugne, July 9, 1853 (*Annuaire de la Société Météorologique de France*, 1, 227). *Astro. Reg.* (5, 179) — C.L. Prince, of Uckfield, writes that, upon June 11, 1867, he saw objects crossing the field of his telescope. They were seeds, in his opinion.

Birmingham *Daily Post* (May 31, 1867):

Mr. Bird, the astronomer, writes that, about 11 A.M., May 30, he saw unknown forms in the sky. In his telescope, which was focussed upon them and upon the planet Venus, they appeared to be twice the size of Venus. They were far away, according to focus; also, it may be accepted that they were far away because an occasional cloud passed between them and this earth. They did not move like objects carried in the wind: all did not move in the same direction, and they moved at different speeds.

"All of them seemed to have hairy appendages, and in many cases a distinct tail followed the object and was highly luminous."

Flashes that have been seen in the sky — and they're from a living island that wags his luminous peninsula. Hair-like substances that have fallen to this earth — a meadow has been shorn from a monster's mane. My animation is the notion that it is better to think in tentative hysteria of pairs of vast things, travelling like a North and South America through the sky, perhaps one biting the other with its Gulf of Mexico, than to go on thinking that all things that so move in the sky are seeds, whereas all things that swim in the sea are not sardines.

In the *Post*, June 3, 1867, Mr. W.H. Wood writes that the objects were probably seeds. *Post*, June 5 — Mr. Bird says that the objects were not seeds. "My intention was simply to describe what was seen, and the appearance was certainly that of meteors." He saves himself, in the annals of extra-geography — "whether they were meteors of the ordinary acceptation, is another matter."

And the planet Venus, and her veil that is dotted with blue-fringed cupids — in the *Astronomical Register* (7, 138), a correspondent writes, from Northampton, that, upon May 2, 1869, he was looking at Venus, and saw a host of shining objects, not uniform in size. He thinks that it is unlikely that so early in the spring could these objects be seeds. He watched them about an hour and twenty minutes — "many of the larger ones were fringed on one side; the fringe appearing somewhat bluish." Or that it is better even to sentimentalize than to go on stupidly thinking that all such things in the sky are seeds, whereas all things in the sea are not the economically adjusting little forms without which critics of underground traffic in New York probably could not express themselves — the planet Venus — she approaches this lordly earth — the blue-fringed ecstasies that suffuse her skies.

With the phenomena of Aug. 7, 1869, I suspect that the "phantom soldiers" that have been seen in the sky, may have been reflections from, or mirages of, things or beings that march, in military formations, in space. In *Popular Astronomy* (3, 159), Prof. Swift writes that, at Mattoon, Ill., during the eclipse of the sun, Aug. 7, 1869, he had seen, crossing the moon, objects that he thought were seeds. If they were seeds, also there happened to be seeds in the sky of Ottumwa, Iowa: here, crossing the visible part of the sun, twenty-five minutes before totality of the eclipse, Prof. Himes and Prof. Zentmayer saw objects that marched, or that moved, in straight, parallel lines (*Cosmos (L.M.)*, 21, 241). In the *Journal of the Franklin Institute* (s. 3, 58, 213), it is said that some of these objects moved in one direction across the moon, and that others moved in another direction across another part of the telescopic field of view, each division moving in parallel lines. If these things were seeds, also there happened to be seeds in the sky, at Shelbyville, Kentucky. Here were seen, by Prof. Winlock, Alvan Clark Jr., and George W. Dean, things that moved across the moon, during the eclipse, in parallel, straight lines (*Pop. Astro.*, 2, 332).

Whatever these things may have been, I offer another datum indicating that the moon is nearby: that these objects probably were not, by coincidence, things in three widely separated skies, parallelness giving them identity in two of the observations; and, if seen, without parallax, from places so far apart, against the moon, were close to the moon; that observation of such detail would be unlikely if they were near a satellite 240,000 miles away — unless, of course, they were mountain-sized.

It may be that out from two floating islands of space, two processions had marched across the moon. *Observatory* (3, 135) — that at St. Paul Junction, Iowa, four persons had seen, without telescopes, a shining object close to the sun and moon, apparently; that, with a telescope, another person had seen another large object, crescentically illuminated, farther from the sun and moon in eclipse. See *Nature* (18, 663) and *Astro. Reg.* (7, 227).

I have many data upon the fall of organic matter from the sky.

Because of my familiarity with many records, it seems no more incredible that up in the seemingly unoccupied sky there should be hosts of living things than that the seemingly blank of the ocean should swarm with life. I have many notes upon a phosphorescence, or electric condition of things that fall from the sky, for instance the highly luminous stones of Dhurmsulla, which were intensely cold —

American Journal of Science, s. 2, 28, 275:

It is said that, according to investigations by Prof. Shepard, a luminous substance was seen falling slowly, by Sparkman R. Scriven, a young man of seventeen, at his home, in Charleston, S.C., Nov. 16, 1857. It is said that the young man saw a fiery, red ball, the size and shape of an orange, strike a fence, breaking, and disappearing. Where this object had struck the fence, was found "a small bristling mass of black fibres." According to Prof. Shepard, it was "a confused aggregate of short clippings of the finest black hair, varying in length from one tenth to one third of an inch." Prof. Shepard says that this substance was not organic. It seems to me that he said this only because of the coercions of his era. My reason for so thinking is that he wrote that when he analysed these hairs they burned away, leaving greyish skeletons, and that they were "composed in part of carbon" and burned with an odour "resembling the bituminous."

For full details of the following circumstances, see *Comptes Rendus* (13, 215) and *B.A. Rept.* (1854, 302):

Feb. 17, 1841 — the fall, at Genoa, Italy, of a red substance from the sky — another fall upon the 18th — a slight quake, at 5 P.M., Feb. 18th — another quake, six hours later — fall of more of the red substance, upon the 19th. Some of this substance was collected and analyzed by M. Canobbia, of Genoa. He says it was oily and red.

CHAPTER 6

In a pamphlet entitled *Wonderful Phenomena* by Eli Curtis, is the report of an occurrence, or of an alleged occurrence, that was investigated by Mr. Addison A. Sawin, a spiritualist. He interpreted in the only way that I know of, and that is the psychochemic process of combining new data with preconceptions with which they seem to have affinity. It is said that, at Warwick, Canada West (Ontario), Oct. 3, 1843, somebody named Charles Cooper heard a rumbling sound in the sky, and saw a cloud, under which were three human forms, "perfectly white," sailing through the air above him, little higher than the tree-tops. It is said that the beings were angels. They were male angels. That is orthodox. The angels wafted through the air, but without motions of their own, and an interesting observation is that they seemed to have belts around their bodies — as if they had been let down from a vessel above, though this poor notion is not suggested in the pamphlet. They moaned. Cooper called to some men who were labouring in another field, and they saw the cloud, but did not see the forms of living beings under it. It is said that a boy had seen the beings in the air, "side by side when he saw them, making a very loud, mournful noise." Another person, who lived six miles away, is quoted: "he saw the clouds and persons, and heard the sound." Mr. Sawin quotes others, who had seen "a very remarkable cloud," and had heard the sounds, but had not seen the angels. He ends up: "Yours, in the glorious hope of the resurrection of the dead." The gloriousness of it is an inverse function of the dolefulness of it: Sunday Schools will not take kindly to the doctrine — be good and you will moan forever. One supposes that the glorious hope coloured the whole investigation.

Some day I shall publish data that lead me to suspect that many appearances upon this earth that were once upon a time interpreted by theologians and demonologists, but are now supposed to be the subject-matter of psychic research, were beings and objects that visited this earth, not from a spiritual existence, but from outer space. That extra-geographic conditions may be spiritual, or of highly attenuated matter, is not my present notion, though that, too, may be some day accepted. Of course all these data suffer, in one way, about as much distortion as they would in other ways, if they had been reported by astronomers or meteorologists. As to all the material in this chapter, I take the position that perhaps there were appearances in the sky, and perhaps they were revelations of, or mirages from, unknown regions and conditions of outer space, and spectacles of relatively nearby inhabited lands, and of space-travellers, but that all reports upon them were products of the assimilating of the unknown with figures and figments of the nearest familiar similarities. Another position of mine that will be found well-taken is that, no matter what my own interpretations or acceptances may be, they will compare favourably, so far as rationality is concerned, with orthodox explanations. There have been many assertions that "phantom soldiers" have been seen in the sky. For the orthodox explanation of the physicists, see David Brewster's *Letters on Natural Magic* (1st ed., 126): a review of the phenomenon of June 23, 1744; that, according to 26 witnesses, some of whom gave sworn testimony before a magistrate, whether that should be mentioned or not, troops of aerial soldiers had been seen, in Scotland, on and over a mountain, remaining visible two hours and then disappearing because of darkness. In James Clarke's *Survey of the Lakes of Cumberland, Westmorland, and Lancashire* (2nd ed., "Book Second," 55) is an account in the words of one of the witnesses. See *Notes and Queries* (s. 1, 7, 304). Brewster says that the scene must have been a mirage of British troops, who, in anticipation of the rebellion of 1745, were secretly manoeuvring upon the other side of the mountain. With a talent for clear-seeing, for which we are notable, except when it comes to some of our own explanations, we almost instantly recognise that, to keep a secret from persons living upon one side of a mountain, it is a very sensible idea to go and manoeuvre upon the other side of the mountain; but then how to keep the secret, in a thickly populated country like Scotland, from persons living upon that other side of the mountain — however there never has been an explanation that did not itself have to be explained.

Or the "phantom soldiers" that were seen at Ujest, Silesia, in 1785 — see Parish's *Hallucination and Illusions* (2nd ed., 309). Parish finds that at the time of this spectacle, there were soldiers, of this earth, marching near Ujest; so he explains that the "phantom soldiers" were mirages of them. They were marching in the funeral procession of General von Cosel. But some time later they were seen again, at Ujest

— and the General had been dead and buried several days, and his funeral procession disbanded — and if a refraction can survive independently of its primary, so may a shadow, and anybody may take a walk where he went a week before, and see some of his shadows still wandering around without him. The great neglect of these explainers is in not accounting for an astonishing preference for, or specialisation in, marching soldiers, by mirages. But if often there be, in the sky, things or beings that move in parallel lines, and, if their betrayals be not mirages, but their shadows cast down upon the haze of this earth, or Brocken spectres, such frequency, or seeming specialisation, might be accounted for.

Sept. 27, 1846 — a city in the sky of Liverpool (*B.A. Rept.*, 1847, Trans., 39). The apparition is said to have been a mirage of the city of Edinburgh. This "identification" seems to have been the product of suggestion: at the time a panorama of Edinburgh was upon exhibition in Liverpool.

Summer of 1847 — see Flammarion's *The Atmosphere* (1873 ed., 153) — story told by M. Grellois: that he was travelling between Ghelma and Bône, when he saw to the east of Bône, upon a gently sloping hill, "a vast and beautiful city, adorned with monuments, domes, and steeples." There was no resemblance to any city known to M. Grellois.

In the *Bull. S.A.F.* (27, 179) is an account of a spectacle that, according to 20 witnesses, was seen for two hours in the sky of Vienne dans le Dauphiné, May 3, 1848. A city — and an army, in the sky. One supposes that a Brewster would say that nearby was a terrestrial city, with troops manoeuvring near it. But also vast lions were seen in the sky — and that is enough to discourage any Brewster. Four months later, according to the London *Times*, Sept. 13, 1848, a still more discouraging — or perhaps stimulating — spectacle was, or was not, seen in Ireland. Early morning of Sept. 9, 1848 — Quigley's Point, Lough Foyle, Ireland — the sky turned dark. It seemed to open. The opening looked reddish, and in the reddish area, appeared a regiment of soldiers. Then came appearances that looked like war vessels under full sail, then a man and woman, and then a swan and a peahen. The "opening" closed, and that was the last of this shocking or ridiculous mixture that nobody but myself would record as being worth thinking about.

"Phantom soldiers" that were seen in the sky, near Banmouth, Dec. 14, 1850 (*B.A. Rept.*, 1852, Trans., 29).

"Phantom soldiers" that were seen at Büderich, Westphalia, Germany, Jan. 22, 1854 (*Notes and Queries*, s. 1, 9, 267).

"Phantom soldiers" that were seen by Lord Roberts of Kandahar (*Forty-One Years in India*, 30th ed., 218), at Mohan, after Feb. 25, 1858. It is either that Lord Roberts saw indistinctly, and described in terms of the familiar to him, or that we are set back in our own notions. According to him, the figures wore Hindoo costumes.

Extra-geography — its vistas and opening and fields — and the Thoreaus that are upon this earth, but undeveloped, because they cannot find their ponds. A lonely thing and its pond, afloat in space — they crossed the moon. In *Cosmos: Revue Encyclopedic* (s. 1, 11, 200), it is said that, night of July 7, 1857, two persons of Chambon had seen forms crossing the moon — something like a human being followed by a pond.

"Phantom soldiers" that were seen, about the year 1860, at Paderborn, Westphalia (Catherine Crowe, *The Night-Side of Nature*, rev. ed., 416).

CHAPTER 7

We attempt to co-ordinate various streaks of data, all of which signify to us that, external to this earth, and in relation with, or relatable to, this earth are lands and lives and a generality of conditions that make of the whole, supposed solar system one globule of circumstances like terrestrial circumstances. Our expressions are in physical terms, though in outer space there may be phenomena known as psychic phenomena, because of the solid substances and objects that have fallen from the sky to this earth, similar to, but sometimes not identified with, known objects and substances upon this earth. Opposing us is the more or less well-established conventional doctrine that has spun like a cocoon around mind upon this earth, shutting off research, and stifling even speculation, shelling away all data of relations and relatability with external existences, a doctrine that, in its various explanations and disregards and denials, is unified in one expression of Exclusionism.

An unknown vegetable substance falls from the sky. The datum is buried: it may sprout some day.

The earth quakes. A luminous object is seen in the sky. Substance falls from the unknown. But the event is catalogued with subterranean earthquakes.

All conventional explanation and all conventional disregards and denials have Exclusionism in common. The unity is so marked, all writings in the past are so definitely in agreement, that I now think of a general era that is, by Exclusionism, as distinctly characterised as ever was the Carboniferous Era.

A pregnant woman stands near Niagara Falls. There are sounds, and they are vast circumstances; but the cells of an unborn being respond, or vibrate, only as they do to disturbances in their own little environment. Horizons pour into a gulf, and thunder rolls upward: embryonic consciousness is no more than to slight perturbations of maternal indigestion. It is Exclusionism.

Stones fall from the sky. To the same part of this earth, they fall again. They fall again. They fall from the same region that, relatively to this part of the earth's surface, is stationary. But to say this leads to the suspicion that it is this earth that is stationary. To think that is to beat

116

against the walls of uterine dogmas — into a partly hairy and somewhat reptilian mass of social undevelopment comes exclusionist explanation suitable for such immaturity.

It does not matter which of our subjects we take up, our experience is unvarying: the standardised explanation will be Exclusionism. As to many appearances in the sky, the way of excluding foreign forces is to say that they are auroras, which are supposed to be mundane phenomena. School children are taught that auroras are electric manifestations encircling the poles of this earth. Respectful urchins are shown an icon by which an electrified sphere does have the polar encirclements that it should have. But I have taken a disrespectful, or advanced, course through the *Monthly Weather Review*, and have read hundreds of times of auroras that were not such polar crownings: of auroras in Venezuela, Sandwich Islands (Hawaii), Cuba, India; of an aurora in Pennsylvania, for instance, and not a sign of it north of Pennsylvania. There are lights in the sky for which "auroral" is as good a name as any that can be thought of, but there are others for which some other names will have to be thought of. There have been lights like luminous surfs beating upon the coasts of this earth's atmosphere, and lights like vast reflections from distant fires; steady pencils of light and pulsating clouds and quick flashes and seeming objects with definite outlines, all in one poverty of nomenclature, for which science is, in some respects, not notable, called "auroral." Nobody knows what an aurora is. It does not matter. This is standardisation, and the essence of this standardisation is Exclusionism.

I see one resolute, unified, unscrupulous exclusion from science of the indications of nearby lands in the sky. It may not be unscrupulousness: it may be hypnosis. I see that all seeming hypnotics, or somnambulists of the past, who have most plausibly so explained, or so denied, have prospered and have had renown. According to my impressions, if a Brewster, or a Swift, or a Newcomb ever had written that there may be nearby lands and living beings in the sky, he would not have prospered, and his renown would be still subject to delay. If an organism flourishes, it is said to be in harmony with environment, or with higher forces. I now conceive of successful and flourishing Exclusionism as an organisation that has been in harmony with higher forces. Suppose we accept that all general delusions function sociologically. Then, if Exclusionism be general delusion; if we shall accept that conceivably the isolation of this earth has been a necessary factor in the development of the whole geo-system, we see that exclusionistic science has faithfully, though falsely, functioned. It would be world-wide crime to spread world-wide too soon the idea that there are other existences nearby and that they have been seen and that sounds from them have been heard: the peoples of this earth must organise themselves before conceiving of, and trying to establish, foreign relations. A premature science of such subjects would be like a United States taking part in a Franco-Prussian War, when such foreign relations should be still far in the future of a nation that has still to concentrate upon its own internal development.

So in the development of all things — or that a stickleback may build a nest, and so may vaguely and not usefully and not explicably at all, in terms of Darwinian evolution, foreshadow a character of coming forms of life; but that a fish should try to climb a tree and to sing to its mate before even the pterodactyl had flapped around with wings daubed with clay would be an unnoticed little clown in cosmic drama. But I do conceive that when the Carboniferous Era is dominant, and when not a discordant thing will be permitted to flourish, though it may adumbrate, restrictions will not last forever, and that the rich and bountiful curse upon rooted things will some day be lifted.

CHAPTER 8

Patched by a blue inundation that had never been seen before — this earth, early in the 60's of the 19th century. Then faintly, from far away, this new appearance is seen to be enveloped with volumes of grey. Flashes like lightning, and faintest of rumbling sounds — then cloud-like envelopments roll away, and a blue formation shines in the sun. Meteorologists upon the moon take notes.

But year after year there are appearances, as seen from the moon, that are so characterised that they may not be meteorologic phenomena upon this earth: changing compositions wrought with elements of blue and of grey; it is like conflict between Synthesis and Dissolution: straight lines that fade into scrawls, but that re-form into seeming moving symbols: circles and squares and triangles abound.

Having had no mean experience with interpretations as products of desires, given that upon the moon communication with this earth should be desired, it seems likely to me that the struggles of hosts of Americans, early in the 60's of the 19th century, were given thought by some lunarians to be manoeuvres directed to them, or attempts to attract their attention. However, having had many impressions upon the resistance that new delusions encounter, so that, at least upon this earth, some benightments have had to wait centuries before finally imposing themselves generally, I'd think of considerable time elapsing before the coming of a general conviction upon the moon that, by means of living symbols, and the firing of explosives, terrestrians were trying to communicate.

Beacon-like lights that have been seen upon the moon. The lights have been desultory. The latest of which I have record was back in the year 1847. But now, if beginning in the early 60's, though not coinciding with the beginning of unusual and tremendous manifestations upon this earth, we have data as if of greatly stimulated attempts to communicate from the moon — why one assimilates one's impressions of such great increase with this or with that, all according to what one's dominant thoughts may be, and calls the product a logical conclusion. Upon the night of May 15, 1864, Herbert Ingall, of Camberwell, saw a little to the west of the lunar crater Picard, in the Mare Crisium, a remarkably bright spot (*Astro. Reg.*, 2, 264).

Oct. 24, 1864 — period of nearest approach by Mars — red lights upon opposite parts of Mars (*C.R.*, 85, 538). Upon Oct. 16, Ingall had again seen the light west of Picard (*Astro. Reg.*, 2, 264). Jan. 1, 1865 — a small speck of light, in darkness, under the east foot of the lunar Alps, shining like a small star, watched half an hour by Charles Gower (*Astro. Reg.*, 3, 255). Jan. 3, 1865 — again the red lights of Mars (*C.R.*, 85, 538). A thread of data appears, as an offshoot from a main streak, but it can not sustain itself. Lights on the moon and lights on Mars, but I have nothing more that seems to signify both signals and responses between these two worlds.

April 10, 1865 — west of Picard, according to Ingall — "a most minute point of light, glittering like a star" (*Astro. Reg.*, 3, 189).

Sept. 5, 1865 — a conspicuous bright spot west of Picard (*Astro. Reg.*, 3, 252). It was seen again by Ingall. He saw it again upon the 7th, but upon the 8th it had gone, and there was a cloud-like effect where the light had been.

Nov. 24, 1865 — a speck of light that was seen by the Rev. W.O. Williams, shining like a small star in the lunar crater Carlini (*Intel. Obs.*, 11, 58).

June 10, 1866 — the star-like light in Aristarchus; reported by Tempel (Denning, *Telescopic Work for Starlight Evenings*, 120).

Astronomically and seleno-meteorologically, nothing that I know of has ever been done with these data. I think well of taking up the subject theologically. We are approaching accounts of a different kind of changes upon the moon. There will be data seeming so to indicate not only persistence but devotedness upon the moon that I incline to think not only of devotedness but of devotions. Upon the 16th of October, 1866, the astronomer Schmidt, of the land of Socrates, announced that the isolated object, in the eastern part of the Mare Serenitatis, known as Linné, had changed. Linné stands out in a blank area like the Pyramid of Cheops in its desert. If changes did occur upon Linné, the conspicuous position seems to indicate selection. Before October, 1866, Linné was well-known as a dark object. Something was whitening an object that had been black.

A hitherto unpublished episode in the history of theologies:

The new prophet who had appeared upon the moon —

Faint perceptions of moving formations, often almost rigorously geometric, upon one part of this earth, and perhaps faintest of signal-like sounds that reached the moon — the new prophet — and that he preached the old lunar doctrine that there is no god but the Earth-god, but exhorted his hearers to forsake their altars upon which had burned unheeded lights, and to build a temple upon which might be recited a litany of lights and shades.

We are only now realising how the Earth-god looks to the beings of the moon — who know that this earth is dominant; who see it frilled with the loops of the major planets; its Elizabethan ruff wrought by the complications of the asteroids; the busy little sun that brushes off the dark.

God of the moon, when mists make it expressionless — a vast, bland, silvery Buddha.

God of the moon, when seeing it clear — when the disguise is off — when, at night, from pointed white peaks drip the fluctuating red lights of a volcano, this earth is the appalling god of carnivorousness.

Sometimes the great roundish earth, with the heavens behind it broken by refraction, looks like something thrust into a shell from external existence — clouds of tornadoes as if in its grasp — and it looks like the fist of God, clutching rags of ultimate fire and confusion.

That a new prophet had appeared upon the moon, and had excited new hope of evoking response from the bland and shining Stupidity that has so often been mistaken for God, or from the Appalling that is so identified with Divinity — from the clutched and menacing fist that has so often been worshipped.

There is no intelligence except era-intelligence. Suppose the whole geo-system be a super-embryonic thing. Then, by the law of the embryo, its parts cannot organise until comes scheduled time. So there are local congeries of development of a chick in an egg, but these local centres can not more than faintly sketch out relations with one another, until comes the time when they may definitely integrate. Suppose that far back in the 19th century there were attempts to communicate from the moon; but suppose that they were premature: then we suppose the fate of the protoplasmic threads that feel out too soon from one part of an egg to another. In October, 1866, Schmidt, of Athens, saw and reported in terms of the concepts of his era, and described in conventional selenographic language. See *B.A. Rept.*

(1867, 6).

Upon December 14, 16, 25, 27, 1866, Linné was seen as a white spot. But there was something that had the seeming more of a design, or of a pattern, an elaboration upon the mere turning to white of something that had been black — a fine, black spot upon Linné; by Schmidt and Buckingham, in December, 1866 (*The Student and Intellectual Observer*, 1, 266). The most important consideration of all is reviewed by Schmidt in the *B.A. Rept.* (1867, 22) — that sunlight and changes of sunlight had nothing to do with the changing appearances of Linné. Jan. 14, 1867 — the white covering, or, at least, seeming of covering, of Linné, had seemingly disappeared — Knott's impression of Linné as a dark spot, but "definition" was poor. Jan. 16 — Knott's very strong impression, which, however, he says may have been an illusion, of a small central dark spot upon Linné. Dawes' observation, of March 15, 1867 — "an excessively minute black dot in the middle of Linné."

A geometric figure that was white-bordered and centred with black, formed and dissolved and formed again.

I have an impression of spectacles that were common in the United States, during the War: hosts of persons arranging themselves in living patterns: flags, crosses, and in one instance, in which thousands were engaged, in the representation of an enormous Liberty Bell. Astronomers have thought of trying to communicate with Mars or the moon by means of great geometric constructions placed conspicuously, but there is nothing so attractive to attention as change, and a formation that could appear and disappear would enchance the geometric with the dynamic. That the units of the changing compositions that covered Linné were the lunarians themselves — that Linné was terraced — hosts of the inhabitants of the moon standing upon ridges of their Cheops of the Serene Sea, some of them dressed in white and standing in a border, and some of them dressed in black, centring upon the apex, or the dark material of the apex left clear for the contrast, all of them unified in a hope of conveying an impression of the geometric, as the product of design, and distinguishable from the topographic, to the shining god that makes the stars of their heaven marginal.

It is a period of great activity — or of conflicting ideas and purposes — upon the moon: new and experimental demonstrations, but also, of course, the persistence of the old. In the *Astronomical Register* (5, 114), Thomas G. Elger writes that upon the 9th of April, 1867, he was surprised to see, upon the dark part of the moon, a light like a star of the 7th magnitude, at 7:30 P.M. It became fainter, and looked almost extinguished at 9 o'clock. Mr. Elger had seen lights upon the moon before, but never before a light so clear — "so conspicuous that it could not possibly have been overlooked." May 7, 1867 — the beacon-like light of Aristarchus — observed by Tempel, of Marseilles, when Aristarchus was upon the dark side of the moon (*Astro. Reg.*, 5, 220). Upon the night of June 10, 1867, Dawes saw three distinct, roundish, black spots near Sulpicius Gallus, which is near Linné; when looked for upon the 13th, they had disappeared (*The Student and Intellectual Observer*, 1, 261).

August 6, 1867 —

And this earth in the sky of the moon — smooth and bland and featureless earth — or one of the scenes that make it divine and appalling — jaws of this earth, as seem to be the rims of more or less parallel mountain ranges, still shining in sunlight, but surrounded by darkness —

And, upon the moon, the assembling of the Chiaroscuroans, or the lunar communicationists who seek to be intelligible to this earth by means of lights and shades, patterned upon Linné by their own forms and costumes. The Great Pyramid of Linné, at night upon the moon — it stands out in bold triangularity pointing to this earth. It slowly suffuses white — the upward drift of white-clad forms, upon the slopes of the Pyramid. The jaws of this earth seem to munch, in variable light. There is no other response. Devotions are the food of the gods.

Upon August 6, 1867, Buckingham saw upon Linné, which was in darkness, "a rising oval spot" (*B.A. Rept.*, 1867, 7). In October, 1867, Linné was seen as a convex white spot (*B.A. Rept.*, 1867, 8).

* * *

Also it may be that the moon is not inhabited, and is not habitable. There are many astronomers who say that the moon has virtually no atmosphere, because when a star is passed over by the moon, the star is not refracted, according to them. See Clerke's *Popular History of Astronomy* (264) — that, basing his calculations upon the fact that a star is never refracted out of place when occulted by the moon, Prof. Comstock, of Washburn Observatory, had determined that this earth's atmosphere is 5,000 times as dense as the moon's.

I did think that in this secondary survey of ours we had pretty well shaken off our old opposition, the astronomers; however, with something of the kindliness that one feels for renewed meeting with the familiar, here we are at home with the same old kind of demonstrations: the basing of laborious calculations upon something that is not so —

See *Monthly Notices* (17: 143, 176; 19, 208; 39, 198; 50, 385) — many instances of stars that have been refracted out of place when occulted by the moon. See the *Observatory* (3, 84; 24: 93, 185, 210, 313, 345, 417), *English Mechanic* (23: 197, 279; 26, 229; 52: 120, 440; 81, 60; 84, 161).

In the year 1821, Gruithuisen announced that he had discovered a city of the moon. He described its main thoroughfare and branching streets. In 1826, he announced that there had been considerable building, and that he had seen new streets. This formation, which is north of the crater Schroeter, has often been examined by disagreeing astronomers: for a sketch of it, in which a central line and radiating lines are shown, see the *English Mechanic* (18, 638). There is one especial object upon the moon that has been described and photographed and sketched so often that I shall not go into the subject. For many records of observations, see the *English Mechanic* and *L'Astronomie*. It is an object shaped like a sword, near the crater Birt. Anyone with an impression of the transept of a cathedral, may see the architectural here. Or it may be a mound similar to the mounds of North America that have so logically been attributed to the Mound Builders. In a letter, published in the *Astronomical Register* (20, 165), Mr. Birmingham calls attention to a formation that suggests the architectural upon the moon — "a group of three hills in a slightly acute-angled triangle, and connected by three lower embankments." There is a geometric object, or marking, shaped like an "X," in the crater Eratosthenes (*Sci. Amer. Supp.*, 59, 24468); striking symbolic-looking thing or sign, or attempt by means of something obviously not topographic, to attract attention upon this earth, in the crater Plinius (*Eng. Mech.*, 35, 34); reticulations, like those of a city's squares, in Plato (*Eng. Mech.*, 64, 252); and there is a structural-looking composition of angular lines in Gassendi (*Eng. Mech.*, 101, 464). Upon the floor of Littrow are six or seven spots arranged in the form of the Greek letter *Gamma* (*Eng. Mech.*, 101, 46). This arrangement may be of recent origin, having been discovered Jan. 31, 1915. The Greek letter makes difficulty only for those who do not want to think easily upon this subject. For a representation of something that looked like a curved wall upon the moon, see *L'Astronomie* (7, 110). As to appearances like viaducts (on Mars), see *L'Astronomie* (7, 213). The lunar craters are not in all instances the simple cirques that they are commonly supposed to be. I have many different impressions of some of them: I remember one sketch that looked like an owl with a napkin tucked under his beak. However, it may be that the general style of architecture upon the moon is Byzantine, very likely, or not so likely, domed with glass, giving the dome-effect that has so often been commented upon.

So then the little nearby moon — it is populated by Lilliputians. However, our experience with agreeing ideas having been what it has been, we suspect that the lunarians are giants. Having reasonably determined that the moon is one hundred miles in diameter, we suppose it is considerably more or less.

* * *

A group of astronomers had been observing extraordinary lights in the lunar crater Plato. The lights had definite arrangement. They were so individualised that Birt and Elger, and the other selenographers, who had combined to study them, had charted and numbered them. They were fixed in position, but rose and fell in intensity.

It does seem to me that we have data of one school of communicationists after another coming into control of efforts upon the moon. At first our data related to single lights. They were extraordinary, and they seem to me to have been signals, but there seemed to be nothing of the organisation that now does seem to be creeping into the fragmentary material that is the best that we can find.

The grouped lights in Plato were so distinctive, so clear and even brilliant, that if such lights had ever shone before, it seems that they must have been seen by the Schroeters, Gruithuisens, Beers and Mädlers, who had studied and charted the features of the moon. For several of Gledhill's observations, from which I derive my impressions of these lights, see *B.A. Rept.* (1871, 80) — "I can only liken them to the small discs of stars, seen in the transit-instrument"; "just like small stars in the transit instrument, upon a windy night!"

In August and September, 1869, occurred a notable illumination of the spots in Group I. It was accompanied by a single light upon a distant spot.

February and March, 1870 — illumination of another group.

April 17, 1870 — another illumination in Plato, but back to the first group.

As to his observations of May 10-12, 1870, Birt gives his opinion that the lights of Plato were not effects of sunlight (*Eng. Mech.*, 14, 194).

Upon the 13th of May, 1870, there was an "extraordinary display," according to Birt: 27 lights were seen by Pratt, and 28 by Elger, but only 4 by Gledhill, in Brighton. Atmospheric conditions may have made this difference, or the lights may have run up and down a scale from 4 to 28. As to independence of sunlight, Pratt says (*B.A. Rept.*, 1871, 88), as to this display, that only the fixed, charted points so shone, and that other parts of the crater were not illuminated, as they would have been to an incidence common throughout. In Pratt's opinion, and, I think, in the opinion of the other observers, these lights were volcanic. It seems to me that this opinion arose from a feeling that there should be something of an opinion: the idea that the lights might have been signals was not expressed by any of these astronomers that I know of. I note that, though many observers were, at this time, concentrating upon this one crater, there are no records findable by me of such disturbance of detail as might be supposed to accompany volcanic action. The clear little lights seem to me to have been anything but volcanic.

The play of these lights of Plato — their modulations and their combinations — like luminous music — or a composition of signals in a code that even in this late day may be deciphered. It was like orchestration — and that something like a baton gave direction to

Light 22, upon August 12, 1870, to shine a leading part — "remarkable increase of brightness." No. 22 subsided, and the leading part shone out in No. 14. It, too, subsided, and No. 16 brightened.

Perhaps there were definite messages in a Morse-like code. There is a chance for the electricity in somebody's imagination to start crackling. Up to April, 1871, the selenographers had recorded 1,600 observations upon the fluctuations of the lights of Plato, and had drawn 37 graphs of individual lights. All graphs and other records were deposited by W.R. Birt in the Library of the Royal Astronomical Society, where presumably they are to this day. A Champollion may some day decipher hieroglyphics that may have been flashed from one world to another.

CHAPTER 9

Our data indicate that the planets are circulating adjacencies. Almost do we now conceive of a difficulty of the future as being not how to reach the planets, but how to dodge them. Especially do we warn aviators away from that rhinoceros of the skies, Mercury. I have a note somewhere upon one of the wickedest-looking horns in existence, sticking out far from Mercury. I think it was Mr. Whitmell who made this observation (*Eng. Mech.*, 100, 364). I'd like to hear Andrew Barclay's opinion on that. I'd like to hear Capt. Noble's.

If sometimes does the planet Mars almost graze this earth, as is not told by the great telescopes, which are only millionaire's memorials, or, at least, which reveal but little more than did the little spy glasses used by Burnham and Williams and Beer and Mädler — but if periodically the planet Mars comes very close to this earth, and, if Mars, an island with perhaps no more surface-area than has England, but likely enough inhabited, like England —

June 19, 1875 — opposition of Mars.

Flashes that were seen in the sky upon the 25th of June, 1875, by Charles Gape, of Scole, Norfolk (*Eng. Mech.*, 21, 488). The Editor of Symons' *Meteorological Magazine* (10, 116), was interested, and sent Mr. Gape some questions, receiving answers that nothing had appeared in the local newspapers upon the subject, and that nothing could be learned of a display of fireworks, at the time. To Mr. Gape the appearances seemed to be meteoric.

The year 1877 — climacteric opposition of Mars.

There were some discoveries.

We have at times wondered how astronomers spend their nights. Of course, according to many of his writings upon the subject, Richard Proctor had an excellent knowledge of whist. But in the year 1877, two astronomers looked up at the sky, and one of them discovered the moons of Mars, and the other called attention to lines on Mars — and, if for centuries, the moons of Mars could so remain unknown to all inhabitants of this earth except, as it were, Dean Swift — why, it is no wonder that we so respectfully heed some of the Dean's other intuitions, and think that there may be Lilliputians, or Brobdingnagians, and other forms not conventionally supposed to be.

As to our own fields of data, I have a striking number of notes upon signal-like appearances upon the moon, in the year 1877, but have notes upon only one occurrence that, in our interests, may relate to Mars. The occurrence is like that of July 31, 1813 and June 19, 1875.

Sept. 5, 1877 — opposition of Mars.

Sept. 7, 1877 — lights appeared in the sky of Bloomington, Indiana. They were supposed to be meteoric. They appeared and disappeared, at intervals of three or four seconds; darkness for several minutes; then a final flash of light. See *Sci. Amer.* (n.s., 37, 193).

* * *

That all luminous objects that are seen in the sky when the planet Venus is nearest may not be Venus; may not be fire-balloons:

In the *Dundee Advertiser,* Dec. 22, 1882, it is said that, between 10 and 11 A.M., Dec. 21, at Broughty Ferry, Scotland, a correspondent had seen an unknown luminous body near and a little above the sun. In the *Advertiser,* Dec. 25, is published a letter from someone who says that this object had been seen at Dundee, also; that quite certainly it was the planet Venus and "no other." In *Knowledge* (2, 489), this story is told by a writer who says that undoubtedly the object was Venus. But in *Knowledge* (3, 13), the astronomer J.E. Gore writes that the object could not have been Venus, which upon this date was 1 h. 33 m., R.A., west of the sun. The observation is reviewed in *L'Astronomie* (2, 108). Here it is said that the position of Mercury accorded better. Reasonably this object could not have been Mercury: several objections are comprehended in the statement that superior conjunction of Mercury had occurred upon December 16.

Upon Feb. 3, 1884, M. Stuyvert, of the Brussels Observatory, saw, upon the disc of Venus, an extremely brilliant point (*Ciel et Terre,* 5, 127). Nine days later, Niesten saw just such a point of light as this, but at a distance from the planet. If no one had ever heard that such things can not be, one might think that these two observations were upon something that had been seen leaving Venus and had then been seen farther along. Upon the 3rd of July, 1884, a luminous object was seen moving slowly in the sky of Norwood, N.Y. It had features that suggest the structural: a globe the size of the moon, surrounded by a ring; two dark lines crossing the nucleus (*Science Monthly*, 2, 136). Upon the 26th of July, 1884, a luminous globe, size of the moon, was seen at Brühl, near Cologne; it seemed to be moving upward from this earth, then was stationary "some minutes," and then continued upward until it disappeared (*Nature*, 30, 360). And in the *English Mechanic* (40, 129), it is not said that a luminous vessel that had sailed out from Venus, in February, visiting this earth, where it was seen in several places, was seen upon its return to the planet, but it is said that an observer in Rochester, N.Y., had, upon August 17, seen a brilliant point upon Venus.

CHAPTER 10

Explosions over the town of Barisal, Bengal, if they were aerial explosions, were continuing. As to some of these detonations that were heard in May, 1874, a writer in *Nature* (53, 197) says that they did seem to come from overhead. For a report upon the Barisal Guns, heard between April 28, 1888, and March 1, 1889, see *Proceedings of the Royal Asiatic Society of Bengal* (1899, 199).

Phenomena at Comrie were continuing. The latest date in Roper's *List of Remarkable Earthquakes* is April 8, 1886, but this list goes on only a few years later. See *Knowledge* (n.s., 6, 145) — shock at Comrie, July 12, 1894 — a repetition upon the corresponding date, the next year. In the *English Mechanic* (74, 155), David Packer says that, upon Sept. 17, 1901, ribbon-like flashes of lightning, which were not ordinary lightning, were seen in the sky (I think of Birmingham) one hour before a shock in Scotland. According to other accounts, this shock was in Comrie and surrounding regions (London *Times,* Sept. 19, 1901).

Smith. Misc. (37, 71):

According to L. Tennyson, Quartermaster's Clerk, at Fort Klamath, Oregon, at daylight, Jan. 8, 1867, the garrison was startled from sleep by what he supposed to be an earthquake and a sound like thunder. Then came darkness, and the sky was covered with black smoke or clouds. Then ashes, of a brownish colour, fell — "as fast as I ever saw it snow." Later there was another shock, described as "frightful." No one was injured, but the sutler's store was thrown a distance of ninety feet, and the vibrations lasted several minutes. Mr. Tennyson thought that somewhere near Fort Klamath, a volcano had broken loose, because, in the direction of the Klamath Marsh, a dark column of smoke was seen. I can find record of no such volcanic eruption. In a list of quakes, in Oregon, from 1846, to 1916, published in the *Bull. Seismo.* (9, 59), not one is attributed to volcanic eruptions. Mr. W.D. Smith, compiler of the list, says, as to the occurrence at Fort Klamath — "If there was an eruption, where was it?" He asks whether possibly it could have been Lassen Peak. But Lassen Peak is, in California, and the explosion upon Jan. 8, 1867, was so close to Fort Klamath that almost immediately ashes fell from the sky.

The following is of the type of phenomena that might be considered evidence of signalling from some unknown world nearby:

La Nature (1881, v. 2, 126) — that, upon June 17, 1881, sounds like cannonading were heard at Gabes, Tunis, and that quaking of the earth was felt, at intervals of 32 seconds, lasting about 6 minutes.

July 30, 1883 — a somewhat startling experience — steamship *Resolute* alone in the Arctic Ocean — six reports like gunfire — *Nature* (53, 295).

In *Nature* (30, 19), a correspondent writes that, upon the 3rd of January, 1869, a policeman in Harlton, Cambridgeshire, heard six or seven reports, as if of heavy guns far away. There is no findable record of an earthquake in England upon this date. In the London *Times*, Jan. 12, 15, and 16, 1869, several correspondents write that upon the 9th of January a loud report had been heard and a shock felt at places near Colchester, Essex, about 30 miles from Harlton. One of the correspondents writes that he had heard the sound but had felt no shock. In the London *Standard*, Jan. 12, the Rev. J.F. Bateman, of South Lopham, Norfolk, writes as to the occurrence upon the 9th — "An extraordinary vibration (described variously by my parishioners as being 'like a gunpowder explosion,' 'a big thunder clap,' and 'a little earthquake' was noticed here this morning about 11:20." In the *Morning Post*, Jan. 14, it is said that at places about twenty miles from Colchester it was thought that an explosion had occurred, upon the 9th, but, inasmuch as no explosion had been heard of, the disturbance was attributed to an earthquake. Night of Jan. 13 — an explosion in the sky, at Brighton (*B.A. Rept.*, 1869, 307). In the *Standard*, Jan. 22, a correspondent writes from Swaffham, Norfolk, that, about 8 P.M., Jan. 15, something of an unknown nature had frightened flocks of sheep, which had burst from their bounds in various places. All these occurrences were in adjoining counties in southeastern England. Something was seen in the sky upon the 13th, and, according to the *Chudleigh Weekly Express*, Jan. 13, 1869, something was seen in the sky, night of the 10th, at Weston-super-Mare, near Bristol, in southwestern England. It was seen between 9 and 10 o'clock, and is said to have been an extraordinary meteor. Five hours later were felt three shocks said to have been earthquakes.

Upon the night of March 17, 1871, there was a series of events in

France, and a series in England. A "meteor" was seen at Tours, at 8 P.M. — at 10:40, a "meteor" that left a luminous cloud over Saintes (Charante-Inferieure) — another at Paris, 11:15, leaving a mark in the sky, of fifteen minutes' duration — another at Tours, at 11:45 P.M. See *Cosmos (L.M.)* (24, 190) and *Comptes Rendus* (72, 788). There were "earthquakes" this night affecting virtually all England north of the Mersey and the Trent, and also southern parts of Scotland. As has often been the case, the phenomena were thought to have been explosions and were then said to have been earthquakes when no terrestrial explosions could be heard of (*Met. Mag.*, 6, 37). There were six shocks near Manchester, between 6 and 7 P.M., and others about 11 P.M.; and in Lancashire about 11 P.M., and continuing in places as far apart as Liverpool and Newcastle, until 11:30 o'clock. The shocks felt about 11 o'clock correspond, in time, with the luminous phenomena in the sky of France, but our way of expressing that these so-called earthquakes in England may have been concussions from repeating explosions in the sky, is to record that, according to correspondence in the London *Times*, there were, upon the 20th, aerial phenomena in the region of Lancashire that had been affected upon the 17th — "sounds that seemed to come from a number of guns at a distance" and "pale flashes of lightning in the sky."

Whether these series of phenomena be relatable to Mars or Martians or not, we note that in 1871 opposition of Mars was upon March 19; and, in 1869, upon Feb. 13; and in 1867 two days after the explosions at Fort Klamath. In our records in this book, similar coincidences can be found up to the year 1879. I have other such records not here published, and others that will be here investigated.

There is a triangular region in England, three points of which appear so often in our data that the region should be specially known to us, and I know it myself as the London Triangle. It is pointed in the north by Worcester and Hereford, in the south by Reading, Berkshire, and in the east by Colchester, Essex. The line between Colchester and Reading runs through London.

Upon Feb. 18, 1884, at West Mersea, near Colchester, a loud report was heard (*Nature*, 53, 4). Upon the 22nd of April, 1884, centring around Colchester, occurred the severest earthquake in England in the 19th century. For several columns of description, see the London

Times, April 23. There is a long list of towns in which there was great damage: in 24 parishes near Colchester, 1250 buildings were damaged. One of the places that suffered most was West Mersea (*Daily Chronicle,* April 28).

There was something in the sky. According to George P. Yeats (*Observations on the Earthquake of Dec. 17, 1896,* 6), there was a red appearance in the sky over Colchester, at the time of the shock of April 22, 1884.

The next day, according to a writer in *Knowledge* (5, 336), a stone fell from the sky, breaking glass in his greenhouse, in Essex. It was a quartz stone, and unlike anything usually known as meteoric.

The indications, according to my reading of the data, and my impressions of such repeating occurrences as those at Fort Klamath, are that perhaps an explosion occurred in the sky, near Colchester, upon Feb. 18, 1884; that a great explosion did occur over Colchester, upon the 22nd of April, and that a great volume of debris spread over England, in a northwesterly direction, passing over Worcestershire and Shropshire, and continuing on toward Liverpool, nucleating moisture and falling in blackest of rain. From the Stonyhurst Observatory, near Liverpool, was reported, occurring at 11 A.M., April 26, the most "extraordinary darkness remembered"; forty minutes later fell rain "as black as ink," and then black snow and black hail (*Nature,* 30, 6). Black hail fell at Chaigley, several miles from Liverpool (*Stonyhurst Magazine,* 1, 267). Five hours later, black substance fell at Crowle, near Worcester (*Nature,* 30, 32). Upon the 28th, at Church Stretton and Much Wenlock, Shropshire, fell torrents of liquid like ink and water in equal proportions (*Field,* 63, 597). In the *Quarterly Journal of the Royal Meteorological Society of London* (11, 7), it is said that, upon the 28th, half a mile from Lilleshall, Shropshire, an unknown pink substance was brought down by a storm. Upon the 3rd of May, black substance fell again at Crowle (*Nature,* 30, 32).

In *Nature* (30, 216), a correspondent writes that, upon June 22, 1884, at Fletching, Sussex, southwest of Colchester, there was intense darkness, and that rain then brought down flakes of soot in such abundance that it seemed to be "snowing black." This was several months after the shock at Colchester, but my datum for thinking that another explosion, or disturbance of some kind, had occurred in the same local sky, is that, as reported by the inmates of one house, a slight shock was felt, upon the 24th of June, at Colchester, showing that the phenomena were continuing. See Roper's *List of Remarkable Earthquakes*.

Was not the loud report heard upon Feb. 18 probably an explosion in the sky, inasmuch as the sound was great and the quake little? Were not succeeding phenomena sounds and concussions and the fall of debris from explosions in the sky, acceptably upon April 22, and perhaps continuing until the 24th of June? Then what are the circumstances by which one small part of this earth's surface could continue in relation with something somewhere else in space?

Comrie, Irkutsk, and Birmingham.

CHAPTER 11

Upon the night if the 13th of July, 1875, at midnight, two officers of the H.M.S. *Coronation,* in the Gulf of Siam, saw a luminous projection from the moon's upper limb (*Nature,* 12, 495). Upon the 14th it was gone, but a smaller projection was seen from another part of the moon's limb. This was in the period of the opposition of Mars.

Upon the night of Feb. 20, 1877, M. Trouvelot, of the Observatory of Meudon, saw, in the lunar crater Eudoxus, which, like almost all other centres of seeming signalling, is in the northwestern quadrant of the moon, a fine line of light (*Astro.,* 4, 212). It was like a luminous cable drawn across the crater.

March 21, 1877 — a brilliant illumination, and not by the light of the sun, according to C. Barrett, in the lunar crater Proclus (*Eng. Mech.,* 25, 89).

May 15 and 29, 1877 — the bright spot west of Picard, (*Eng. Mech.,* 25, 335).

The changes upon Linné were first seen by Schmidt, in 1866, near the time of opposition of Mars. In May, 1877, Dr. Klein announced that a new object had appeared upon the moon. It was close to the centre of the visible disc of the moon, and was in a region that had been most carefully studied by the selenographers. In the *Observatory* (1, 238) is Neison's report from his own memoranda. In the years 1874 and 1875, he had studied this part of the moon, but had not seen this newly reported object in the crater Hyginus, or the object Hyginus N, according to the selenographers' terminology. In the *Astronomical Register* (17, 204), Neison lists, with details, 20 minute examinations of this region, from July, 1870, to August, 1875, in which this conspicuous object was not recorded.

June 14, 1877 — a light on the dark part of the moon, resembling a reflection from a moving mirror, reported by Prof. Henry Harrison (*Sidereal Messenger,* 3, 150). June 15 — the bright spot west of Picard, according to Birt (*Jour. B.A.A.,* 19, 376). Upon the 16th, Prof. Harrison thought that again he saw the moving light of the 14th, but shining faintly. In the *English Mechanic* (25, 432), Frank Dennett writes, as to an observation of June 17, 1877 — "I fancied I could detect a minute point of light shining out of the darkness that filled Bessel."

These are data of extraordinary activity upon the moon preceding the climacteric opposition of Mars, early in September, 1877.

Now we have an account of an occurrence during an eclipse of the moon:

On the night of the eclipse (Aug. 23, 1877) a ball of fire, of the apparent size of the moon, was seen, at ten minutes to eleven, dropping apparently from cloud to cloud, and the light flashing across the road (*Astro. Reg.*, 16, 75).

Astro. Reg. (17, 201):

Nov. 13, 1877 — Hyginus N standing out with such a prominence as to be seen at the first glance;

Nov. 14, 1877 — not a trace of Hyginus N, though seeing was excellent:

Oct. 3, 1878 — the most conspicuous of all appearances of Hyginus N;

Oct. 4, 1878 — not a trace of Hyginus N.

Upon the night of Nov. 1, 1879, again in the period of opposition of Mars (opposition November 12) again the bright spot west of Picard (*Jour. B.A.A.*, 19, 376). But I have several records of observations upon this appearance not in times of opposition of Mars. Whether there be any relation with anything else or not, at 5:30, morning of Nov. 1, 1879, a "vivid flash" was seen and a shock was felt at West Cumberland (*Nature*, 21, 19).

In the autumn of the year 1883, began extraordinary atmospheric effects in the sky of this earth. For Prof. John Haywood's description of similar appearances upon the moon, Nov. 4, 1883, and March 29, 1884, see the *Sidereal Messenger* (3, 121). They were misty light-effects upon the dark part of the moon, not like "earthshine." Our expression is that so close is the moon to this earth that it, too, may be affected by phenomena in the atmosphere of this earth.

Something like another luminous cable, or like a shining wall, that was seen in Aristarchus, by Trouvelot, Jan. 23, 1880, (*Astro.*, 4, 215); a speck of light in Marius, Jan. 13, 1881, by A.S. Williams (*Eng. Mech.*, 32, 494); unexplained light in Eudoxus, by Trouvelot, May 4, 1881 (*Astro.*, 4, 213); an illumination in Kepler, by Morales, Feb. 5, 1884 (*Astro.*, 9, 149).

In *Knowledge* (7, 224), William Gray writes that, upon Feb. 19,

1885, he saw, in Hercules, a dull, deep, reddish appearance. In *L'Astronomie* (4, 227), Lorenzo Kropp, an astronomer of Paysandu, Uruguay, writes that, upon Feb. 21, 1885, he had seen, in Cassini, a formation not far from Hercules, both of them in the northwestern quadrant of the moon, a reddish smoke or mist. He had heard that several other persons had seen, not a misty appearance, but a star-like light here, and upon the 22nd he had seen a definite light, himself, shining like the planet Saturn.

May 11, 1885 — two lights upon the moon (*Astro.*, 9, 73).

May 11, 1886 — two lights upon the moon (*Astro.*, 6, 312).

CHAPTER 12

That through lenses rimmed with horizons, inhabitants of this earth have seen revelations of other worlds — that atmospheric strata of different densities are lenses — but that the faults of the wide glasses in the observatories are so intensified in atmospheric revelations that all our data are distortions. Our acceptance is that every mirage has a primary; that in human mind all poetry is based upon observation, and that imagery in the sky is similarly uncreative. If a mirage can not be traced to the known upon this earth, one supposes that it is either a derivation from the unknown upon this earth, or from the unknown somewhere else. We shall have data of a series of mirages in Sweden, or upon the shores of the Baltic, from Oct., 1881, to Dec., 1888. I take most of the data from *Nature* (26, 209; 28, 158; 31, 42; 32: 112, 231, 279, 541, 552; 34, 108; 38, 304), *Knowledge* (2, 223), *Cosmos: Les Mondes* (s. 4, 11, 336), and *L'Astronomie* (7, 432), published in this period. I have no data of such appearances in this region either before or after this period: the suggestion in my own mind is that they were not mirages from terrestrial primaries, or they would not be so confined to one period, but were shadows or mirages from something that was in temporary suspension over the Baltic and Sweden, all details distorted and reported in terms of familiar terrestrial appearances.

Oct. 10, 1881 — that at Rugenwalde, Pomerania, the mirage of a village had been seen: snow-covered roofs from which hung icicles; human forms distinctly visible. It was believed that the mirage was a representation of the town of Nexo, on the island of Bornholm. Rugenwalde is on the Baltic, and Nexo is about 100 miles northwest, in the Baltic (*Cosmos (L.M.)*, s. 4, 56, 494).

The first definite account of the mirages of Sweden, findable by me, is published in *Nature* (26, 209), where it is said that preceding instances had attracted attention — that, in May, 1882, over Lake Orsa, Sweden, representations of steamships had been seen, and then "islands in the lakes, covered with more or less vegetation." Night of May 19, 1883 — beams of light at Ludvika, Sweden — they looked like a representation of a lake in moonshine, with shores covered with trees, showing faint outlines of farms (*Monthly Weather Review*, 11, 121; *Nature*,

28, 134). May 28, 1883 — at Finsbo, Sweden — changing scenes, at short intervals: mountains, lakes, and farms (*Nature*, 28, 158). Oct. 16, 1884 — Lindesberg — a large town, with four-storied houses, a castle and a lake (*Nature*, 31, 42). May 22, 1885 — Gothland — a town surrounded by high mountains, a large vessel in front of the town (*Nature*, 32, 112). June 15, 1885 — near Oxelosund — two wooded islands, a construction upon one of them, and two warships (*Cosmos (L.M.)*, s. 4, 1, 677). It is said that at the time two Swedish warships were at sea, but were at considerable distance north of Oxelosund. Sept. 12, 1885 — Valla — a representation that is said to have been a "remarkable mirage" but that is described as if the appearances were cloud-forms — several monitors, one changing into a spouting whale, and the other into a crocodile — then forests — dancers — a wooded island with buildings and a park (*Nature*, 32, 541). Sept. 29, 1885 — again at Valla — between 8 and 9 o'clock, P.M.; a lurid glare upon the northwestern horizon; a cloud bank — animals, groups of dancers, a forest, and then a park with paths (*Nature*, 32, 552). July 15, 1888 — Hudikswall — a tempestuous sea, and a vessel upon it; a small boat leaving the vessel (*Astro.*, 7, 392). Upon Oct. 8, 1888, at Merekŭla, on the Baltic, but in Estonia, was seen a mirage of a city that lasted an hour. It is said that some buildings were recognised, and that the representation was identified with St. Petersburg, which is over 100 miles eastwards on the Baltic coast (*Astro.*, 7, 432).

* * *

That a large, substantial mass, presumably of land, can be in at least temporary suspension over a point upon this earth's surface, and not fall, and be, in ordinary circumstances, invisible —

In *L'Astronomie* (6, 426), MM. Codde and Payan, both of them astronomers, well-known for their conventional observations and writings, publish accounts of an unknown body that appeared upon the sun's limb, for twenty or thirty seconds, after the eclipse of August 19, 1887. They saw a round body, apparent diameter about one tenth of the apparent diameter of the sun, according to the sketch that is published. In *L'Astronomie*, these two observers write separately, and, in the city of Marseilles, their observations were made at a distance apart. But the unknown body was seen by both upon the same part of the sun's limb. So it is supposed that it could not have been a balloon, nor a circular cloud, nor anything else very near this earth. But many astronomers in other parts of Europe were watching this eclipse, and it seems acceptable that others, besides two in Marseilles, continued to look, immediately after the eclipse; but from nowhere else came a report upon this object, so that all indications are that it was far from the sun and near Marseilles, but farther than clouds or balloons in this local sky. I can draw no diagram that can satisfy all these circumstances, except by supposing the sun to be only a few thousand miles away.

* * *

If little black stones fall four times, in eleven years, to one part of this earth's surface, and fall nowhere else, we are, in conceiving of a fixed origin somewhere above a stationary earth, at least conceiving in terms of data, and, whether we are fanatics or not, we are not of the type of other upholders of stationariness of this earth, who care more for Moses than they do for data. I'd not like to have it thought that we are not great admirers of Moses, sometimes.

The rock that hung in the sky of Serbia —

Upon October 13, 1872, a stone fell from the sky, to this earth, near the town of Soko-Banja, Serbia. If it were not a peculiar stone, there is no force to this datum. It is said that it was unknown stone. A name was invented for it. The stone was called *banjite,* after the town near which it fell.

Seventeen years later (Dec. 1, 1889) another rock of *banjite* fell in Serbia, near Jelica.

For Meunier's account of these stones, see *L'Astronomie* (9, 272) and *Comptes Rendus* (92, 331). Also, see *La Nature* (1881, v. 1, 192). According to Meunier these stones did fall from the sky; indigenous to this earth there are no such stones; nowhere else have such stones fallen from the sky; they are identical in material; they fell seventeen years apart.

* * *

At times when we think favourably of this work of ours, we see in it a pointing-out of an evil of modern specialisation. A seismologist studies earthquakes, and an astronomer studies meteors; neither studies both earthquakes and meteors, and consequently each, ignorant of the data collected by the other, sees no relation between the two phenomena. The treatment of the event in Serbia, Dec. 1, 1889, is an instance of conventional scientific attempts to understand something by separately, or specially, focussing upon different aspects, and not combining into an inclusive concept. Meunier writes only upon the stones that fell from the sky, and does not mention an earthquake at the time. Milne, in his "Catalogue of Destructive Earthquakes," lists the occurrence as an earthquake, and does not mention stones that fell from the sky (*B.A. Rept.*, 1911, 735). All combinations greatly affect the character of components: in our combination of two aspects, we see that the phenomenon was not an earthquake, as earthquakes are commonly understood, though it may have been meteoric; but was not meteoric, in ordinary terms of meteors, because of the unlikelihood that meteors, identical in material, should, seventeen years apart, fall upon the same part of this earth's surface, and nowhere else.

This occurrence was of course an explosion in the sky, and its vibrations were communicated to the earth below, with all the effects of any other kind of earthquake. Back in our earliest confusion of the data of a century's first quarter, we had awareness of this combination and its conventional misinterpretation: that many concussions that have been communicated from explosions in the sky have been catalogued in lists of subterranean earthquakes. We are farther along now, in our data of the 19th century, and now we come across awareness, in other minds, of this distinguishment. At 8:20 A.M., Nov. 20, 1887, was heard and felt something that was reported from many places in the region that is known to us as the London Triangle, as an earthquake, though in some towns it was thought that a great explosion, perhaps in London, had occurred. It was reported from Reading, and from places where the concussion was greatest. There were several accounts of slight alarm among sheep, which are sensitive to meteors and earthquakes. But, in Symons' *Met. Mag.* (23, 153), Mr. H.G. Fordham wrote that the occurrence was not an earthquake, that a meteor had exploded. He had very little to base this opinion upon: out of scores of descriptions, he had record of only two assertions that something had been seen in the sky. Nevertheless, because the sound was so much greater than the concussion, Mr. Fordham came to his conclusion.

In Symons' *Met. Mag.* (23, 154), Dr. R.H. Wake writes that, upon the evening of Nov. 3, 1888, in a region about four miles wide and ten or fifteen miles long, in the Thames Valley (near Reading) flocks of sheep had rushed from their folds in a common alarm. About a year later, in the Chiltern Hills, which extend in a northeasterly direction from the Thames Valley, near Reading, there was another such occurrence. In the London *Standard*, Nov. 7, 1889, the Rev. J. Ross Barker, of Chesham, a town about 25 miles northeast of Reading, writes that, upon Oct. 25, 1889, many flocks of sheep, in a region of 30 square miles, had, by common impulse, broken from their folds. Mr. Barker asks whether anyone knew of a meteor or of an earthquake at the time. In Symons' *Met. Mag.* (24, 161), Mr. Symons accepts that all three of these occurrences were effects of meteoric explosions in the sky. The phenomena are insignificant relatively to some that we have considered: the significance is in this definite recognition in orthodoxy, itself, that some supposed earthquakes, or effects of supposed earthquakes, are reactions to explosions in the sky.

Chapter 13

Exploding monasteries that shoot out clouds of monks into cyclonic formations with stormy nuns similarly dispossessed — or collapsing monasteries — sometimes slowly crumbling confines of the cloistered — by which we typify all things: that all developments pass through a process of walling-away within shells that will break. Once upon a time there was a shell around the United States. The shell broke. Some other things were smashed.

The doctrines of great distances among heavenly bodies, and of a moving earth are the strongest elements of Exclusionism: the mere idea of separations by millions of miles discourages thoughts of communication with other worlds; and only to think that this earth shoots through space at a velocity of 19 miles a second puts an end to speculation upon how to leave it and how to return. But, if these two conventions be features of a walling-away like that of a chick within its shell, or that of the United States within its boundaries, and if some day all such confinements of the embryonic break, our own prophecy, in the vague terms of all successful prophecies, is that a matured view of astronomic phenomena will be from a litter of broken demonstrations.

Our expression now is upon the function of Isolation in Development. Specially it is not ours, because I think we learned it from the biologists, but we are applying it generally. If the general expression be accepted, we conceive that functionally have the astronomers taught that planets are millions of miles away, and that this earth moves at such terrific velocity that it is encysted with speed. Whether isolations function or not, that exclusions that break down are typical of all developments is signified by data upon all growing things, beginning with the aristocratic seeds, which, however, liberalise to intercourse with mean materials or die. All animal-organisms are at first walled away. In human circumstances conditions are the same. The development of every science has been a series of temporary exclusions, and the story of every industry tells of inventions that were resisted, but that were finally admitted. At the beginning of the nineteenth century, Hegel published his demonstration that there could be only seven planets: too late to recall his work, he learned that Ceres had been discovered. It is our expression that the mental state of Hegel partook of a general spirit of his time, and that it was necessary, or that it functioned, because early astronomers could scarcely have systematised their doctrine had they been bewildered by seven or eight hundred planetary bodies; and that, besides the functions of the astronomers, according to our expressions, there was also their usefulness in breaking down the walls of the older, and outlived, orthodoxy. We conceive that it is well that a great deal of experience should be withheld from children, and that, any way, in their early years, they are sexually isolated, for instance, and our idea is that our data have been held back by no outspoken conspiracy, but by an inhibition similar to that by which a great deal of biology, for instance, is not taught to children. But, if we think of something of this kind, equally acceptable is it that even in the face of orthodox principles, these data have been preserved in orthodox publications, and that, in the face of supposed principles of Darwinism, as applied generally they have survived, though not in harmony with their environment.

Tons of paper have been consumed by calculations upon the remoteness of stars and planets. But I can find nothing that has been calculated, or said, that is sounder than Mr. Shaw's determination that the moon is 37 miles away. It is that the Vogels and the Struves and the Newcombs have been functionally hypnotised and have usefully spread the embryonic delusion that there is a vast, untraversible expanse of space around this earth, or that they have had some basis that it has been my misfortune to be unable to find, or that there is no pleasant and unaccusatory way of explaining them.

April 10, 1874 — a luminous object that exploded in the sky of Kuttenburg, Bohemia. It is said that the glare was like sunlight, and that the "terrifying flash" was followed by a detonation that rumbled about a minute. April 9, 1876 — an explosion that is said to have been violent, at Iglö (Spisska Nova Ves, Slovakia), near the town of Rosenau, Hungary (Roznava, Slovakia). See *B.A. Rept.* (1877, 146).

These two objects which appeared in virtually the same local sky of this earth — point of explosion 250 miles apart — came from virtually the same point in the sky: constellation of Cassiopeia; different by two degrees in right ascension, and with no difference in declination. About the same time in the evening: one at 8:09 P.M., and the other at 8:20 P.M. Same night in the year, according to extra-terrestrial calendars: the year 1876 was a leap year.

If they had been ordinary meteors, by coincidence two ordinary meteors of the same stream might, exactly two years apart, come from almost the same point in the heavens and strike almost the same point over this earth. But they were two of the most extraordinary occurrences in the records of explosions in the sky. Coincidences multiply, or these objects did come from the not far-distant constellation of Cassiopeia, and their striking so closely together indicates that this earth is stationary; and something of the purposeful may be thought of. Serially related to these events, or representing some more coincidence, there had been, upon June 9, 1866, a tremendous explosion in the sky of Knyahinya, Hungary, and about a thousand stones had fallen from the sky (*B.A. Rept.*, 1867, 430). Rosenau and Knyahinya are about 75 miles apart. Of course one can very much extend our own circumscribed little notions, and think of firing projectiles from beyond the stars, just as one can think of unknown lands as being not in the immediate sky of Serbia or Birmingham or Comrie, but as being beyond the nearby stars, reducing everything more than we have reduced — but the firing of stones to this earth seems crude to me. Of course, objects, or fragments of objects made of steel, like the manufactured steel of this earth, have fallen to this earth, and are now in collections of "meteorites." There is a story in a book that is not very accessible to us, because it can't be found along with *C.R.*, or *Eng. Mech.*, or *L'Astro.*, of tablets of stone that were once upon a time fired to this earth. It may be that inhabitants of this earth have been receiving instructions ever since, engravings arriving very badly damaged, however.

I have data upon repeating appearances, said to have been "auroral," in a local sky. If they were auroral, repetitions at regular intervals and so localised are challengers to the most resolute of explainers. If they were of extra-mundane origin, they indicate that this earth is stationary. The regularity is suggestive of signalling. For instance — a light in the sky of Lyons, N.Y., Dec. 9, 1891, Jan. 5, Feb. 2, Feb. 29, March 27, April 23, 1892. In the *Scientific American* (n.s., 66, 293), Dr. M.A. Veeder writes that, from December 9, 1891, to April 23,

1892, there had been a bright light that he calls "auroral" in the sky of Lyons, every 27th night. He associates the lights with the sun's synodic period, and says that upon each of the days preceding a nocturnal display, there had been a disturbance in the sun. How a disturbance in the sun could, at night, sun somewhere near the antipodes of Lyons, New York, so localise its effects, one can't clear up. In *Nature* (46, 29), Dr. Veeder associates the phenomena with the synodic period of the sun, but he says that this period is of 27 days, 6 hours, and 40 minutes, noting that this period is inconsistent with the phenomena at Lyons, making more than a day's difference in the time of his records. This precise determination is more of the "exact science" that is driving some of us away from refinements into hoping for caves. Different parts of the sun move at different rates: I have read of sun spots that moved diagonally across the sun.

In *Nature* (15, 451), a correspondent writes that, at 8:55 P.M., he saw a large red star in Serpens, where he had never seen such an appearance before — Gunnersbury, March 17, 1877. Ten minutes later, the object increased and decreased several times, flashing like the revolving light of a lighthouse, then disappearing. This correspondent writes that, about 10 P.M., he saw a great meteor. He suggests no relation between the two appearances, but there may have been relation, and there may be indication of something that was stationary at least one hour over Gunnersbury, because the object said to have been a "meteor" was first seen at Gunnersbury. In the *Observatory* (1, 19), Capt. Tupman writes that, at 9:57 P.M., a great meteor was first seen at Frome, Tetbury, and Gunnersbury. The red object might not have been in the local sky of Gunnersbury; might have been in the constellation Serpens, unseen in all the rest of the world.

There is a great field of records of "meteors" that, with no parallax, or with little parallax, or with little parallax that may be accounted for by supposing that observations were not quite simultaneous, have been seen to come as if from a star or from a planet, and that may have come from such points, indicating that they are not far away. For instance, *B.A. Rept.* (1879, 77) — the great meteor of Sept. 5, 1868. It was seen, at Zurich, Switzerland, to come from a point near Jupiter; at Tremont, France, origin was so close to Jupiter that this object and the planet were seen in the same telescopic field; at

Bergamo, Italy, it was seen five or six degrees from Jupiter. Zurich is about 140 miles from Bergamo, and Tremont is farther from Zurich and Bergamo than that.

So there are data that indicate that objects have come to this earth from planets or from stars, enforcing our idea that the remotest planet is not so far from this earth as the moon is said, conventionally, to be; and that the stars, all equi-distant from this earth might be reached by travelling from this earth. One notices that I always conclude that, if phenomena repeatedly occur in one local sky of this earth, their origin is traceable to a fixed place over a stationary earth. The fixed place over this earth is indicated, but that fixed place — island of space, foreign coast, whatever it may be — may be conceived of as accompanying this earth in its rotations and revolutions around the sun. Accepting that nothing much is known of gravitation; that gravitational astronomy is a myth; that attraction may extend but a few miles around this earth, if I can think of something hanging unsupported in space, I always think of an island, say, over Birmingham, or Irkutsk, or Comrie, as soon flying off by the centrifugal force of a rotating earth, or as being soon left behind in a rush around the sun. Nevertheless there is good room for discussion here. But when it comes to other orders of data, I find one convergence toward the explanation that this earth is stationary. But the subject is supposed to be sacred. One must not think that this earth is stationary. One must not investigate. To think upon this subject, except as one is told to think, is, or seems to be considered, impious.

But how can one account for an earth that moves?

By thinking that something started it and that nothing ever stopped it.

Earth that doesn't move?

That nothing ever started it.

Some more sacrilege.

CHAPTER 14

If a grasshopper could hop on a cannon ball, passing overhead, I could conceive, perhaps, how something, from outer space, could flit to a moving earth, explore a while, and then hop off.

But suppose we have to accept that there have been instances of just such enterprise and agility, relatively to the planet Venus. Irrespective of our notion that it may be that sometimes a vessel sails to this earth from Venus and returns, there are striking data indicating that, whether conceivable or not, luminous objects have appeared from somewhere, or presumably from outer space, and have been seen temporarily suspended over the planet Venus. This is in accord with our indications that there are regions in the sky suspended over and near this earth. It looks bad for our inference that this earth is stationary, but it is the supposed rotary motion of this earth more than the supposed orbital motion that seems to us would dislodge such neighbouring bodies; and all astronomers, except those who say that Venus rotates in about 24 hours, say that Venus rotates in about 224 days, a velocity that would generate little centrifugal force.

I have a note upon a determined luminosity that was bent upon Saturn, as its objective. In the *English Mechanic* (63, 496), a correspondent writes that, upon July 13, 1896, he saw, through his telescope, from 10 until after 11:15, P.M., after which the planet was too near the horizon for good seeing, a luminous object moving near Saturn. He saw it pass several small stars. "It was certainly going toward Saturn at a good rate." There may be swifts in the sky that can board planets. If they can swoop on and off an earth moving at a rate of 19 miles a second, disregarding rotation, because entrance at a pole may be thought of, why, then, for all I know smaller things do ride on cannon balls. Of course if our data that indicate that the supposed solar system, or the geo-system, is to an enormous degree smaller than is conventionally taught be accepted, the orbital velocity of Venus is far cut down.

About the last of August, 1873 — Brussels; eight o'clock in the evening — rising above the horizon, into a clear sky, was seen a star-like object. It mounted higher and higher, until, about ten minutes later, it disappeared (*La Nature,* 1873, v. 2, 239). It seems that this conspicuous object did appear in a local sky, and was therefore not far from this earth. If it were not a fire-balloon, one supposes that it did come from outer space, and then returned.

Perhaps a similar thing that visited the moon, and was then seen sailing away — in the *Astronomical Register* (23, 205), Prof. Schafarik, of Prague, writes that upon April 24, 1874, he saw "an object of so peculiar a character that I do not know what to make of it." He saw a dazzling white object slowly traversing the disc of the moon. He had not seen it approaching the moon. He watched it after it left the moon. Sept. 27, 1881 — South Africa — an object that was seen near the moon by Col. Markwick — like a comet but moving very rapidly (*Journal of the Liverpool Astronomical Society*, 7, 106).

Our chief interest is in objects, like ships, that have "boarded" this moving earth with the agility of a Columbus who could dodge a San Salvador and throw out an anchor to an American coast screeching past him at a rate of 19 miles a second, or in objects that have come as close as atmospheric conditions, or unknown conditions, would permit to the bottom of a kind of stationary sea. We now graduate Capt. Noble to the extra-geographic fold. In *Knowledge* (4, 173), Capt. Noble writes that, at 10:35 P.M., night of August 28, 1883, he saw in the sky something like a "new and most glorious comet." First he saw something like the tail of a comet, or it was like a search-light, according to Capt. Noble's sketch of it in *Knowledge.* Then Capt. Noble saw the nucleus from which this light came. It was a brilliant object. Upon page 207, W.K. Bradgate writes that, at 12:40 A.M., August 29, at Liverpool, he saw an object like the planet Jupiter, a ray of light emanating from it. Upon the nights of Sept. 11 and 13, Prof. Swift saw, at Rochester, New York, an unknown object like a comet, perhaps in the local sky of Rochester, inasmuch as it was reported from nowhere else (*Observatory*, 6, 345). In *Knowledge* (4, 219), Mrs. Harbin writes that, upon the night of Sept. 21, at Yeovil, she saw the same brilliant searchlight-like light that had been seen by Capt. Noble, but that it had disappeared before she could turn her telescope upon it. And several months later (Nov., 1883) a similar object was seen obviously not far away, but in the local sky of Puerto Rico and then of Ohio (*American Meteorological Journal*, 1, 110; and, *Scientific American*, n.s., 50: 40, 97). It may be better not to say at this time that we have data for thinking that a vessel carrying something like a searchlight, visited this earth, and explored for several months over regions as far apart as England and Puerto Rico. Just at present it is enough to record that something that was presumably not a fire-balloon appeared in the sky of England, close to this earth, if seen nowhere else, and in two hours traversed the distance of about 200 miles between Sussex and Liverpool.

Aug. 22, 1885 — Saigon, Cochin-China (Vietnam) — according to Lieut. Réveillère, of the vessel *Guiberteau* — object like a magnificent red star, but larger than the planet Venus — it moved no faster than a cloud in a moderate wind; observed seven or eight minutes, then disappearing behind clouds (*C. R.,* 101, 680).

In this book it is my frustrated desire to subordinate the theme of this earth's stationariness. My subject is New Lands — things, objects, beings that are, or may be, the data of coming expansions —

But the stationariness of this earth can not be subordinated. It is crucial.

Again — there is no use discussing possible explorations beyond this earth, if this earth moves at a rate of 19 miles a second, or 19 miles a minute.

As to voyagers who may come to or near this earth from other planets — how could they leave and return to swiftly moving planets? According to our principles of Extra-geography, the planets move part of the time with the revolving stars, the remotest planets remaining in, under, or near one constellation years at a time. Anything that could reach, and then travel from, a swiftly revolving constellation in the ecliptic could arrive at a stellar polar region, where, relatively to a central, stationary body, there is no motion.

CHAPTER 15

It may be that we now add to our sins the horse that swam in the sky. For all I know, we contribute to a wider biology. In the New York *Times,* July 8, 1878, is published a dispatch from Parkersburg, West Virginia: that, about July 1, 1878, three or four farmers had seen, in a cloudless sky, apparently half a mile away, "an opaque substance." It looked like a white horse, "swimming in the clear atmosphere." It is said to have been a mirage of a horse in some distant field. If so, it is interesting not only because it was opaque, but because of a selection or preference: the field itself was not miraged.

Black bodies and the dark rabbles of the sky — and that rioting things, from floating anarchies, have often spotted the sun. Then, by all that is compensatory, in the balances of existence, there are disciplined forces in space. In the *Scientific American* (n.s., 45, 291), it is said that, according to newspapers of Delaware, Maryland, and Virginia, figures had been seen in the sky in the latter part of September, and the first week in October, 1881, reports that "exhibit a mediæval condition of popular intelligence in the rural districts scarcely less than marvellous." The writer suggests that, though probably something was seen in the sky, it was only an aurora. Our own intelligence and that of astronomers and meteorologists and everybody else with whom we have had experience had better not be discussed, but the accusation of mediævalism is something that we're sensitive about, and we hasten to the *Monthly Weather Review,* and if that doesn't give us a modern touch, I mistake the sound of it. *Monthly Weather Review* (9: Sept., 1881, 24; and, Oct., 1881, 21) — an auroral display in Maryland and New York, upon the 23rd of September; all other auroras far north of the three states in which it was said phenomena were seen. October — no auroras until the 18th; that one in the north. There was a mirage upon Sept. 23, but at Indianola; two instances in October, but late in the month, and in northern states.

It is said, in the *Scientific American,* that according to the Warrenton (Va.) *Solid South,* a number of persons had seen white-robed figures in the sky, at night. The story in the *Richmond Dispatch* (Oct. 7, 1881) is that many persons had seen, or had thought they had seen, an alarming sight in the sky, at night: a vast number of armed, uniformed soldiers drilling. Then a dispatch from Wilmington,

Delaware — platoons of angels marching and countermarching in the sky, their white robes and helmets gleaming. Similar accounts came from Laurel and Talbot. Several persons said they had seen, in the sky, the figure of President Garfield, who had died not long before. Our general acceptance is that all reports upon such phenomena are coloured in terms of appearances and subjects uppermost in minds.

L'Astronomie (7, 392):

That, about the first of August, 1888, at Vidorec, near Warasdin, Hungary, several divisions of infantry, led by a chief, who waved a flaming sword, had been seen in the sky, three consecutive days, marching several hours a day. The writer in *L'Astronomie* says that in vain does one try to explain that this appearance was a mirage of terrestrial soldiers marching at a distance from Warasdin, because widespread publicity and investigation had disclosed no such soldiers. Even if there had been terrestrial soldiers near Warasdin repeating mirages localised would call for explanation.

But that there may be space-armies, from which reflections or shadows or Brocken spectres are sometimes cast — a procession that crossed the sun: forms that moved, or that marched, sometimes four abreast; observation by M. Bruguière, at Marseilles, April 15 and 16, 1883 (*Astro.*, 5, 70). An army that was watched, forty minutes, by M. Jacquot, July 15 and 16, 1886 (*Astro.*, 5, 70) — things or beings that seemed to march and to counter-march: all that moved in the same direction, moved in parallel lines. In *L'Année Scientifique et Industrielle* (29, 8), there is an account of observations by M. Trouvelot, Aug. 29, 1871. He saw objects, some round, some triangular, and some of complex forms. Then occurred something that at least suggests that these things were not moving in the wind, nor sustained in space by the orbital forces of meteors; that each was depending upon its own powers of flight, and that an accident occurred to one of them. All of them, though most of the time moving with great rapidity, occasionally stopped, but then one of them fell toward the earth, and the indications are that it was a heavy body, and had not been sustained by the wind, which would scarcely suddenly desert one of its flotsam and continue to sustain all the others. The thing fell, oscillating from side to side like a disc falling through water.

New York *Sun*, March 16, 1890 — that, at 4 o'clock, in the

afternoon of March 12th, in the sky of Ashland, Ohio, was seen a representation of a large, unknown city. By some persons it was supposed to be a mirage of the town of Mansfield, thirty miles away; other observers thought that they recognized Sandusky, sixty miles away. '"The more superstitious declare that it was a vision of the New Jerusalem."

May have been a revelation of heaven, and for all I know heaven may resemble Sandusky, and those of us who have no desire to go to Sandusky may ponder that point, but our own expression is that things have been pictured in the sky, and have not been traced to terrestrial origins, but have been interpreted always in local terms. Probably a living thing in the sky — seen by farmers — a horse. Other things, or far-refracted images, or shadows — and they were supposed to be vast lions or soldiers or angels, all according to preconceived ideas. Representations that have been seen in India — Hindoo costumes described upon them. Suppose that, in the afternoon of January 17, 1892, there was a battle in the sky of Montana — we know just about in what terms the description would be published. Brooklyn *Eagle,* Jan. 18, 1892 — mirage in the sky of Lewiston, Montana — Indians and hunters alternately charging and retreating. The Indians were in superior numbers and captured the hunters. Then details — hunters tied to stakes; the piling of faggots; etc. "So far as could be ascertained last night, the Indians on the reservations are peaceable." I think that we're peaceable enough, but, unless the astronomers can put us on reservations, where we'll work out expressions in beads and wampum instead of data, we'll have to carry on a conflict with the vacant minds to which appear mirages of their own emptiness in the sometimes swarming skies.

Altogether there are many data indicating that vessels and living things of space do come close to this earth, but there is absence of data of beings that have ever landed upon this earth, unless someone will take up the idea that Kaspar Hauser, for instance, came to this earth from some other physical world. Whether spacarians have ever dredged down here or not, or "sniped" down here, pouncing, assailing, either wantonly, or in the interests of their sciences, there are data of seeming seizures and attacks from somewhere, and I have strong objections against lugging in the fourth dimension, because then I am no better off, wondering what the fifth and sixth are like.

In *La Nature* (1888, v. 2, 66), M. Adrian Arcelin writes that, while excavating near de Solutré, in August, 1878, upon a day, described as *superbe,* sky clear to a degree said to have been *parfaitement,* several dozen sheets of wrapping paper upon the ground suddenly rose. Nearby were a dozen men, and not one of them had felt a trace of wind. A strong force had seized upon these conspicuous objects, touching nothing else. According to M. Arcelin, the dust on the ground under and around was not disturbed. The sheets of paper continued upward, and disappeared in the sky.

A powerful force that swooped upon a fishing vessel, raising it so far that when it fell back it sank — see London *Times,* Sept. 24, 1875. A quarter of a mile away were other vessels, from which set out rescuers to the sailors who had been thrown into the sea. There was no wind: the rescuers could not use sails, but had to row their boats.

Upon Oct. 2, 1875, a man was trundling a cart from Schaffhausen, near Beringen, Germany. His right arm was perforated from front to back, as if by a musket ball (*Popular Science Monthly,* 15, 566). This man had two companions. He had heard a whirring sound, but his companions had heard nothing. At one side of the road there were labourers in a field, but they were not within gunshot distance. Whatever the missile may have been, it was unfindable.

La Nature (1879, v. 1, 366) quotes the *Courrier des Ardennes* as to an occurrence in the Commune Signy-le-Petit, Easter Sunday, 1879 — a conspicuous, isolated house — suddenly its slate roof shot into the air, and then fell to the ground. There had not been a trace of wind. The writer of the account says that the force, which he calls a *trouble inoui* had so singled out this house that nothing in its surroundings beyond a distance of thirty feet had been disturbed.

Scientific American (n.s., 43, 24) — that, according to the *Plaindealer,* of East Kent, Ontario, two citizens of East Kent were in a field, and heard a loud report. They saw stones shooting upward from a field. They examined the spot, which was about 16 feet in diameter, finding nothing to suggest an explanation of the occurrence. It is said that there had been neither a whirlwind nor anything else by which to explain.

It may be that witnesses have seen human beings dragged from their own existence either into the objectionable fourth dimension, perhaps then sifting into the fifth, or up to the sky by some exploring thing. I have data, but they are from the records of psychic research. For instance, a man had been seen walking along a road — sudden disappearance. Explanation — that he was not a living human being, but an apparition that had disappeared. I have not been able to develop such data, finding, for instance, that someone in the neighbourhood had been reported missing; but it may be that we can find material in our own field.

Upon December 10, 1881, Walter Powell and two companions ascended from Bath in the Government balloon *Saladin* (Valentine and Tomlinson, *Travels in Space,* 227). The balloon descended at Bridport, coast of the English Channel. Two of the aeronauts got out, but the balloon, with Powell in it, shot upward. There was a report that the balloon had been seen to fall in the English Channel, near Bridport, but according to Capt. Temple, one of Powell's companions, probably something thrown from the balloon had been seen to fall.

A balloon is lost near or over the sea. If it should fall into the sea it would probably float and for considerable time be a conspicuous object; nevertheless the disappearance of a balloon last seen over the English Channel, can not, without other circumstances, be considered very mysterious. Now one expects to learn of reports from many places of supposed balloons that had been seen. But the extraordinary circumstance is that reports came in upon a luminous object that was seen in the sky at the time that this balloon disappeared. In the London *Times,* it is said that a luminous object had been seen, evening of the 13th, moving in various directions in the sky near Cherbourg. It is said that upon the night of the 16th three customhouse guards, at Laredo, Spain, had seen something like a balloon in the sky, and had climbed a mountain in order to see it better, but that it had shot out sparks and had disappeared — and had been reported from Bilbao, Spain, the next day. In the *Morning Post,* it is said that this luminous display was the chief feature; that it was this sparkling that had made the object visible. In the *Standard,* Dec. 16, is an account of something that was seen in the sky, five o'clock, morning of Dec. 15, by Capt. Mc. Bain, of the steamship *Countess of Aberdeen,* off the coast of Scotland, 25 miles from Montrose. Through glasses, the object seemed to be a light attached to something thought to be the car of a balloon, increasing and decreasing in size — a large light — "as large as the light at Girdleness." It moved in a direction opposite to that of the wind, though possibly with wind of an upper stratum. It was visible half an hour, and when it finally disappeared, was moving toward Bervie, a town on the Scottish coast about 12 miles north of Montrose. In the *Morning Post* it is said that the explanation is simple: that someone in Monfreith, 8 miles from Dundee, had, late in the evening of the 15th, sent up a fire-balloon, "which had been carried along the coast by a gentle breeze, and, after burning all night, extinguished and collapsed off Montrose, early on Thursday morning (16th)." This story of a balloon that wafted to Montrose, and that was evidently traced until it collapsed near Montrose does not so simply explain an object that was seen 25 miles from Montrose. In the *Standard*, Dec. 19, it is said that two bright lights were seen over Dartmouth Harbour, upon the 11th.

Walter Powell was Member of Parliament for Malmesbury, and had many friends, some of whom started immediately to search. His relatives offered a reward. A steamboat searched the Channel, and did not give up until the 13th; fishing vessels kept on searching. A "sweeping expedition" was organized, and the coast guard was doubled, searching the shore for wreckage, but not a fragment of the balloon, nor from the balloon, except a thermometer in a bag, was found.

In *L'Astronomie* (5, 312), Prof. Paroisse of the College Bar-sur-Aube, quotes a witness of a *curieux phénomène* that occurred in a garden, May, 22, 1886 — cloudless sky; wind *trés faible*. Within a small circle in the garden were some baskets and ashes and a cold frame that weighed sixty kilograms. These things suddenly rose from the ground. At a height of about forty feet, they remained suspended about two minutes, then falling back to the place from which they had risen. Not a thing outside this small circle had been touched by the seizure. The witness said that they felt no disturbance in the air.

Scientific American (n.s., 55, 65) — that in June, 1886, according to the London *Times* (June 17, 1886), "a well known official" was entering Pall Mall, when he felt a violent blow on the shoulder and heard a crackling sound. There was no one in sight except a distant policeman. At home, he found that the nap of his coat looked as if a hot wire had been pressed against the cloth, in a long, straight line. No missile was found, but it was thought that something of a meteoritic nature had struck him.

Charleston News and Courier (Nov. 25, 1886) — that, at Edina, Mo., Nov. 23, a man and his three sons were pulling corn on a farm. Nothing is said of meteorologic conditions, and, for all I know, they may have been pulling corn in a violent thunderstorm. Something that is said to have been lightning flashed from the sky. The man was injured slightly, one son killed, the other seriously injured — the third had disappeared. "What has become of him is not known, but it is supposed that he was blinded or crazed by the shock, and wandered away."

Brooklyn *Eagle* (March 17, 1891) — that, at Wilkes-Barre, Pa., March 16th, two men were "lifted bodily and carried some distance" in a whirlwind. It was a powerful force, but nothing else was affected by it. Upon the same day, there was an occurrence in Brooklyn. In the *New York Times* (March 17, 1891), it is said that two men, Smith Morehouse, of Orange Co., N.Y., and William Owen, of Sussex Co., N.J., were walking along Vanderbilt Avenue, Brooklyn, about 1:50 P.M., on the 16th, when a terrific explosion occurred close to the head of Morehouse, injuring him and stunning Owen, the flash momentarily blinding both. Morehouse's face was covered with marks like powder-marks, and his tongue was pierced. With no one else to accuse, the police arrested Owen, but held him upon the technical charge of intoxication. Morehouse was taken to a hospital, where a splinter of metal, considered either brass or copper, but not a fragment of a cartridge, was removed from his tongue. No other material could be found, though an object of considerable size had exploded. Morehouse's hat had been perforated in six places by unfindable substances. According to witnesses there had been no one within a hundred feet of the men. One witness had seen the flash before the explosion, but could not say whether it had been from something falling or not. In the Brooklyn *Eagle* (March 17, 1891), it is said that neither of the men had a weapon of any kind, and that there had been no disagreement between them. According to a witness, they had been under observation at the time of the explosion, her attention having been attracted by their rustic appearance.

There is an interesting merging here of the findable and the unfindable. I suppose that no one will suppose that someone threw a bomb at these men. But enough substance was found to exclude the notion of "lightning from a clear sky." Something of a meteoritic nature seems excluded.

Chapter 16

Out from a round, red planet, a little white shaft — a fairy's arrow shot into an apple. June 10, 1892 — a light like a little searchlight, projecting from the limb of Mars. Upon July 11 and 13, it was seen again, by Campbell and Hussey (*Nature*, 50, 499).

Aug. 3, 1892 — climacteric opposition of Mars.

Upon August 12, 1892, flashes were seen by many persons, in the sky of England. See *Eng. Mech.* (56: 12, 15, 37). At Manchester, so like signals they were, or so unlike anything commonly known as "auroral" were they, that Albert Buss mistook them for flashes from a lighthouse. They were seen at Dewsbury; described by a correspondent to the *English Mechanic,* who wrote: "I have never heard of such an appearance of aurora." "Rapid flashes" reported from Loughborough.

* * *

A shining triangle in a dark circle.

In *L'Astronomie* (7, 75), Dr. Klein publishes an account of de Speissen's observation of Nov. 23, 1887 — a luminous triangle on the floor of Plato. Dr. Klein says it was an effect of sunlight.

In this period, there were in cities of the United States, some of the most astonishing effects at night, in the history of this earth. If Rigel should run for the Presidency of Orion, and if the stars in the great nebula should start to march, there would be a spectacle like those that Grover Cleveland called forth in the United States, in this period.

So then — at least conceivably — something similar upon the moon. Flakes of light moving toward Plato, this night of Nov. 23, 1887, from all the other craters of the moon; a blizzard of shining points gathering into light-drifts in Plato; then the denizens of Aristarchus and of Kepler, and dwellers from the lunar Alps, each raising his torch, marching upon a triangular path, making the triangle shine in the dark — conceivably. Other formations have been seen in Plato, but, according to my records, this symbol that shone in the dark had never been seen before, and has not been seen since.

About two years later — a demonstration of a more exclusive kind — assemblage of all the undertakers of the moon. They stood in a circular formation, surrounded by virgins in their nightgowns — and in nightgowns as nightgowns should be. An appearance in Plinius, Sept. 13, 1889, was reported by Prof. Thury, of Geneva — a black spot with an "intensely white" border (*Nature*, 41, 183; *Bull. S.A.F.*, 6, 461).

January 28, 1889 — a black spot that was seen for the first time, by Gaudibert, near the centre of Copernicus (*Astro.*, 9, 235). May 11, 1889 — an object as black as ink upon a rampart of Gassendi (*Astro.*, 8, 275). It had never been reported before; at the time of the next lunation, it was not seen again. March 30, 1889 — a new black spot in Plinius (*Astro.*, 9, 187).

The star-like object in Aristarchus — it is a long time since latest preceding appearance, (May 7, 1867). Then it can not be attributed to commonplace lunar circumstances. The light was seen Nov. 7, 1891, by M. d'Adjuda, of the Observatory of Lisbon — "a very distinct, luminous point" (*Astro.*, 11, 33).

Upon April 1, 1893, a shaft of light was seen projecting from the moon, by M. de Moraes, in the Azores. A similar appearance was seen, Sept. 25, 1893, at Paris, by Mr. Gaboreau (*Astro.*, 13, 34).

* * *

Another association like that of 1884 — in the *English Mechanic* (55, 310), a correspondent writes that, upon May 6, 1892, he saw a shining point (not polar) upon Venus. Upon the 13th of August, 1892, the same object — conceivably — was seen at a short distance from Venus — an unknown, luminous object, like a star of the 7th magnitude that was seen close to Venus, by Prof. Barnard (*Astronomische Nachrichten,* no. 4106, c. 25).

Upon August 24, 1895, in the period of primary maximum brilliance of Venus, a luminous object, it is said, was seen in the sky, in day time, by someone in Donegal, Ireland. Upon this day, according to the *Scientific American* (n.s., 73, 374), a boy, Robert Alcorn, saw a large luminous object falling from the sky. It exploded near him. The boy's experience was like Smith Morehouse's. He put his hands over his face: there was a second explosion, shattering his fingers. According to

Prof. George M. Minchin, no substance of the object that had exploded could be found. Whether there be relation or not, something was seen in the sky of England a week later. In the London *Times*, Sept. 4, 1895, Dr. J.A.H. Murray writes that, at Oxford, a few minutes before 8 P.M., August 31, 1895, he saw in the sky a luminous object, considerably larger than Venus at greater brilliance, emerge from behind tree tops, and sail slowly eastward. It moved as if driven in a strong wind, and disappeared behind other trees. "The fact that it so perceptibly grew fainter as it receded seems to imply that it had not a very great elevation, and so far favours a terrestrial origin, though I am quite unable to conceive how anything artificial could present the same appearance." In the *Times*, of the 6th, someone who had read Dr. Murray's letter says that, about the same time, same evening, he, in London, had seen the same object moving eastward so slowly that he had thought it might be a fire-balloon from a neighbouring park. Another correspondent, who had not read Dr. Murray's letter, his own dated Sept. 3, writes from a place not stated that about 8:20 P.M., Aug. 31, he had seen a star-like object, moving eastward, remaining in sight four or five minutes. Then someone who, about 8 P.M., same evening, while driving to the Scarborough station, had seen "a large shooting star," astonishing him, because of its leisurely rate, so different from the velocity of the ordinary "shooting star." There are two other accounts of objects that were seen in the sky, at Bath and at Ramsgate, but not about this time, and I have looked them up in local newspapers, finding that they were probably meteors.

In the *Oxford Times*, Sept. 7, Dr. Murray's letter to the London *Times* is reprinted, with this comment — "We would suggest to the learned doctor that the supposed meteor was one of the fire-balloons let off with the allotments show."

Let it be that when allotments are shown, balloons are always sent up, and that this Editor did not merely have a notion to this effect. Our data are concerned with an object that was seen, at about the same time, at Oxford, about 50 miles southeast of Oxford, and about 170 miles northeast of Oxford, with a fourth observation that we can not place.

And, in broader terms, our data are concerned with a general expression that objects like ships have been seen to sail close to this earth at times when the planet Venus is nearest this earth. Sept. 18, 1895 — inferior conjunction of Venus.

Still in the same period, there were, in London, two occurrences perhaps like that at Donegal. London *Morning Post*, Nov. 16, 1895—that, at noon, Nov. 15, an "alarming explosion" occurred somewhere near Fenchurch Street, London. No damage was done; no trace could be found of anything that had exploded. An hour later, near the Mansion House, which is not far from Fenchurch Street, occurred a still more violent explosion. The streets filled with persons who had run from buildings, and there was investigation, but not a trace could be found of anything that had exploded. It is said that somebody saw "something falling." However, the deadly explainers, usually astronomers, but this time policemen, haunt or arrest us. In the *Daily News*, Nov. 16, 1895, though it is not said that a trace of anything that had exploded had been found, it is said that the explanation by the police was that somebody had mischievously placed in the streets fog-signals, which had been exploded by passing vehicles.

Observations by Müller, of Nymegen, Holland — an unknown luminous object that, about three weeks later, was seen near Venus (*Monthly Notices*, 57, 276).

Upon the 28th of April, 1897, Venus was in inferior conjunction. In *Popular Astronomy* (5, 54), it is said that many persons had written to the Editor, telling of "airships" that had been seen, about this time. The Editor writes that some of the observations were probably upon the planet Venus, but that others probably related to toy balloons, "which were provided with various colored lights."

The first group of our data, I take from dispatches to the New York *Sun*, April 2, 11, 16, 18, 1897. First of April — "the mysterious light" in the sky of Kansas City — something like a powerful searchlight. "It is directed toward the earth, and is travelling east at the rate of sixty miles an hour." A week later, something was seen in Chicago. "Chicago's alleged airship is believed to be a myth in spite of the fact that a great many persons say they have seen the mysterious night wanderer. A crowd gazed at strange lights from the top of a downtown skys-craper, and Evanston students declare they saw the swaying red and green lights." April 15 — reported from Denton, Texas, but this time as a dark object that passed across the moon. Reports from other towns in Texas: Fort Worth, Dallas,

Marshall, Ennis, and Beaumont — "It was shaped like a Mexican cigar, large in the middle and small at both ends, with great wings resembling those of an enormous butterfly. It was brilliantly illuminated by the rays of two great searchlights, and was sailing in a southeasterly direction with the velocity of the wind, presenting a magnificent spectacle."

New York Herald, April 11 — that, at Chicago, night of April 9-10, "until two o'clock in the morning thousands of amazed spectators declared that the lights seen to the northwest were those of an airship or some other floating object, miles above the earth ... Some declare they saw two cigar-shaped objects and great wings." It is said that a white light, a red light, and a green light had been seen.

There does seem to be an association between this object and the planet Venus, which upon this night was less than three weeks from nearest approach to this earth. Nevertheless this object could not have been Venus, which had set hours earlier. Prof. Hough, of the Northwestern University, is quoted — that the people had mistaken the star *Alpha Orionis* (Betelgeuse) for an airship. Prof. Hough explains that astronomic effects may have given a changing red and green appearance to this star. *Alpha Orionis* as a northern star is some more astronomy by the astronomers who teach astronomy daytimes and then relax when night comes. That atmospheric conditions could pick out this one star and not affect other brilliant stars in Orion is more astronomy. At any rate the standardised explanation that the thing was Venus disappears.

There were other explainers — someone who said that he knew of an airship (terrestrial one) that had sailed from San Francisco and had reached Chicago.

Herald (April 12, 1897) — said that the object had been photographed in Chicago: "a cigar shaped, silken bag," with a framework — other explanations and identifications, not one of them applying to this object, if it be accepted that it was seen in places as far apart as Illinois and Texas. It is said that, upon March 29th, the thing had been seen in Omaha, as a bright light sailing to the northwest, and that, for a few moments, upon the following night, it had been seen in Denver. It is said that, upon the night of the 9th, despatches had bombarded the newspaper offices of Chicago, from many places in

Illinois, Indiana, Missouri, Iowa, and Wisconsin.

Prof. George Hough maintains "that the object seen is *Alpha Orionis*."

April 14 — story, veritable observation, yarn, hoax — despatch from Carlinville, Illinois — that upon the afternoon of the 11th, the airship had alighted upon a farm, but had sailed away when approached — "cigar-shaped, with wings and a canopy or top."

April 15 — shower of telegrams — developments of jokers and explainers — thing identified as an airship invented by someone in Dodge City, Kansas; identified as an airship invented by someone in Brule, Wisconsin — stories of letters found on farms, purporting to have been dropped by the unknown aeronauts (terrestrial ones) — jokers in various towns, sending up balloons with lights attached — one laborious joker who rigged up something that looked like an airship and put it in a vacant lot and told that it had fallen there — yarn or observation, upon a "queer-looking boat" that had been seen to rise from the water in Lake Erie — continued reports upon a moving object in the sky, and its red and green lights.

Against such an alliance as this, between the jokers and the astronomers, I see small chance for our data. The chance is in the future. If, in April, 1897, extra-mundane voyagers did visit this earth, likely enough they will visit again, and then the alliance against the data may be guarded against.

New York *Herald* (April 20) — that, upon the 19th, about 9 P.M., at Sistersville, W.Va., a luminous object had approached the town from the northwest, flashing brilliant red, white, and green lights. "An examination with strong glasses left the impression of a huge cone shaped arrangement 180 feet long, with large fins on either side."

My own general impression:

Night of October 12, 1492 — if I have that right. Some night in October, 1492, and savages upon an island-beach are gazing out at lights that they have never seen before. The indications are that voyagers from some other world are nearby. But the wise men explain. One of the most nearly sure expressions in this book is upon how they explain. They explain in terms of the familiar. For instance, after all that is spiritual in a fish passes away, the rest of him begins to shine nights. So there are three big, old, dead things out in the water —

CHAPTER 17

There have been published several observations upon a signal-like regularity of the Barisal Guns, which, because unaccompanied by phenomena that could be considered seismic, may have been detonations in the sky, and which, because, according to some hearers, they seemed to come from the sky, may have come from some region stationary in the local sky of Barisal. In *Nature* (61, 127), appears a report by Henry S. Schurr, who investigated the sounds in the years 1890-91:

"These Guns are always heard in triplets, ie. three guns are always heard, one after the other, at regular intervals, and though several guns may be heard the number is always three or a multiple of three. Then the interval between the three is always constant, ie. the interval between the first and the second is the same as the interval between the second and the third, and this interval is usually three seconds, though I have timed it up to ten seconds. The interval, however, between the triplets varies, and varies largely, from a few seconds up to hours and days. Sometimes only one series of triplets is heard in a day; at others, the triplets follow with great regularity, and I have counted as many as forty-five of them, one after the other, without a pause."

In vols. 16 and 17, *Ciel et Terre*, M. Van den Broeck published a series of papers upon the mysterious sounds that had been heard in Belgium.

July, 1892 — heard near Brée, by Dr. Raeymaekers, of Antwerp — detonations at regular intervals of about 12 seconds, repeated about 20 times.

Aug. 5, 1892 — near Dunkirk, by Prof. Gérard, of Brussels — four reports like sounds of cannons.

Aug. 17, 1893 — between Ostend and Ramsgate, by Prof. Gérard — a series of distinct explosions — state of the sky giving no reason to think that they were meteorological manifestations.

Sept. 5, 1893 — at Middelkirke — loud sounds of remarkable intensity.

Sept. 8, 1893 — English Channel near Dover — by Prof. Gérard — an explosive sound.

In *Ciel et Terre* (16, 485), M. Van den Broeck records an experience of his own. Upon June 25, 1894, at Louvain, he had heard detonations like discharges of artillery: he tabulates the intervals in a series of sounds. If there is signalling from some unknown region over Belgium, and not far from the surface of this earth, or from extra-mundane vessels, and if there were something of the code-like, resembling the Morse alphabet, perhaps, in this series of sounds, there can be small hope of interpreting such limited material, but there may be suggestion to someone to record all sounds and their intervals and modulations, if, with greater duration, such phenomena should ever occur again. The intervals were four minutes, then twenty minutes, then three minutes; then three minutes, four, three-quarters, three-and three-quarters, three-quarters.

Sept. 16, 1895 — a triplet of detonations, heard by M. de Schryvere, of Brussels.

There were attempts to explain. Some of M. Van den Broeck's correspondents thought that there had been firing from forts on the coast of England, and somebody thought that the phenomena should be attributed to gravitational effects of the moon. Upon Sept. 13, 1895, four shocks were felt and sounds heard at Southampton: a series of three and then another (*Nature*, 52, 552); but I have no other notes upon sounds that were heard in England at this time, except the two explosions that were explained by the police of London. However, M. Van den Broeck says that Mr. Harmer, of Alderburgh, Suffolk, had, about the first of November, heard booming sounds that had been attributed to cannonading at Harwich. Mr. Harmer had heard other sounds that had been attributed to cannonading somewhere else. He could not offer a definite opinion upon the first sounds, but had investigated the others, learning that the attribution was a mistake.

It was M. de Schryvere's opinion that the triplet of detonations that he had heard was from vessels in the North Sea. But now, according to developments, the sounds of Belgium cannot very well be attributed to terrestrial cannonading in or near Belgium: in *Ciel et Terre* (16, 614) are quoted two artillery officers who had heard the sounds, but could not so trace them: one of these officers had heard a series of detonations with intervals of about two minutes. A variety of explanations was attempted, but in conventional terms, and if these localised, repeating sounds did come from the sky, there's nothing to it but a new variety of attempted explanations, and in most unconventional terms. There are recorded definite impressions that the sounds were in the sky: Prof. Pelseneer's *positivement aérien*. In *Ciel et Terre* (17, 4), M. Van den Broeck announced that General Hennequin, of Brussels, had co-operated with him, and had sent enquiries to army officers and other persons, receiving thirty replies. Some of these correspondents had heard detonations at regular intervals. It is said that the sounds were like cannonading, but not in one instance were the sounds traced to terrestrial gunfire.

January 24, 1896 — a triplet of triplets — between 2:30 and 3:30 P.M. — by M. Overloop, of Middelkirke, Belgium — three series of detonations, each of three sounds.

The sounds went on, but, after this occurrence, there seems to me to be little inducement to continue upon this subject. This is indication that from somewhere there has been signalling: from extra-mundane vessels to one another, or from some unknown region to this earth, as nearly final as we can hope to find. There are persons who will see nothing but a susceptibility to the mysticism of numbers in a feeling that there is significance in threes of threes. But, if there be attempt in some other world to attract attention upon this earth, it would have to be addressed to some state of mind that would feel significances. Let our three threes be as mystic as the eleven horns on Daniel's fourth animal; if throughout nature like human nature there be only superstition as to such serialisation, that superstition, for want of something more nearly intelligent, would be a susceptibility to which to appeal, and from which response might be expected. I think that a sense of mystic significance in the number three may be universal, because upon this earth it is general, appearing in theologies, in the balanced composition of all the arts, in logical demonstrations, and in the indefinite feelings that are supposed to be superstitious.

The sounds went on, as if there were experiments, or attempts to communicate by means of other regularisations and repetitions. Feb. 18, 1896 — a series of more than 20 detonations, at intervals of two or three minutes, heard at Ostend, by M. Putzeys, an engineer of Brussels. Four or five sounds were heard at Ostend by someone else:

repeated upon the 21st of February. Heard by M. Overloop, at Ostend, April 6: detonations at 11:57:30 A.M., and at 12:01:32 P.M. Heard the next day, by M. Overloop, at Blankenberghe, at 2:35 and 2:51 P.M.

The last occurrence recorded by M. Van den Broeck was upon the English Channel. May 23, 1896: detonations at 3:20 and 3:40 P.M., I have no more data, as to this period, myself, but I have notes upon similar sounds, by no means so widely reported and commented upon, in France and Belgium about 15 years later. One notices that the old earthquake-explanation as to these sounds has not appeared.

But there were other phenomena in England, in this period, and to considerable degree they were conventionally explained. They were not of the type of the Belgian phenomena, and, because manifestations were seen and felt, as well as heard, they were explained in terms of meteors and earthquakes. But in this double explanation, we meet a divided opposition, and no longer are we held back by the uncompromising attempt by exclusionist science to attribute all disturbances of this earth's surface to subterranean origin. The admission by Symons and Fordham that we have recorded, as to occurrences of 1887-89, has survived.

The earliest of accounts that I have read of the quakes in the general region of Worcester and Hereford (London Triangle) that associated with appearances in the sky, was published by two church wardens in the year 1661, as to occurrences of October, 1661, and is entitled, *A True and Perfect Relation of the Terrible Earthquake.* It is said that monstrous flaming things were seen in the sky, and that phenomena below were interesting. We are told, "truly and perfectly," that Mrs. Margaret Petmore fell in labour and brought forth three male offspring all of whom had teeth and spoke at birth. Inasmuch as it is not recorded what the infants said, and whether in plain English or not, it is not so much an extraordinary birth such as, in one way or another, occurs from time to time, that affronts our conventional notions, as it is the idea that there could be relation between the abnormal in obstetrics and the unusual in terrestrics. The conventional scientist has just this reluctance towards considering shocks of this earth and phenomena in the sky at the same time. If he could accept with us that there often has been relation, the seeming discord would turn into a commonplace, but with us he would never again want to hear of extraordinary detonating meteors exploding only by coincidence over a part of this earth where an earthquake was occurring, or of concussions of this earth, time after time, in one small region, from meteors that, only by coincidence, happened to explode in one little local sky, time after time. Give up the idea that this earth moves, however, and coincidences many times repeated do not have to be lugged in.

Our subject now is the supposed earthquake centring around Worcester and Hereford, Dec. 17, 1896; but there may have been related events, leading up to this climax, signifying long duration of something in the sky that occasionally manifested relatively to this corner of the London Triangle. Mrs. Margaret Petmore was too sensational a person for our liking, at least in our colder and more nearly scientific moments, so we shall not date so far back as the time of her performance; but the so-called earthquakes of Oct. 6, 1863, and of Oct. 30, 1868, were in this region, and we had data for thinking that they were said to be earthquakes only because they could not be traced to terrestrial explosions.

At 5:45 P.M., Nov. 2, 1893, a loud sound was heard at a place ten miles northeast of Worcester, and no shock was felt (*Nature*, 49, 34); however at Worcester and in various parts of the west of England and in Wales a shock was felt.

According to James G. Wood, writing in Symons' *Met. Mag.* (29, 8), at 9:30 P.M., January 25, 1894, at Llanthomas and Clifford, towns less than 20 miles west of Hereford, a brilliant light was seen in the sky, an explosion was heard, and a quake was felt. Half an hour later, something else occurred: according to Denning (*Nature*, 49, 325), it was in several places, near Hereford and Worcester, supposed to be an earthquake. But, at Stokesay Vicarage, Shropshire (Symons' *Met. Mag.*, 29, 9), was seen the same kind of an appearance as that which had been seen at Llanthomas and Clifford, half an hour before: an illumination so brilliant that for half a minute everything was almost as visible as by daylight.

In *English Mechanic* (74, 155), David Packer calls attention to "a strange meteoric light" that was seen in the sky, at Worcester, during the quake of Dec. 17, 1896. I should say that this was the severest shock felt in the British Isles, in the 19th century, with the exception of the shock of April 22, 1884, in the eastern point of the London Triangle. There was something in the sky. In *Nature* (55, 178), J. Lloyd Bozward writes that, at Worcester, a great light was seen in the sky, at the time of the shock, and that, in another town, "a great blaze" had been seen in the sky. In Symons' *Met. Mag.* (31, 183) are recorded many observations upon lights that were seen in the sky. In an appendix to his book, *The Hereford Earthquake of 1896,* Dr. Charles Davison says that at the time of the quake (5:30 A.M.) there was a luminous object in the sky, and that it "traversed a large part of the disturbed area." He says that it was a meteor, and an extraordinary meteor that lighted up the ground so that one could have picked up a pin. With the data so far considered, almost anyone would think that of course an object had exploded in the sky, shaking the earth underneath. Dr. Davison does not say this. He says that the meteor only happened to appear over a part of this earth where an earthquake was occurring "by a strange coincidence."

Suppose that, with ordinary common sense, he had not lugged in his "strange coincidence," and had written that of course the shock was concussion from an explosion in the sky —

Shocks that had been felt before midnight, Dec. 17, and at 1:30 or 1:45, 2, 3, 3:30, 4, 5, and 5:20, and then others at 5:40 or 5:45 and at 6:15 o'clock — and were they, too, concussions, but fainter and from remoter explosions in the sky — and why not, if of course the great shock at 5:30 o'clock was from a great explosion in the sky — and by what multiplication of strangeness of coincidence could detonating meteors, or explosions of any other kind, so localise in the one little sky of Worcester, if this earth be a moving earth — and how could their origin be otherwise than a fixed region nearby?

In some minds it may be questionable that the earth could be so affected as it was at 5:30 A.M., Dec. 17, 1896, by an explosion in the sky. Upon Feb. 10, 1896, a tremendous explosion occurred in the sky of Madrid: throughout the city windows were smashed; a wall in the building occupied by the American Legation was thrown down. The people of Madrid rushed to the streets, and there was a panic in which many were injured. For five hours and a half, a luminous cloud of debris hung over Madrid, and stones fell from the sky.

Suppose, just at present, we disregard all the Worcester-

Hereford phenomena except those of Dec. 17, 1896. Draw a diagram, illustrating a stream of meteors pursuing this earth, now supposed to be rotating and revolving, for more than 400,000 miles in its orbit, and curving around gracefully and unerringly after the rotating earth, so as to explode precisely in this little local sky and nowhere else. But we can't think very reasonably even of a flock of birds flying after and so precisely pecking one spot on an apple thrown in the air by somebody. Another diagram — stationary earth — bombardment of any kind one chooses to think of — same point hit every time — thinkable.

The phenomena associate with an opposition of Mars. Dec. 10, 1896 — opposition of Mars.

But we have gone on rather elaborately with perhaps an insufficiency to base upon. We cannot say, directly, that all the phenomena of the night Dec. 16-17, 1896, were shocks from explosions in the sky: only during the greatest of the concussions was something seen, or was something near enough to be seen.

We apply the idea of diagrams to another series of occurrences in this period. Now draw a diagram relatively to the sky of Florida, and see just what the explanation of coincidence demands or exacts. But then consider the diagram as one of the earth that does not move and of something that is fixed over a point upon its surface. Things can be thought of as coming down from somewhere else to one special sky of this earth, as logically as precariously placed objects on one special window sill sometimes come down to a special neighbour.

In the *Monthly Weather Review* (23, 57) is a report, by the Director of the Florida Weather Service, upon "mysterious noises" and luminous effects in the sky of Florida. According to investigation, these phenomena did occur in the sky of Florida, about 11:30 A.M., Feb. 7, 1895, again at 5:30 A.M., morning of the 8th, and again between 6 and 10 o'clock, night of the 8th. The Editor of the *Review* thinks that three meteors may have exploded so in succession in the sky of Florida, and nowhere else, by coincidence.

Chapter 18

Char me the trunk of a redwood tree. Give me pages of white chalk cliffs to write upon. Magnify me thousands of times, and replace my trifling immodesties with a titanic megalomania — then I might write largely enough for our subjects. Because of accessibility and abundance of data, our accounts deal very much with the relatively insignificant phenomena of Great Britain. But our subject, if not so restricted, would be the violences that have screamed from the heavens, lapping up villages with tongues of fire. If, because of appearances in the sky, it be accepted that some of the so-called earthquakes of Italy and South America represented relations with regions beyond this earth, then it is accepted that some of this earth's greatest catastrophes have been relations with the unknown and the external. We have data that seem to be indications of signalling, but not unless we can think that foreign giants have hurled explosive mountains at this earth can we see such indications in all the data.

Our data do seem to fall into two orders of phenomena: sounds of Melida, Barisal, and Belgium, and nothing falling from the sky, and nothing seen in the sky, and excellently supported observations for accepting a signal-like intent in intervals and groupings of sounds, at least in Barisal and Belgium; and the unregularised phenomena of Worcester-Hereford, Colchester, Comrie, and Birmingham, in which appearances are seen in the sky, or in which substances fall from the sky, and in which effects upon this earth, not noted at all in Belgium and Bengal, are great, and sometimes tremendous. It seems that extra-geography divides into the extra-sociologic and the extra-physical; and in the second type of phenomena, we suppose the data are of physical relations between this earth and other worlds. We think of a difference of potential. There were tremendous detonations in the sky at the times of the falls of the little black stones of Birmingham and Wolverhampton, and the electric manifestations, according to descriptions in the newspapers, were extraordinary, and great volumes of water fell. Consequently the events were supposed to be thunderstorms. I suppose, myself, that they were electric storms, but electric storms that represented difference in potential between this earth and some region that was fixed, at least eleven years, over

Birmingham and Wolverhampton, bringing down stones and volumes of water from some other world, or bringing down stones, and dislodging intervening volumes of water, such as we have many data for thinking exist in outer space, sometimes in bodies of warm or hot water, and sometimes as great masses, or fields, of ice.

Let two objects be generically similar, but specifically different and a relation that may be known as a difference of potential, though that term is usually confined to electric relations, generates between them. Quite as the Gulf Stream — though there are no reasons to suppose that there is such a Gulf Stream as one reads of — represents a relation between bodies of water heated differently, given any two worlds, alike in general constitution, but differing, say, electrically, and given proximity, we conceive of relations between them other than gravitational.

But this cloistered earth, and its monkish science — shrinking from, denying, or disregarding, all data of external relations, except some one controlling force that was once upon a time known as Jehovah, but that has been re-named Gravitation —

That the electric exchanges that were recognized by the ancients, but that were anthropomorphically explained by them, have poured from the sky and have gushed to the sky, afferently and efferently, between this earth and the nearby planets, or between this mainland and its San Salvadors, and have been recognized by the moderns, or the neo-ancients, but have been meteorologically and seismologically misconstrued by them.

When a village spouts to the sky, it is said to have been caught up in a cyclone: when unknown substances fall from the sky, not much of anything is said upon the subject.

Lost tribes and nations that have disappeared from the face of this earth — that the skies have reeked with terrestrial civilizations, spreading out in celestial stagnations, where their remains to this day may be. The Mayans — and what became of them? Bones of the Mayans, picked white as frost by space-scavengers, spread upon existence like the pseudo-breath of Death, crystallized on a sky-pane. Three times gaps wide and dark obscure the history of Egypt — and that these abysses were gulfed by disappearances — that some of the eliminations from this earth may have been upward translations in functional suctions. We conceive of Supervision upon this earth's development, but for it the names Jehovah and Allah seem old-fashioned — that the equivalence of wrath, but like the storms of cells that, in an embryonic thing, invade and destroy cartilage-cells, when they have outlived their usefulness, have devastated this earth's undesirables. Likely enough, or not quite likely enough, one of these earlier Egypts was populated by sphinxes, if one can suppose that some of the statuary still extant in Egypt were portraitures. This is good, though also not so good, orthodox Evolutionary doctrine — that between types occur transitionals —

That Elimination and Redistribution swept an earlier Egypt with suctions — because it is written, in symbols of embryonic law, that life upon this earth must form onward — and the crouching sphinx on the sands of Egypt, blinking the mysticism of her morphologic mixtures, would perhaps detain forever the less interesting type that was advancing —

That often has Clarification destroyed transitionals, that they shall not hold back development.

One conceives of their remains, to this day, wafting still in the currents of the sky: floating avenues of frozen sphinxes, solemnly dipping in cosmic undulations, down which circulate processions of Egyptian mummies.

An astronomer upon this earth notes that things in parallel lines have crossed the sun.

We offer this contribution as comparing favourably with the works of any other historian. We think that some of the details may need revision, but that what they typify is somewhere nearly acceptable.

Latitudes and longitudes of bones, not in the sky, but upon the surface of this earth. Baron Toll and other explorers have, upon the surface of this earth, kicked their way through networks of ribs and protrusions of skulls and stacks of vertebrae, as numerous as if from dead land they sprouted there (*Geographical Journal*, 16, 95). Anybody who has read of these tracts of bones upon the northern coast of Siberia, and of some of the outlying islands that are virtually composed of bones cemented with icy sand, will agree with me that there have been cataclysms of which conventionality and standardi-sation tell us nothing. Once upon a time, some unknown force translated, from somewhere, a million animals to Colorado, where their remains now form great bone-quarries. Very largely do we express a reaction against dogmatism, and sometimes we are not dogmatic, ourselves. We don't know very positively whether at times the animal life of some other world has been swept away from that world or not, eventually pouring from the sky of Siberia and of Colorado, in some of the shockingest floods of mammoths from which spattered cats and rabbits, in cosmic scenery, or not. All that we can say is that when we turn to conventionality it is to blankness or suppression. Every now and then, to this day, occurs an alleged fall of blood from the sky, and I have notes upon at least one instance in which the microscopically examined substance was identified as blood. But now we conceive of intenser times, when every now and then a red cataract hung in the heavens like the bridal veil of the goddess of murder. But the science of today is a soporific like the idealism of Europe before the War broke out. Science and idealism — wings of a vampire that lulls consciousness that might otherwise foresee catastrophe. Showers of frogs and showers of fishes that occur to this day — that they are the dwindled representatives to this day of the cataclysms of intenser times when the skies of this earth were darkened by afferent clouds of dinosaurs. We conceive of intenser times, but we conceive of all times as being rhythmic times. We are too busy to take up alarmism, but, if Rome, for instance, never was destroyed by terrestrial barbarians, if we can not very well think of Apaches seizing Chicago, extra-mundane vandals may often have swooped down upon this earth, and they may swoop again; and it may be a comfort to us, some day, to mention in our last gasp that we told about this.

History, geology, palæontology, astronomy, meteorology — that nothing short of cataclysmic thinking can break down these united walls of Exclusionism.

Unknown monsters sometimes appear in the ocean. When, upon the closed system of normal preoccupations, a story of a sea serpent appears, it is inhospitably treated. To us of the wider cordialities, it has recommendations for kinder reception. I think that we shall be noted in recognitions of good works for our bizarre charities. Far back in the topography of the nineteenth century, Richard Proctor was almost submerged in an ocean of smugness, but now and then he was a little island emerging from the gently alternating doubts and satisfactions of his era, and by means of several papers upon the "sea serpent" he so protruded and gave variety to a dreary uniformity. Proctor reviewed some of the stories of "sea serpents." He accepted some of them. This will be news to some conventionalists. But the mystery that he could not solve is their conceivable origin. To be sure this earth may not be round, or top-shaped, and may tower away somewhere, perhaps with the great Antarctic plateau at its foothills, to a gigantic existence commensurate throughout with sea monsters that some-times reach regions unknown to us. Judging by our experience in other fields of research, we suspect that this earth never has been traversed except in conventional trade-routes and standard explorations. One supposes that enormous forms of life that have appeared upon the surface of the ocean did not come from conditions of great pressure below the surface. If there is no habitat of their own, in unknown seas of this earth, the monsters fell from the sky, surviving for a while. In his day, Charles Lyell never said a more preposterous thing than this — however, we have no idea that mere preposterousness is a criterion.

Then at times the things have fallen upon land, presumably. To scientific minds in their present anæmia of malnutrition, we offer new nourishment. There are materials for a science of neo-palæontology — as it were — at least a new view of animal-remains upon this earth. Remains of monsters, supposed to have lived geologic ages ago, are sometimes found, not in ancient deposits, but upon, or near, the surface of the ground, sometimes barely covered. I have notes upon a great pile of bones, supposed to be the remains of a whale, out in open view in a western desert.

In the American Museum of Natural History, New York City, is the mummified body of a monster called a *trachodon*, found in Converse County, Wyoming. It was not found upon the surface of the ground, which is bad for our attempts to stimulate palæontology. But the striking datum to me is that the only other huge mummy that I know of is another *trachodon*, now in the Museum of Frankfort. If only extraordinarily would geologic processes mummify remains of a huge animal, doubly extraordinarily would two animals of the same species be so exclusively affected. One at least gives some consideration to the idea that these *trachodons* are not products of geologic circumstances, but were affected, in common, by other circumstances. By inspiration, or progressive deterioration, one then conceives of the things as having wafted and dried in space, finally falling to this earth. Our swooping vandals are relieved with showering mummies. Life is turning out to be interesting.

Organic substances like life-fluids of living things have rained from the sky. However, it is enough for our general purposes to make acceptable simply that unknown substances have, in large quantities, fallen from the sky. That is neo-ism enough, it seems to me. I consider, myself, all such data relatively to this earth's stationariness or possible motions. In *Ciel et Terre* (22, 198), it is said that, about 2 P.M., June 8, 1901, a glue-like substance fell at Sart. The story is told by an investigator, M. Michael, a meteorologist. He says that he saw this substance falling from the sky, but does not give an estimate of duration: he says that he arrived during the last five minutes of the shower. Editors and extra-geographers can't help trying to explain. The Editor of *Ciel et Terre* writes that, three days before, there had been, at Antwerp, a great fire, in which, among other substances, a large quantity of sugar had been burned. He asks whether there could be any connection. Antwerp is about 80 miles from Sart.

Sept. 2, 1905 — the tragedy of the space-pig:

In the *English Mechanic* (86, 100), Col. Markwick writes that, according to the *Cambrian Natural Observer* (1905: 30, 32- 34), something was seen in the sky, at Llangollen, Wales, Sept. 2, 1905. It is described as an intensely black object, about two miles above the earth's surface, moving at the rate of about twenty miles an hour. Col. Markwick writes: "Could it have been a balloon?" We give Col. Markwick good rating as an extra-geographer, but of the early or differentiating type, a transitional, if not a sphinx: so he was not quite developed enough to publish the details of this object. In the *Cambrian Natural Observer* (1905, 35) — the journal of the Astronomical Society of Wales — it is said that, according to accounts in the newspapers, an object had appeared in the sky, at Llangollen, Wales, Sept. 2, 1905. At the schoolhouse, in Vroncysylite — I think that's it: with all my credulity, some of these Welsh names look incredible to me, in my notes — the thing in the sky had been examined through powerful field glasses.

We are told that it had short wings, and flew, or moved, in a way described as "casually inclining sideways." It seemed to have four legs and looked to be about ten feet long. According to several witnesses it looked like a huge, winged pig, with webbed feet. "Much speculation was rife as to what the mysterious object could be."

Five days later, according to a member of the Astronomical Society of Wales — see *Cambrian Observer* (1905, 30) — a purple-red substance fell from the sky, at Llanelly, Wales.

I don't know that my own attitude toward these data is understood, and I don't know that it matters in the least; also from time to time my own attitude changes: but very largely my feeling is that not much can be, or should be, concluded from our meagre accounts, but that so often are these occurrences, in our fields, reported, that several times every year there will be occurrences that one would like to have investigated by someone who believes that we have written nothing but bosh, and by someone who believes in our data almost religiously. It may be that, early in February, 1892, a luminous thing travelled back and forth, exploring for ten hours in the sky of Sweden. The story is copied from a newspaper, and ridiculed, in the *English Mechanic* (55, 34). Upon March 7, 1893, a luminous object shaped like an elongated pear was seen in the sky of Val-de-la-Haye, by M. Raimond Coulon (*Astro.*, 12, 196). M. Coulon's suggestion is that the light may have been a signal suspended from a balloon. The signal-idea is interesting.

In the summer of 1897, several weeks after Prof. Andrée and his two companions had sailed in a balloon, from Amsterdam Island, Spitzbergen, it was reported that a balloon had been seen in British Columbia. There was wide publicity: the report was investigated. It may be that had a terrestrial balloon escaped from somewhere in the United States or Canada, or if there had been a balloon-ascension at this time, the circumstances would have been reported: it may well be that the object was not Andrée's balloon. President Bell, of the National Geographic Society, heard of this object, and heard that details had been sent to the Swedish Foreign Office, and cabled to the American Minister, at Stockholm, for information. He publishes his account in the *National Geographic Magazine* (9, 102). He was referred to the Swedish Consul, at San Francisco. In reply to inquiry, the Consul telegraphed the following data, which had been collected by the President of the Geographical Society of the Pacific:

"Statement of a balloon passing over the Horse-Fly Hydraulic Mining Camp, in Caribou, British Columbia, 52°, 20', and Longitude 120°, 30' —

"From letters of J.B. Robson, Manager of the Caribou Mining Co., and of Mrs. Wm. Sullivan, the blacksmith's wife, there, and a statement of Mr. John J. Newsome, San Francisco, then at camp. About 2 or 3 o'clock, in the afternoon, between fourth and seventh of August last, weather calm and cloudless, Mrs. Sullivan, while looking over the Hydraulic Bank, noticed a round, grayish-looking object in the sky, to the right of the sun. As she watched, it grew larger and was descending. She saw the larger mass of the balloon above, and a smaller mass apparently suspended from the larger. It continued to descend, until she plainly recognized it as a balloon and a large basket hanging thereto. It finally commenced to swing violently back and forth, and move very fast toward the eastward and northward. Mrs. Sullivan called her daughter, aged 18, and about this time Mrs. Robson and her daughter were observing it."

If someone saw a strange fish in the ocean, we'd like to know — what was it like? Stripes on him — spots — what? It would be unsatisfactory to be told over and over only that a dark body had crossed some waves. In *Cosmos (L.M.)* (s. 4, 39, 356), a satisfactory correspondent writes that, at Lille, France, Sept. 4, 1898, he saw a red object in the sky. It was like the planet Mars, but was in the position of no known planet. He looked through his telescope, and saw a rectangular object, with a violet-coloured band on one side of it, and the rest of it striped with black and red. He watched it ten minutes, during which time it was stationary; then, like the object that was seen at the time of the Powell-mystery, it cast out sparks and disappeared.

In the *English Mechanic* (75, 417), Col. Markwick writes that, upon May 10, 1902, a friend of his had seen in the sky, in South Devon, a great number of highly coloured objects like little suns or toy balloons. "Altogether beats me," says Col. Markwick.

Upon March 2, 1899, a luminous object in the sky, from 10 A.M., until 4 P.M., was reported from El Paso, Texas. Mentioned in the *Observatory* (22, 247) — supposed to have been Venus, even though

Venus was then two months past secondary maximum brilliance. That seems reasonable enough, in itself, but there are other data for thinking that an unknown, luminous body was at this time in the especial sky of the southernmost states. In the *Monthly Weather Review*, (27, 110), it is said, at Prescott, Arizona, Dr. Warren E. Day had seen a luminous object, upon the 8th of March, "traveling with the moon" all day, until 2 P.M. It is said that, the day before, this object had been seen close to the moon, by Mr. G.O. Scott, at Tonto, Arizona. Dr. Day and Mr. Scott were voluntary observers for the Weather Review. This association with the moon and this localisation of observation are puzzling.

La Nature (1899, v. 2, Supp., 94) — that at Luzarches, France, upon the 28th of October, 1899, M. A. Garrie had seen, at 4:50 P.M., a round, luminous object, about the size of the moon, rising above the horizon. He watched it for 15 minutes, as it moved away, diminishing to a point. It may be that something from external regions was for several weeks in the especial sky of France. In *La Nature* (1900, v. 1, Supp., 10), someone writes that he had seen, Nov. 15, 1899, 7 P.M., at Dourite (Dordogne) an object like an enormous star, at times white, then red, and sometimes blue, but moving like a kite. It was in the south. He had never seen it before. Someone, in the issue of December 30th (*La Nature*, 1900, v. 1, Supp., 18) , says that, without doubt it was the star Formalhaut, and asks for precise position. Issue of Jan. 20, 1900 (*La Nature*, 1900 v. 1, Supp., 30)— the first correspondent says that the object was in the southwest, about 35 degrees above the horizon, but moving so that the precise position could not be stated. The kite-like motion may have been merely seeming motion — object may have been Formalhaut, though 35 degrees above the horizon seems to me to be too high for Formalhaut — but, then, like the astronomers, I'm likely at times to expose what I don't know about astronomy. Formalhaut is not an enormous star. Eighteen are brighter.

May 1, 1908, between 8 and 9 P.M., at Vittel, France — an object, with a nebulosity around it, diameter equal to the moon's, according to a correspondent to *Cosmos (L.M.)* (s. 4, 58, 535). At 9 o'clock a black band appeared upon the object, and moved obliquely across it, then disappearing. The Editor thinks that the object was the planet Venus, under extraordinary meteorologic conditions.

Dark object, by Prof. Brooks, July 21, 1896 (*Eng. Mech.*, 64, 12);

dark object, by Guthman, Aug. 22, 1896 (*Sci. Amer. Supp.*, 67, 362); two luminous objects, by Prof. Swift, evidently in a local sky of California, because unseen elsewhere in California, Sept. 20, and one of them again, Sept. 21, 1896 (*Astro. Jour.*, 17: 8, 103); "Waldemath's second moon," Feb. 5, 1898 (*Eng. Mech.*, 66, 596; 67: 545, 546); unknown object, March 30, 1908 (*Observatory*, 31, 215); dark object, Nov. 10, 1908 (*Bull. S.A.F.*, 23, 74).

CHAPTER 19

Cold Harbor, Hanover Co., Virginia — two men in a field — "an apparently clear sky." In the *Monthly Weather Review* (28, 292), it is said that upon Aug. 7, 1900, two men were struck by lightning. The Editor says that the weather map gave no indication of a thunderstorm, nor of rain, in this region at the time.

In July, 1904, a man was killed on the summit of Mt. San Gorgonio, near the Mojave Desert. It is said that he was killed by lightning. Two days later, upon the summit of Mt. Whitney, 180 miles away, another man was killed "by lightning" (*Ciel et Terre,* 29, 120).

It is said, in *Ciel et Terre* (17, 40), that in the year 1892, nineteen soldiers were marching near Bourges, France, when they were struck by an unknown force. It is said that in known terms there is no explanation. Some of the men were killed, and the others struck insensible. At the inquest it was testified that there had been no storm, and that nothing had been heard.

If there occur upon the surface of this earth pounces from blankness and seizures by nothings, and "sniping" with bullets of unfindable substance, we nevertheless hesitate to bring witchcraft and demonology into our fields. Our general subject now is the existence of a great deal that may be nearby, or temporarily nearby, ordinarily invisible, but occasionally revealed by special circumstances. A background of stars is not to be compared, in our data, with the sun for a background, as a means of revelations. We accept that there are sunspots, but we gather from general experience and special instances that the word "sunspot" is another of the standardising terms like "auroral" and "meteoric" and "earthquakes." See Webb's *Celestial Objects* for some observations upon large definite obscurations called "sunspots" but which were as evanescent against the sun as would be islands and jungles of space, if intervening only a few moments between this earth and the swiftly moving sun. According to Webb, astronomers have looked at great obscurations upon the sun, have turned away, and then looked again, finding no trace of the phenomena. Eclipses are special circumstances, and rather often have large, unknown bulks been revealed by different light-effects during eclipses. For instance, upon Jan. 22, 1898, Lieut. Blackett, R.N., assisting Sir Norman Lockyer, at Viziadrug, India, during the total eclipse of the sun, saw an unknown body between Venus and Mars (*Journal of the Leeds Astronomical Society*, no. 14, 23). We have had other instances, and I have notes upon still more. The photographic plate is a special condition, or sensitiveness. In *Knowledge* (16, 234), a correspondent writes that, in August, 1893, in Switzerland, moon-lighted night, he had exposed a photographic plate for one hour. Upon the photograph, when developed, were seen irregular, bright markings, but there had been no lightning to this correspondent's perceptions.

The details of the sheep-panic of Nov. 3, 1888, are extraordinary. The region affected was much greater than was supposed by the writer whom we quoted in an earlier chapter. It is said in another account in Symons' *Meteorological Magazine* (23, 154), that, in a tract of land twenty-five miles long and eight miles wide, thousands of sheep had, by simultaneous impulse, burst from their bounds; and had been found the next morning, widely scattered, some of them still panting with terror under hedges, and many crowded into corners of fields. See London *Times*, Nov. 20, 1888. An idea of the great number of flocks affected is given by one correspondent who says that malicious mischief was out of the question, because a thousand men could not have frightened and released all these sheep. Someone else tries to explain that, given an alarm in one flock, it might spread to the others. But all the sheep so burst from their folds at about eight o'clock in the evening, and one supposes that many folds were far from contiguous, and one thinks of such contagion requiring considerable time to spread over 200 square miles. Something of an alarming nature and of pronounced degree occurred somewhere near Reading, Berkshire, upon this evening. Also there seems to be something of special localisation: the next year another panic occurred in Berkshire not far from Reading.

I have a datum that looks very much like the revelation of a ghost-moon, though I think of it myself in physical terms of light-effects. In *Country Queries and Notes* (1: 138, 417), it is said that, in the sky of Gosport, Hampshire, night of Sept. 14, 1908, was seen a light that came as if from an unseen moon. It may be that I can record that there was a moon-like object in the sky of the Midlands and the south of England, this night, and that, though to human eyesight, this world, island of space, whatever it may have been, was invisible, it was, nevertheless, revealed. Upon this evening of Sept. 14, 1908, David Packer, then in Northfield, Worcestershire, saw a luminous appearance that he supposed was auroral, and photographed it. When the photograph was developed, it was seen that the "auroral" light came from a large, moon-like object. A reproduction of the photograph is published in the *English Mechanic* (88, 211). It shows an object as bright and as well-defined as the conventionally accepted moon, but only to the camera had it revealed itself, and Mr. Packer had caught upon film a space-island that had been invisible to his eyes. It seems so, anyway.

In *Country Queries and Notes* (1, 328), it is said that, upon Aug. 2, 1908, at Ballyconneely, Connemara coast of Ireland, was seen a phantom city of different-sized houses, in different styles of architecture; visible three hours. It is said that no doubt the appearance was a mirage of some city far away — far away, but upon this earth, of course. This apparition is not of the type that we consider so especially of our own data. The so-called mirages that so especially interest are interesting to us not in themselves, but in that they belong to the one order of phenomena or evidence that unifies so many fields of our data: that is, repetitions in a local sky, signifying the fixed position of something relatively to a small part of this earth's surface. We can not think that mirages, terrestrial or extra-terrestrial, could so repeat. But if in the local sky of this earth there be a fixed region, perhaps not a city, but something of rugged and featureful outlines, with projections that might look architectural, reflections from it, shadows, or Brocken spectres repeating always in one special sky are thinkable except by the Chinese-minded who regard all our data as "foreign devils." The writer in *Country Queries and Notes* says — "Circumstantial accounts have been published of the city of Bristol being distinctly recognized in a mirage seen occasionally in North America." If we shall accept that anywhere in North America repeated representations of the same city or city-like scene have appeared in the same local sky, I prefer, myself, a foreign devil of thought, and its significance, whether hellish or not, that this earth is stationary, to such a domestic vagrant of a thought as the idea that mirage could so pick out the city of Bristol, or any other city, over and over, and also invariably pick out for its screen the same local sky, thousands of miles, or five miles away.

In the *English Mechanic* (66, 81), a correspondent to the *Weekly Times and Echo* (September 5, 1897) is quoted. He had just returned from the Yukon. Early in June, 1897, he had seen a city pictured in the sky of Alaska. "Not one of us could form the remotest idea what part of the world this settlement could be in. Some guessed at Toronto, others Montreal, and one of us even suggested Peking (Beijing). But whether this city exists in some unknown world on the other side of the North Pole or not remains to be proved. Nevertheless, it is a fact that this wonderful mirage occurs from time to time yearly, and we were not the only ones who witnessed the spectacle. Therefore it is evident that it must be the reflection of some place built by the hands of men." According to this correspondent, the "mirage" did not look like one of the cities named, but like "some immense city of the past."

In the New York *Tribune*, Feb. 17, 1901, it is said that Indians of Alaska had told of an occasional appearance, as if of a city, suspended in the sky, and that a prospector named Willoughby, having heard the stories, had investigated, in the year 1887, and had seen the spectacle. It is said that, having several times attempted to photograph the scene, Willoughby did finally at least show an alleged photograph of an aerial city. In *Alaska* (1st ed., 86; 2nd ed., 140), Miner Bruce say that Willoughby, one of the early pioneers in Alaska, after whom Willoughby Island is named, had told him of the phenomenon, and that, early in 1889, he had accompanied Willoughby to the place over which the mirage was said to repeat. It seems that he saw nothing himself, but he quotes a member of the Duc d'Abruzzi's expedition to Mt. St. Elias, summer of 1897, Mr. C.W. Thornton, of Seattle, who saw the spectacle, and wrote — "It required no effort of the imagination to liken it to a city, but was so distinct and plain that it required instead faith to believe that it was not in reality a city." Bruce publishes a reproduction of Willoughby's photograph, and says that the city was identified as Bristol, England. So definite, or so un-mirage-like, is this reproduction, trees and many buildings shown in detail, that one supposes that the original was a photograph of a good-sized terrestrial city, perhaps Bristol, England.

In chapter ten, of his book, *Wonders of Alaska*, Alexander Badlam tries to explain. He publishes a reproduction of Willoughby's photograph: it is the same as Bruce's, except that all buildings are transposed, or are negative in positions. Badlam does not like to accuse Willoughby of fraud: his idea is that some unknown humorist had sold Willoughby a dry plate, picturing part of the city of Bristol. My own idea is that something of this kind did occur, and that this photograph, greatly involved in accounts of repeating mirages, had nothing to do with mirages. Badlam then tells of another photograph. He tells that two men, near the Muir Glacier, had, by means of a pan of quicksilver, seen a reflection of an unknown city somewhere, and that their idea was that it was at the bottom of the sea near the glacier, reflecting in the sky, and reflecting back to and from the quicksilver. That's complicated. A photographer named Isaiah West Taber then announced that he had photographed this scene, as reflected in a pan of quicksilver. Badlam publishes a reproduction of Taber's photograph, or alleged photograph. This time, for anybody who prefers to think that there is, somewhere in the sky of Alaska, a great, unknown city, we have a most agreeable photograph: exotic-looking city; a structure like a coliseum, and another prominent building like a mosque, and many indefinite, mirage-like buildings. I'd like to think this photograph genuine, myself, but I do conceive that Taber could have taken it photographing a panorama that he had painted. Badlam's explanation is that mirages of glaciers are common, in Alaska, and that they look architectural. Some years ago, I read five or six hundred pounds of literature upon the Arctic, and I should say that far-projected mirages are not common in the Arctic: mere looming is common. Badlam publishes a photograph of a mirage of Muir Glacier. The looming points of ice do look Gothic, but they are obviously only loomings, extending only short distances from primaries, with no detachments from primaries, and not reflecting in the sky.

For the first identification of the Willoughby photograph as a photograph of part of the city of Bristol, see the New York *Times*, Oct. 20, 1889. That this photograph was somebody's hoax seems to be acceptable. But it is not similar to the frequently reported scene in the sky of Alaska, according to descriptions. In the New York *Times*, Oct. 31, 1889, is an account, by Mr. L.B. French, of Chicago, of the spectral representation, as he saw it, near Mt. Fairweather. "We could plainly see houses, well-defined streets, and trees. Here and there rose tall spires over huge buildings which appeared to be ancient mosques or cathedrals ... It did not look like a modern city — more like an ancient European city."

Jour. R.M.S., (27, 158):

That, every year, between June 21 and July 10, a "phantom city" appears in the sky, over a glacier in Alaska; that features of it had been recognised as buildings in the city of Bristol, England, so that the "mirage" was supposed to be a mirage of Bristol. It is said that for generations these repeating representations had been known to the Alaskan Indians, and that, in May, 1901, a scientific expedition from San Francisco would investigate. It is said that, except for slight changes, from year to year, the scene was always the same.

La Nature (1901, v. 1, 303):

That a number of scientists had set out from Victoria, B.C., to Mt. Fairweather, Alaska, to study the repeating mirage of a city in the sky, which had been reported by the Duc d'Abruzzi, who had seen it and sketched it.

CHAPTER 20

Night of Dec. 7, 1900 — for seventy minutes a fountain of light played upon the planet Mars.

Prof. Pickering — "absolutely inexplicable" (*Sci. Amer.*, n.s., 84, 179).

It may have been a geyser of messages. It may be translated some day. If it were expressed in imagery befitting the salutation by a planet to its dominant, it may be known some day as the most heroic oration in the literature of the geo-system. See Lowell's account in *Popular Astronomy* (10, 187). Here are published several of the values in a possible code of long flashes and short flashes. Lowell takes a supposed normality for unity, and records variations of two-thirds, one-and-one-third, and one-and-a-half. If there be, at Flagstaff, Arizona, records of all the long flashes and short flashes that were seen, for seventy minutes, upon this night of Dec. 7, 1900, it is either that the greetings of an island of space have been hopelessly addressed to a continental stolidity, or there will have to be the descent, upon Flagstaff, Arizona, by all the amateur Champollions of this earth, to concentrate in one deafening buzz of attempted translation.

It was at this time that Tesla announced that he had received, upon his wireless apparatus, vibrations that he attributed to the Martians. They were series of triplets.

* * *

It is our expression that, during eclipses and oppositions and other notable celestial events, lunarians try to communicate with this earth, having a notion that at such times the astronomers of this earth may be more nearly alert.

An eclipse of the moon, March 10-11, 1895 — not a cloud; no mist — electric flashes like lightning, reported from a ship upon the Atlantic (*Eng. Mech.*, 61, 100).

During the eclipse of the sun, July 29, 1897, a strange image was taken on a sensitive plate, by Mr. L.E. Martindale, of St. Mary's, Ohio. It looks like a record of knotted lightning. See *Photography* (27, 355).

In the *Bull. S.A.F.* (17: 205, 315, 447), it is said that upon the first and the third of March, 1903, a light like a little star, flashing intermittently, was seen by M. Rey, in Marseilles, and by Maurice Gheury, in London, in the lunar crater Aristarchus. March 28, 1903 — opposition of Mars.

* * *

In *Cosmos (L.M.)* (s. 4, 49, 259), M. Desmoulins writes, from Argenteuil, that upon August 9, 1903, at 11 P.M., moving from north to south, he saw a luminous object. The planet Venus was at primary greatest brilliance upon August 13, 1903. In three respects it was like other objects that have been observed upon this earth at times of the nearest approach of Venus: it was a red object; it appeared only in a local sky, and it appeared in the time of the visibility of Venus. With M. Desmoulins were four persons, one of whom had field glasses. The object was watched twenty minutes, during which time it travelled a distance estimated at five or six kilometers. It looked like a light suspended from a balloon, but, through glasses, no outline of a balloon could be seen, and there were no reflections of light as if from the opaque body of a balloon. It was a red body, with greatest luminosity in its nucleus. The Editor of *Cosmos* writes that, according to other correspondents, this object had been seen, at 11 P.M., July 19th and 26th, at Chatou. Argenteuil and Chatou are four or five miles apart, and both are about five miles from Paris. All three of these dates were Sundays, and even though nothing like a balloon had been seen through glasses, one naturally supposes that somebody near Paris had been amusing himself sending up fire-balloons, Sunday evenings. The one great resistance to all that is known as progress is what one "naturally supposes."

In the *English Mechanic* (81, 220), Arthur Mee writes that several persons, in the neighbourhood of Cardiff, had, upon the night of March 29, 1905, seen in the sky, "an appearance like a vertical beam of light, which was not due (they say) to a searchlight, or any such cause." There were other observations, and they remind us of the observations of Noble and Bradgate, Aug. 28-29, 1883: then upon an object that cast a light like a searchlight; this time an association between a light like a searchlight, and a luminosity of definite form. In the *Cambrian Natural Observer* (1905, 32), are several accounts of a more definite-looking appearance that was seen, this night, in the sky of Wales — "like a long cluster of stars, obscured by a thin film or mist." It was seen at the time of the visibility of Venus, then an "evening star" — about 10 P.M. It grew brighter, and for about half an hour looked like an incandescent light. It was a conspicuous and definite object, according to another description — "like an iron bar, heated to an orange-coloured glow, and suspended vertically."

Three nights later, something appeared in the sky of Cherbourg, France — *L'Astre Cherbourg* — the thing that appeared, night after night, in the sky of the city of Cherbourg, at a time when the planet Venus was nearest (inferior conjunction April 26, 1905).

Flammarion, in the *Bull. S.A.F.* (19, 243), says that this object was Venus. He therefore denies that it had moved in various directions, saying that the supposed observations to this effect were illusions. In *L'Illustration* (125, 254), he tells the story in his own way, and says some things that we are not disposed to agree with, but he also says that the ignorance of some persons is *inénarrable*. In *Cosmos (L.M.)* (s. 4, 42, 420), a few weeks after the occurrence, it is said that many correspondents had written to inquire as to *L'Astre Cherbourg*. The Editor gives his opinion that the object was either Jupiter or Venus. Throughout our Venus-visitor expression, the most important point is appearance in a local sky. That unifies this expression with other expressions, all of them converging into our general extra-geographic acceptances. The Editor of *Cosmos* says that this object, which was reported from Cherbourg, was reported from other towns as well. He probably means to say that it was seen simultaneously in different towns. For all guardians of this earth's isolation, this is a convenient thing to say: the conclusion then is that the planet Venus, exceptionally bright, was attracting unusual attention generally, and that there was nothing in the especial sky of Cherbourg. But we have learned that standardising disguisements often obscure our data in later accounts, and we have formed the habit of going to contemporaneous sources. We shall find that the newspapers of the time reported a luminous object that appeared, night after night, only over the city of Cherbourg, as the name by which it was known indicates. It was a reddish object. The Editor of *Cosmos* explains that atmospheric conditions could give this colouration to Venus. I suppose this could be so occasionally: not night after night, I should say. We shall find that this object, or a similar object, was reported from other places, but not simultaneously with its appearance over Cherbourg.

In the *Journal des Debats*, the first news is in the issue of April 4, 1905. It is said that a luminous body was appearing, every evening, between 8 and 10:30 P.M., over the city of Cherbourg.

These were about the hours of the visibility of Venus. In this period, Venus set at 9:30 P.M., and Jupiter at 8 P.M. It is enough to make any conventionalist feel most reasonable, though he'd feel that way anyway, in thinking that of course then this object was Venus. In my own earlier speculations upon this subject, this one datum stood out so that had it not been for other data, I'd have abandoned the subject. But then I read of other occurrences: time after time has something been seen in the local sky of this earth, sometimes so definitely seen to move, not like Venus, but in various directions, that one has to think that it was not Venus, though appearing at the time of visibility of Venus. Between these appearances and visibility of Venus there does seem to be relation.

In the *Journal*, it is said that *L'Astre Cherbourg* had an apparent diameter of 15 centimeters, and a less definite margin of 75 centimeters — seemed to be about a yard wide — meaningless of course. In the *Bull. S.A.F.*, it is said that, according to reports, its form was oval. In the *Journal des Debats*, we are told that, at first the thing was supposed to be a captive balloon but that this idea was given up because it appeared and disappeared.

Journal des Debats, April 12, 1905:

That every evening the luminous object was continuing to appear above Cherbourg; that many explanations had been thought of: by some persons that it was the planet Jupiter, and by others that it was a comet but that no one knew what it was. The comet-explanation is of course ruled out. The writer in the *Journal* expresses regret that neither the Meteorological Bureau nor the Observatory of Paris had sent anybody to investigate, but says that the *préfet maritime*, of Cherbourg had commissioned a naval officer to investigate. In *Le Temps*, of the 12th, is published an interview with Flammarion, who complains some more against general *inénarrable-ness*, and says that of course the object was Venus. The writer in *Le Temps* says that soon would the matter be settled, because the commander of a war ship had undertaken to decide what the luminous body was.

Le Figaro, April 13, 1905:

The report of Commander de Kerillis, of the *Chasseloup-Laubut* — that the position of *L'Astre Cherbourg* was not the position of Venus, and that the disc did not look like the crescentic disc of Venus, but that observations had been made from a vessel, under unfavourable conditions, and that the commander and his colleagues did not offer a final opinion.

I think that there was *inénarrable-ness* all around. Given visibility, I can't think what the unfavourable conditions could have been. Given, however, observations upon something that all astronomers in the world would say could not be, one does think of the dislike of a naval officer, who, though he probably knew right ascension from declination, was himself no astronomer, to commit himself. In *Le Temps*, and other newspapers published in Paris, it is said that, according to the naval officers, the object might have been a comet, but that they would not positively commit themselves to this opinion, either.

I think that somebody should be brave; so, though not positively, of course, I incline, myself, to relate these appearances over Cherbourg with the observations in Wales, upon March 29th; also I suggest that there is another report that may relate. In *Le Temps*, April 12, it is said that, at midnight, April 9-10, a luminous body, like *L'Astre Cherbourg*, was seen in the sky of Tunis. Though it was visible several minutes, it is said that this object was probably a meteor.

Every night, from the first to the eleventh of April, a luminous body appeared in the sky of Cherbourg. Then it was seen no longer. It may have been seen sailing away, upon its final departure from the sky of Cherbourg. In *Le Figaro*, April 15, it is said that, upon the night of the eleventh of April, the guards of La Blanche Lighthouse had seen something like a lighted balloon in the sky. Supposing it was a balloon, they had started to signal to it, but it had disappeared. It is said that the lighthouse had been out of communication with the mainland, and that the guards had not heard of *L'Astre Cherbourg*.

* * *

In the London *Times,* Nov. 23, 1905, a correspondent writes that, at East Liss, Hants., which is about 40 miles from Reading, he and his gamekeeper had, about 3:30 P.M., Nov. 17th, heard a loud, distant rumbling. According to this hearer, the rumbling seemed to be a composition of triplets of sound. We shall accept that three sounds were heard, but we have no other assertion that each sound was itself so sub-serialised. This correspondent's gamekeeper said he had heard similar sounds at 11:30 A.M., and at 1:30 P.M. It is said that the sounds were not like gunfire, and that the direction from which they seemed to come, and the time in the afternoon, precluded the explanation of artillery-practice at Aldershot or Portsmouth. Aldershot is about 15 miles from East Liss, and Portsmouth about 20.

Times, Nov. 24 — that the "quake" had been distinctly felt in Reading, about 3:30 P.M., Nov. 17th. *Times,* Nov. 25 — heard at Reading, at 11:30, 1:30, and 3:30 o'clock, Nov. 17th.

Reading Standard, Nov. 25, 1905:

That consternation had been caused in Reading, upon the 17th, by sounds and vibrations of the earth, about 11:30 A.M., 1:30 P.M., and 3:30 P.M. It is said that nothing had been seen, but that the sounds closely resembled those that had been heard during the meteoric shower of 1866.

Mr. H.G. Fordham appears again. In the *Times,* Dec. 1, he writes that the phenomena pointed clearly to an explosion in the sky, and not to an earthquake of subterranean origin. "The noise and shock experienced are, no doubt, attributable to the explosion (or to more than one explosion) of a meteorite, or bolide, high up in the atmosphere, and setting up a wave (or waves) of sound and aerial shock. It is probable, indeed, that many a good phenomenon having this source is wrongly ascribed to slight and local earthshock."

Mr. Fordham wrote this, but he wrote no more, and I think that somewhere else something else was written, and that, in the year 1905, it had to be obeyed; and that it may be interpreted in these words — "Thou shalt not." Mr. Fordham did not inquire into the reasonableness of thinking that, only by coincidence, meteors so successively exploded, in a period of four hours, in one local sky of this earth, and nowhere else; and into the inference, then, as to whether this earth is stationary or not.

We have data of a succession occupying far more than four hours.

In the *Times,* Mrs. Lane of Petersfield, 20 miles from Portsmouth, writes that, at 11:30 A.M., and at 3:30 P.M., several days before the 17th, she had heard detonations, then hearing them again, upon the 17th. Mrs. Lane thinks that there must have been artillery-practice at Portsmouth. It seems clear that there was no cannonading anywhere in England, at this time. It seems clear that there was signalling from some other world.

In the *English Mechanic* (82, 433), Joseph Clark writes that, a few minutes past 3 P.M., upon the 18th a triplet of detonations was heard at Somerset — "as loud as thunder, but not exactly like thunder."

Reading Observer, Nov. 25, 1905 — that, according to a correspondent, the sounds had been heard again, at Whitechurch (20 miles from Reading) upon the 21st, at 1:35 P.M., and 3:08 P.M. The sounds had been attributed to artillery-practice at Aldershot, but the correspondent had written to the artillery commandant, at Bulford Camp, and had received word that there had been no heavy firing at the times of his inquiry. The Editor of the *Observer* says that he, too, had written to the commandant, and had received the same answer.

I have searched widely. I have found record of nobody's supposition that he had traced these detonations to origin upon this earth.

CHAPTER 21

In Coconino County, Arizona, is an extraordinary formation. It is known as Coon Butte and as Crater Mountain. Once upon a time, something gouged this part of Arizona. The cavity in the ground is about 3,800 feet in diameter, and it is approximately 600 feet deep, from the rim of the ramparts to the floor of the interior. Out from this cavity had been hurled blocks of limestone, some of them a mile or so away, some of these masses weighing probably 5,000 tons each. And in the formation, and around it, have been found either extraordinary numbers of meteorites, or fragments of one super-meteorite. Barringer, in his report to the Academy of Natural Science of Philadelphia (*Proceedings of the Academy of Natural Sciences of Philadelphia*, 57, 861), says that, of the traffickers in this meteoritic material, he knew of two men who had shipped away fifteen tons of it. But Barringer's minimum estimate of a body large enough so to gouge the ground is ten million tons.

It was supposed that a main mass of meteoritic material was buried under the floor of the formation, but this floor was drilled, and nothing was found to support this supposition. One drill went down 1020 feet, going through 100 feet of red sandstone, which seems to be the natural, undisturbed sub-structure. The datum that opposes most strongly the idea that this pit was gouged by one super-meteorite is that in it and around it at least three kinds of meteorites have been found: they are irons, masses of iron-shale, and shale-balls that are so rounded and individualised that they cannot be thought of as fragments of a greater body, and cannot be very well thought of as great drops of molten matter cast from a main, incandescent mass, inasmuch as there is not a trace of igneous rock such as would mark such contact.

There are data for thinking that these three kinds of objects fell at different times, presumably from origin of fixed position relatively to this point in Arizona. With the formation, shales were found, buried at various distances, as if they had fallen at different times, for instance seven of them in a vertical line, the deepest buried 27 feet down; also shales outside the formation were found buried. But, quite as if they had fallen more recently, the hundreds of irons were found upon the surface of the ground, or partly covered, or wholly covered, but only with superficial soil.

There is no knowing when this great gouge occurred, but cedars upon the rim are said to be 700 years old.

In terms of our general expression upon differences of potential, and of electric relations between nearby worlds, I think of a blast between this earth and a land somewhere else, and of something that was more than a cyclone that gouged this pit.

Other meteorites have been found in Arizona: the 85-pound iron that was found at Weaver, near Wickenburg, 130 miles from Crater Mountain, in 1898, and the 960-pound mass, now in the National Museum, said to have been found at Peach Springs, 140 miles from Crater Mountain. These two irons indicate nothing in particular; but, if we accept that somewhere else in Arizona there is another deposit of meteorites, also extraordinarily abundant, such abundance gives something of commonness of nature if not of commonness of origin to two deposits. There are several large irons known as the Tucson meteorites, one weighing 632 pounds and another 1514 pounds, now in museums. They came from a place known as Iron Valley, in the Santa Rita Mountains, about 30 miles south of Tucson, and about 200 miles from Crater Mountain. Iron Valley was so named because of the great number of meteorites found in it. According to the people of Tucson, this fall occurred about the year 1660. See *Amer. Jour. Sci.* (s. 2, 13, 290).

Upon June 24, 1905, Barringer found, upon the plain, about a mile-and-a-half northwest of Crater Mountain, a meteorite of a fourth kind. It was a meteoritic stone, "as different from all the other meteoric specimens ... which have come from this locality, as one specimen can be from another." Barringer thinks that it fell, about the 15th of January, 1904. Upon a night in the middle of January, 1904, two of his employees were awakened by a loud hissing sound, and saw a meteor falling north of the formation. At the same time, two Arizona physicians, north of the formation, saw the meteor falling south of them. For analysis and description of this object, see *Amer. Jour. Sci.* (s. 4, 21, 347). Barringer, who believes that once upon a time one super-meteorite, of which only a very small part has ever been found, gouged this hole in the ground, writes — "That a small stony meteorite should have fallen on almost exactly the same spot on this earth's surface as the great Canon Diablo iron meteorite fell many centuries ago, is certainly a most remarkable coincidence. I have stated the facts as accurately as possible, and I have no opinion to offer as to whether or not these involve anything more than a coincidence."

Other phenomena in Arizona:

Upon Feb. 24, 1897, a great explosion was heard over the town of Tombstone. It is said that a fragment of a meteor fell at St. David (*Monthly Weather Review*, 25, 56). Yarnell, Arizona, Sept. 12, 1898 — "a deep, thundering noise" that was heard between noon and 1 P.M. The noise proceeded "from the Granite Range, between the station (Yarnell) and Prescott. From all accounts a large meteor struck the earth at this time" (*Monthly Weather Review*, 26, 463).

Upon July 19, 1912, at Holbrook, Arizona, about 60 miles from Crater Mountain, occurred a loud detonation and one of the most remarkable falls of stones recorded. See *Amer. Jour. Sci.* (s. 4, 34, 437). Some of the stones are very small. About 14,000 were collected. Only twice, since the year 1800, have stones in greater numbers fallen from the sky to this earth, according to conventional records.

About a month later (Aug. 18) there was another concussion at Holbrook. This was said to be an earthquake (*Bull. Seismo.*, 2, 209).

CHAPTER 22

The climacteric opposition of Mars, of 1909 — the last in our records — the next will be in 1924 —

Aug. 8, 1909 — see *Jour. R.M.S.* (35, 298) — flashes in a clear sky that were seen in Epsom, Surrey, and other places in the southeast of England. They could not be attributed to lightning in England. The editor in the *Journal* finds that there was a storm in France, more than one hundred miles away. For an account of these flashes, tabulated at Epsom — "night was fine and starlight" — Symons' *Met. Mag.* (44, 147). During each period of five minutes, from 10 to 11:15, P.M., the number of flashes — 16-14-20-31-15-26-12-20-30-18-27-22-14-12-10-21-8-5-3-1-0-1-0-0. With such a time-basis, I can see no possibility of detecting anything of a code-like significance. I do see development. There were similar observations at times in the favourable oppositions of Mars of 1875 and 1877. In 1892, such flashes were noted more particularly. Now we have them noted and tabulated, but upon a basis that could be of interest only to meteorologists. If they shall be seen in 1924, we may have observation, tabulation, and some marvellously different translations of them. After that there will be some intolerably similar translations, suspiciously delayed in publication.

Sept. 23, 1909 — opposition of Mars.

Throughout our data, we have noticed successions of appearances in local skies of this earth, that indicate that this earth is stationary, but that also relate to nearest approaches of Mars. Upon the night of Dec. 16-17, 1896, concussion after concussion was felt at Worcester, England; a great "meteor" was seen at the time of the greatest concussion. Mars was seven days past opposition. We thought it likely enough that explosion after explosion had occurred over Worcester, and that something in the sky had been seen only at the time of the greatest, or the nearest, explosion. We did not think well of the conventional explanation that only by coincidence had a great meteor exploded over a region where a series of earthquakes was occurring, and exactly at the moment of the greatest of these shocks.

In November, 1911, Mars was completing his cycle of changing proximities of a duration of fifteen years, and was duplicating the relationship of the year 1896. About 10 o'clock, night of Nov. 16, 1911, a concussion that is conventionally said to have been an earthquake occurred in Germany and Switzerland. But plainly there was an explosion in the sky. In the *Bulletin of the Seismological Society of America* (3, 190), Count Montessus de Ballore writes that he had examined 112 reports upon flashes and other luminous appearances in the sky that had preceded the "earthquake" by a few seconds. He concludes that a great meteor had only happened to explode over a region where, a few seconds later, there was going to be an earthquake. "It therefore seems highly probable that the earthquake coincided with a fall of meteors or of shooting stars."

The duplication of the circumstances of Dec., 1896, continues. If of course this concussion in Germany and Switzerland was the effect of something that had exploded in the sky — of what were the concussions that were felt later, the effects? De Ballore does not mention anything that occurred later. But, a few minutes past midnight, and then again, at 3 o'clock, morning of the 17th, there were other, but slighter, shocks. Only at the time of the greatest shock was something seen in the sky. *Nature* (88, 116) — that this succession of phenomena did occur. We relate the phenomena to the planet Mars, but also we ask — how, if most reasonably, all three of these shocks were concussions from explosions in the sky, if of course one of them was, meteors could ever so hound one small region upon a moving earth, or projectiles be fired with such specialisation and preciseness? November 17th, 1911 was seven days before the opposition of Mars. Though the opposition occurred upon the 24th of November, Mars was at minimum distance upon the 17th.

No matter how difficult of acceptance our own notions may be, they are opposed by this barbarism, or puerility, or pill that can't be digested:

Seven days from the opposition of Mars, in 1896, a great meteor exploded over a region where there had been a succession of earthquakes — by coincidence;

Seven days from the next similar opposition of Mars, a great meteor exploded over a region where there was going to be a succession of earthquakes — by coincidence.

* * *

The Advantagerians of the moon — that is the cult of lunar communicationists, who try to take advantage of such celestial events as oppositions and eclipses, thinking that astronomers, or night watchmen, or policemen of this earth might at such times look up at the sky —

A great luminous object, or a meteor, that was seen at the time of the eclipse of June 28, 1908 — "as if to make the date of the solar eclipse more notable," says W.F. Denning (*Observatory*, 31, 287).

Not long before the opposition of Mars, in 1909, the bright spot west of Picard was seen twice: March 26 and May 23 (*Jour. B.A.A.*, 19, 375).

Nov. 16, 1910 — an eclipse of the moon, and a "meteor" that appeared, almost at the moment of totality (*Eng. Mech.*, 92, 430). It is reported, in *Nature* (85, 118), as seen by Madame de Robeck, at Naas, Ireland, "from an apparent radiant just below the eclipsed moon." The thing may have come from the moon. Seemingly with the same origin, it was seen far away in France. In *La Nature* (1910, v. 2, 415), it is said that, at Besançon, France, during the eclipse, was seen a meteor like a superb rocket, "qui serait partie de la lune." There may have been something occurring upon the moon at the time. In the *Jour. B.A.A.* (21, 99), it is said that Mrs. Albright had seen a luminous point upon the moon throughout the eclipse.

* * *

Our expression is that there is an association between reported objects, like extra-mundane visitors, and nearest approaches by the planet Venus to this earth. Perhaps unfortunately this is our expression, because it makes for more restriction than we intend. The objects, or the voyagers, have often been seen during the few hours of visibility of Venus, when the planet is nearest. "Then such an object is Venus," say the astronomers. If anybody wonders why, if these seeming navigators can come close to this earth — as they do approach, if they appear only in a local sky — they do not then come all the way to this earth, let him ask a sea captain why said captain never purposely descends to the bottom of the ocean, though travelling often not far away. However, I conceive of a great variety of extra-mundanians, and I am now collecting data for a future expression — that some kinds of beings from outer space can adapt to our conditions, which may be like the bottom of a sea, and have been seen, but have been supposed to be psychic phenomena.

Upon Oct. 31, 1908, the planet Venus was four months past inferior conjunction, and so had moved far from nearest approach, but there are vague stories of strange objects that had been seen in the skies of this earth — localised in New England — back to the time of nearest approach. In the New York *Sun*, Nov. 1, 1908, is published a dispatch, from Boston, dated Oct. 31. It is said that, near Bridgewater, at 4 o'clock in the morning of Oct. 31, two men had seen a spectacle in the sky. The men were not astronomers. They were undertakers. There may be a disposition to think that these observers were not in their own field of greatest expertness, and to think that we are not very exacting as to the sources of our data. But we have to depend upon undertakers, for instance: early in our investigations, we learned that the prestige of astronomers has been built upon their high moral character, all of them most excellently going to bed soon after sunset, so as to get up early and write all day upon astronomical subjects. But the exemplary in one respect may not lead to much advancement in some other respect. Our undertakers saw, in the sky, something like a searchlight. It played down upon this earth, as if directed by an investigator, and then it flashed upward. "All of the balloons in which ascensions are made in this State were accounted for today and a search through southeastern Massachusetts failed to reveal any further traces of the supposed airship." It is said that "mysterious bright lights," believed to have come from a balloon, had been reported from many places in New England. The week before, persons at Ware had said that they had seen an illuminated balloon passing over the town, early in the morning. During the summer such reports had come from Bristol, Conn., and later from Pittsfield, Mass., and from White River Junction, Vt. "In all these cases, however, no balloon could be found, all the known airships being accounted for at the time." In the New York *Sun*, Dec. 13, 1909, it is said that, during the autumn of 1908, reports had come from different places in Connecticut, upon a mysterious light that moved rapidly in the sky.

Venus moved on, travelling around the sun, which was revolving around this earth, or travelling any way to suit anybody. In December, 1909, the planet was again approaching this earth. So close was Venus to this earth, upon the 15th of December, 1909, crowds stood, at noon, in the streets of Rome, watching it, or her, (New York *Sun,* Dec. 16). At 3 o'clock, afternoon of December 24th crowds stood in the streets of New York, watching Venus (New York *Tribune,* Dec. 25). One supposes that upon these occasions Venus may have been within several thousand miles of this earth. At any rate I have never heard of one fairly good reason for supposing otherwise. If again something appeared in local skies of this earth, or in the skies of New England, and sometimes during the few hours of the visibility of Venus, the object was or was not Venus, all according to the details of various descriptions, and the credibility of the details. The searchlight, for instance; more than one light; directions and motions. Venus, at the time, was several hours after sunset, slowly descending in the southwest: primary maximum brilliance Jan. 8th, 1910; inferior conjunction Feb. 12th.

There is an amusing befuddlement to clear away first. Upon the night of September 8, 1909, a luminous object had been seen sailing over New England, and sounds from it, like sounds from a motor, had been heard. Then Mr. Wallace Tillinghast, of Worcester, Mass., announced that this light had been a lamp in his "secret aeroplane," and that upon this night he had travelled, in said "secret aeroplane," from Boston to New York, and back to Boston. At this time the longest recorded flight, in an aeroplane, was Farman's, of 111 miles, from Rheims, August, 1909; and, in the United States, according to records, it was not until May 29, 1910, that Curtiss flew from Albany to New York City, making one stop in the 150 miles, however. So this unrecorded flight made some stir in the newspapers. Mr. Tillinghast meant his story humorously of course. I mention it because, if anybody should look the matter up, he will find the yarn involved in the newspaper accounts. If nothing else had been seen, Mr. Tillinghast might still tell his story, and explain why he never did anything with his astonishing "secret aeroplane;" but something else was seen, and upon one of the nights in which it appeared, Tillinghast was known to be in his home.

According to the New York *Tribune,* Dec. 21, 1909, Immigration Inspector Hoe, of Boston, had reported having seen, at one o'clock in the morning of December 20, "a bright light passing over the harbor" and had concluded that he had seen an airship of some kind.

New York *Tribune,* Dec. 23 — that a "mysterious airship" had appeared over the town of Worcester, Mass., "sweeping the heavens with a searchlight of very high power." It had come from the southeast, and travelled northwest, then hovering over the city, disappearing in the direction of Marlboro. Two hours later, it returned. "Thousands thronged the streets to watch the mysterious visitor." Again it hovered, then moving away, heading first to the south and then to the east.

The next night, something was seen, at 6 o'clock, at Boston. "The searchlights shot across the sky line." "As it flew away to the north, queries began to pour into the newspaper offices and the police stations, regarding the remarkable visitation." It is said that an hour-and-a-half later, an object that was supposed to be an airship with a powerful searchlight, appeared in the sky, at Willimantic, Conn., "hovering" over the town about 15 minutes. In the New York *Sun,* Dec. 24, are more details. It is said that, at Willimantic, had been seen a large searchlight, approaching from the east, and that then dark outlines of something behind the searchlight had been seen. Also, in the *Sun,* it is said that whatever it may have been that was seen at Boston, it was a dark object, with several red lights and a searchlight, approaching Boston from the west, hovering for 10 minutes, and then moving away westward. From Lynn, Mass., it was described as "a long black object," moving in the direction of Salem, and then returning, "at a high speed." It is said that the object had been seen at Marlboro, Mass., nine times since Dec. 14.

New York *Tribune,* Jan. 1, 1910 — dispatch from Huntington, West Virginia, Dec. 31, 1909 — "Three huge lights of almost uniform dimensions appeared in the early morning sky, in this neighborhood, today. Joseph Green, a farmer, declared that they were meteors, which fell on his farm. An extensive search of his land by others who saw the lights was fruitless, and many persons believe that an airship had sped over the country."

In the *Tribune,* Jan. 13, 1910, it is said that, at 9 o'clock, morning of Jan. 12, an airship had been seen at Chattanooga, Tenn. "Thousands saw the craft, and heard the chugging of the engine." Later the object was reported from Huntsville, Alabama. New York *Tribune*, Jan. 15 — dispatch from Chattanooga, Jan. 14 — "For the third successive day a mysterious white air craft passed over Chattanooga about noon today. It came from the north and was travelling southeast, disappearing over Missionary Ridge. On Wednesday, it came south and then on Thursday it returned north."

In the middle of December, 1909, someone had won a prize for sailing a dirigible from St. Cyr to the Eiffel Tower and back.

St. Cyr is several miles from Paris.

Huntsville, Alabama, and Chattanooga, Tennessee, are 75 miles apart.

An association between the planet Venus and "mysterious visitors" either illumines or haunts our data. In the New York *Tribune,* Jan. 29, 1910, it is said that a luminous object, thought to be Winnecke's comet, had been seen, Jan. 28, near Venus; reported from the Manila Observatory.

I have another datum that perhaps belongs to this series of events. Every night, from the 14th to the 23rd of December, 1909, if we accept the account from Marlboro, a luminous object was seen travelling, or exploring, in the sky of New England. Certainly enough it was no "secret airship" of this earth, unless its navigator went to extremes with the notion that the best way to keep a secret is to announce it with red lights and a searchlight. However, our acceptance depends upon general data as to the development of terrestrial aeronautics. But upon the night of December 24th, the object was not seen in New England, and it may have been travelling or exploring somewhere else. Night of the 24th — Venus in the southwest in the early hours of the evening. In the *English Mechanic* (104, 71), a correspondent, who signs himself "Rigel," writes that, upon Dec. 24, at 8:30 o'clock in the evening, he saw a luminous object appear above the northeastern horizon and slowly move southward, until 8:50 o'clock, then turning around, retracing, and disappearing whence it came, at two minutes past nine. The correspondent is James Ferguson, Rossbrien, Limerick, Ireland. He writes frequently upon astronomical and meteorological subjects, and is still contributing to the somewhat enlightened columns of the *English Mechanic.*

* * *

Nov. 19, 1912 — explosive sounds reported from Sunninghill, Berkshire. No earthquake was recorded at the Kew Observatory, and, in the opinion of W.F. Denning (*Nature,* 9: 365, 417), the explosion was in the sky. It was a terrific explosion, according to the Westminster *Gazette* (Nov. 19). There was either one great explosion that rumbled and echoed for five minutes, or there were repeated detonations, resembling cannonading — "like a tremendous discharge of big guns" according to reports from Abingdon, Lewes, and Epsom. Sunninghill is about ten miles from Reading, and Abingdon is near Reading, but the sound was heard in London, and down by the English Channel, and even in the island of Alderney. In the *Gazette,* Nov. 28, Sir George Fordham (H.G. Fordham) writes that, in his opinion, it was an explosion in the sky. He says — "The phenomena of air-shock have never, I believe, been fully investigated." His admissions and his omissions remain the same as they have since the occurrences of the year 1889. He does not mention that, according to Philip T. Kenway, of Hambledon, near Godalming, about thirty miles southeast of Reading, the sounds were heard again the next day, from 1:45 P.M. to 2 P.M. Mr. Kenway thinks that there had been big-gun firing at Portsmouth (Westminster *Gazette,* Nov. 21). In the London *Standard,* a correspondent, writing from Dorking, says that the phenomena of the 19th were like concussions from cannonading — "at regular intervals" — "at quick intervals, lasting some seconds each time, for five minutes, by the clock."

It develops that Reading was the centre over which the detonations occurred. In the Westminster *Gazette,* Nov. 30, it is said that the shocks had been felt in Reading, upon the 19th, 20th, and 21st. Only from Reading have I record of phenomena upon the 21st. Mr. H.L. Hawkins, Lecturer in Geology, of the Reading University, writes that according to his investigations there had been no gun-firing in England, to which the detonations could be attributed. He says that Fordham's explanation was in accord with his own investigations, or that detonations had occurred in the sky. He writes that, inasmuch as the detonations had occurred upon three successive days, a shower of meteors, of long duration, would have to be supposed. How he ever visualised that unerring shower, striking one point over this earth's surface, and nowhere else, day after day, if this earth be a rotating and revolving body, I can not see. If he should say that by coincidence this repetition could occur, then by what coincidence of coincidences could the same repetitions have occurred in this same local sky, centring around Reading, seven years before? The indications are that this earth is stationary, no matter how unreasonable that may sound.

In the Westminster *Gazette,* Dec. 9, W.F. Denning writes that without doubt the phenomena were "meteoric explosions." But he alludes to the "airquake and strange noises" that were heard upon the 19th. He does not mention the detonations that were heard upon the following days. Not one of these writers mentions the sounds that were heard in Reading, in November, 1905.

London *Standard,* Nov. 23, 1912 — that, according to Lieut. Col. Trewman, of Reading, the sounds had been heard at Reading, at 9 A.M., upon the 19th; 1:45 P.M., the 20th; 3:30 P.M., the 21st.

CHAPTER 23

"Unknown Aircraft Over Dover."

According to the Dover correspondent to the London *Times* (Jan. 6, 1913), something had been seen, over Dover, heading from the sea.

In the London *Standard,* Jan. 24, 1913, it is said that, upon the morning of Jan. 4, an unknown airship had been seen, over Dover, and that, about the same time, the lights of an airship had been seen over the Bristol Channel. These places are several hundred miles apart.

London *Times,* Jan. 21 — report by Capt. Lindsay, Chief Constable of Glamorganshire: that, about five o'clock, in the afternoon of Jan. 17, he saw an object in the sky of Cardiff, Wales. He says that he called the attention of a bystander, who agreed with him that it was a large object. "It was much larger and moved faster than the Willows airship, and left in its trail a dense volume of smoke ... It disappeared quickly."

The next day, according to the *Times* (Jan. 22, 1913), there were other reports: people in Cardiff, saw something that was lighted or that carried lights, moving rapidly in the sky. In the *Times,* of the 28th, it is said that an airship that carried a brilliant light had been seen in Liverpool. "It is stated at the Liverpool Aviation School that none of the airmen there were out on Saturday night." Dispatches from town after town — a travelling thing in the sky, carrying a light, and also a searchlight that swept the ground. It is said that a vessel, of which the outlines had been clearly seen, had appeared in the sky of Cardiff, Newport, Neath, and other places in Wales. In the *Standard,* Jan. 31, is published a list of cities where the object had been seen. Here a writer tries to conclude that some foreign airship had made half a dozen visits to England and Wales, or had come once, remaining three weeks; but he gives up the attempt, thinking that nothing could have reached England and have sailed away half a dozen times without being seen to cross the coast; thinking that the idea of anything having made one journey, and remaining three weeks in the air deserved no consideration.

If the unknown object did carry something like a searchlight, an idea of its power is given in an account in the Cardiff *Evening Express and Evening Mail,* Jan. 25, 1913 — "Last evening brilliant lights were to be seen sweeping skywards, and now, this evening, the lights grow bolder. Streets and houses in the locality of Totterdown were suddenly illuminated as brilliant piercing lights were to be seen sweeping upwards, giving the many spectators fine views of the hills beyond." In the *Express,* Feb. 6, is a report upon this light like a searchlight, and the object that flashed it, by the police of Dulais Valley. Also there is an account by a police sergeant, of a luminous thing that was for a while stationary in the sky, and then moved away (*Cardiff Evening Express and Evening Mail,* Feb. 6, 1913).

Still does the conventional explanation, or suggestion, survive. It is said that members of the staff of the *Evening Express* had gone to the roof of the newspaper building, but had seen only the planet Venus, which was brilliant at this time.

Then writes a correspondent, to the *Express,* that the object could not have been Venus, because he had seen it travelling at a rate of 20 or 30 miles an hour, and had heard sounds from it (*Cardiff Evening Express and Evening Mail,* Feb. 10, 1913). Someone else writes that not possibly could the thing be Venus: he had seen it as "a bright red light, going very fast." Still someone else says that he had seen the seeming vessel upon the 5th of February, and that it had suddenly disappeared.

There is a hiatus. Between the 5th and the 21st of February, nothing like an airship was seen in the sky of England and Wales. If we can find that somewhere else something similar was seen in the sky, in this period, one supposes that it was the same object, exploring or manoeuvring somewhere else. It seems however that there were several of these objects, because of simultaneous observations at places far apart. If we can find that, during the absence from England and Wales, similar objects were seen somewhere else, a great deal of what we try to think upon the subject will depend upon how far from Great Britain they were seen. It seems incredible that the planet Venus should deceive thousands of Britons, up to the 5th of February, and stop her deceptions abruptly upon that date, and then abruptly resume deceptions upon the 21st, in places at a distance apart. These circumstances oppose the idea of collective hallucinations, by which some writers in the newspapers tried to explain. If they were hallucinations, the hallucinations renewed collectively, upon the 21st, in towns one hundred miles apart. One extraordinary association is that all appearances, except the first, were in hours of visibility of Venus, then an "evening star."

Upon the night of the 21st, a luminous object was reported from towns in Yorkshire and from towns in Warwickshire, two regions about one hundred miles apart; about 10 P.M. All former attempts to explain had been abandoned, and the general supposition was that German airships were manoeuvring over England. But not a thing had been seen to cross the coast of England, though guards were patrolling the coasts, especially commissioned to watch for foreign airships. Sailors in the North Sea, and people in Holland and Belgium had seen nothing that could be thought a German airship sailing to or from England. A writer in *Flight* takes up as especially mysterious the appearance far inland, in Warwickshire. Then came reports from Portsmouth, Ipswich, Hornsea, and Hull, but, one notes, no more, at this time, from Wales. Also in Ipswich, which is more than a hundred miles from the Yorkshire towns, a luminous object was seen upon the night of the 21st. *Ipswich Evening Star,* Feb. 25 — something that carried a searchlight that had been seen upon the nights of the 21st and 24th, moving in various directions, and then "dashing off towards the southwest at lightning speed" — that, at Hunstanton, had been seen three bright lights travelling from the eastern sky, remaining in sight 30 minutes, stationary, or hovering over the town, and then disappearing in the northwest. *Portsmouth Evening News,* Feb. 25 — that soon after 8 P.M., evening of the 24th, had been seen a very bright light, appearing and disappearing, remaining over Portsmouth about one hour, and then moving away. Portsmouth and Ipswich are about 120 miles apart. In the London newspapers, it is said that, upon the evening of the 25th, crowds stood in the streets of Hull, watching something in the sky, "the lights of which were easily distinguishable." Hull is about 190 miles northeast of Portsmouth. *Hull Daily Mail,* Feb. 26 — that a crowd had watched a light high in the air. It is said that the light had been stationary for almost half an hour and had then shot away northward. In the *Times,* Feb. 28, are published reports upon "the clear outline of an airship, which was carrying a dazzling searchlight," from Portland, Burcleaves, St. Alban's Head, Papplewick, and the Orkneys. The last account, after a long interval, that I know of, is another report from Capt. Lindsay: that, about 9 o'clock, evening of April 8th, he and many persons had seen, over Cardiff, something that carried a brilliant light and travelled at a rate of sixty or seventy miles an hour.

Upon April 24, 1913, the planet Venus was at inferior conjunction.

In the *Times,* Feb. 28, it is said that a fire-balloon had been found in Yorkshire, and it is suggested that someone had been sending up fire-balloons.

In the *Bull. S.A.F.* (27, 179), it is said that the people of England were as credulous as the people of Cherbourg, and had permitted themselves to be deceived by the planet Venus.

If German airships were manoeuvring over England, without being seen either approaching or departing, appearing sometimes far inland in England without being seen to cross the well-guarded coasts, it was secret manoeuvring, inasmuch as the accusation was denied in Germany (*Times,* Feb. 26 and 27, 1913). It was then one of the most brilliantly proclaimed of secrets, or it was concealment under one of the most powerful searchlights ever seen. Possibly an airship from Germany could appear over such a city as Hull, upon the east coast of England, without being seen to arrive or to depart, but so far from Germany is Portsmouth, for instance, that one does feel that something else will have to be thought of. The appearances over Liverpool and over towns in Wales might be attributed to German airships by someone who had not seen a map since he left school. There were more observations upon sudden appearances and disappearances than I have recorded: stationariness often occurred.

The objects were absent from the sky of Great Britain, from Feb. 5 to Feb. 21.

According to data published by Prof. Chant, in the *Journal of the Royal Astronomical Society of Canada* (7, 147), the most extraordinary procession in our records was seen, in the sky of Canada, upon the night of Feb. 9, 1913. Either groups of meteors, in one straight line, passed over the city of Toronto, or there was a procession of unknown objects, carrying lights. According to Prof. Chant, the spectacle was seen from the Saskatchewan to Bermuda, but if this long route was traversed, data do not so indicate. The supposed route was diagonally across New York State, from Buffalo, to a point near New York City, but from New York State are recorded no observations other than might have been upon ordinary meteors, this night. A succession of luminous objects passed over Toronto, night of Feb. 9, 1913, occupying from three to five minutes in passing, according to different estimates. If one will think that they were meteors, at least one will have to think that no such meteors had ever been seen before. In the *Journal* (7, 405), W.F. Denning writes that, though he had been watching the heavens since the year 1865, he had never seen anything like this. In most of the observations, the procession is described as a whole — "like an express train, lighted at night" — "the lights were at different points, one in front, and a rear light, then a succession of lights in the tail." Almost all of the observations relate to the sky of Toronto and not far from Toronto. It is questionable that the same spectacle was seen in Bermuda, this night. The supposed long flight from the Saskatchewan to Bermuda might indicate something of a meteoric nature, but the meteor-explanation must take into consideration that these objects were so close to this earth that sounds from them were heard, and that, without succumbing to gravitation, they followed the curvature of this earth at a relatively low velocity that can not compare with the velocity of ordinary meteors.

If now be accepted that again, the next day, objects were seen in the sky of Toronto, but objects unlighted, in the daytime — I suppose that to some minds will come the thought that this is extraordinary, and that almost immediately the whole subject will then be forgotten. Prof. Chant says that, according to the Toronto *Daily Star*, unknown objects, but dark objects this time, were seen at Toronto, in the afternoon of the next day — "not seen clearly enough to determine their nature, but they did not seem to be clouds or birds or smoke, and it was suggested that they were airships cruising over the city." Toronto *Daily Star*, February 10 — "They passed from west to east in three groups of two each, and then returned west in a more scattered formation, about seven or eight in all."

Chapter 24

August 1914 — this arena-like earth, with its horizon banking high into a Coliseum, when seen from not too far above — faint, rattling sounds of the opening of boundaries — tawny formations slinking into the arena — their crouchings and seizures and crunchings. Aug. 13, 1914 — things that were gathering in the skies. They were seen by G.W. Atkins, of Elstree, Herts., and were seen again upon the 16th and the 17th (*Observatory*, 37, 358). Sept. 9, 1914 — a host in the sky; watched several hours by W.H. Steavenson (*Jour. B.A.A.*, 25, 36). There were round appearances, but some of them were shaped like dumb bells. They were not seeds, snowflakes, insects, nor anything else that they "should" have been, according to Mr. Steavenson. He says that they were large bodies.

Oct. 10, 1914 — a ship that was seen in the sky — or "an absolutely black, spindle-shaped object" crossing the sun. It was seen, at Manchester, by Albert Buss (*Eng. Mech.*, 100, 256). "Its extraordinarily clear-cut outline was surrounded by a kind of halo, giving one the impression of a ship ploughing her way through the sea, throwing up white-foamed waves with her prow."

Enjar Mikkelsen (*Lost in the Arctic*, 345):

"During the last few days (Oct.-Nov., 1911) we have been much tumbled up and down in our minds, owing to a remarkable occurrence, somewhat in the nature of Robinson Crusoe's encounter with the footprint in the sand. Our advanced load has been attacked — an empty petroleum cask is found riddled with tiny holes, such as would be made by a charge of shot! Now a charge of shot is scarcely likely to materialise out of nowhere; one is accustomed to associate the phenomenon with the presence of human beings. It is none of our doing — then whose doing is it? We hit upon the wildest theories to account for it, as we sit in the tent turning the mysterious object over and over. No beast of our acquaintance could make all those little round holes; what animal could even open its jaws so wide? And why should anybody take the trouble to make a target of our gear? Are there Eskimos about — Eskimos with guns? There are no footprints to be seen: it could scarcely have been an animal — the whole thing is highly mysterious."

Jan. 31, 1915 — a symbolic-looking formation upon the moon — six or seven lights, in Littrow, arranged like the Greek letter *Gamma* (*Eng. Mech.*, 101, 46).

Feb. 13, 1915 — Steep Island, Chusan Archipelago (Zhoushan Qundao, China) — a lighthouse-keeper complained to Capt. W.F. Tyler, R.N., that a British warship had fired a projectile at the lighthouse. But no vessel had fired a shot, and it is said that the object must have been a meteor (*Nature*, 97, 17).

In the middle of February, 1915, the planet Venus was about two-months-and-a-half past inferior conjunction. If objects like navigating constructions were seen in the sky, at this time, there may be an association, but I am turning against that association, feeling that it is harmful to our wider expression that extra-mundane vessels have been seen in the sky of this earth, and that they come from regions at present unknown. New York *Tribune*, Feb. 15, 1915 — that, at 10 P.M., Feb. 14, three aeroplanes had been seen to cross the St. Lawrence river, near Morristown, N.Y., according to reports, but that, in the opinion of the Dominion Police, nothing but fire-balloons had been seen. It is said that two "responsible residents" had seen two of the objects cross the river, between 8 and 8:30 P.M., and then return five hours later. In the Canadian Parliament, Prime Minister Robert Borden had said that, at 9 P.M., he had been called by the Mayor of Brockville, telling him that three aeroplanes with "powerful search-light" had crossed the St. Lawrence. The story is told in the New York *Herald* (February 15, 1915). Here it is said that, according to the Chief of Police, of Ogdensburg, N.Y., a farmer, living five miles from Ogdensburg, had reported having seen an aeroplane, upon the 12th. Then it is said that the mystery had been solved: that, while celebrating the one hundredth anniversary of peace between the United States and Canada, some young men in Morristown had sent up paper balloons, which had exploded in the sky, after 9 P.M., night of the 14th. New York *Times* (February 15, 1915) — that the objects had been seen first at Gananoque, Ontario. Here it is said that the balloon-story is absurd. According to the Dominion Observatory, the wind was, at the time, blowing from the east, and the objects had travelled toward the northeast. It is said that one of the objects had, for several minutes, turned a powerful searchlight upon the town of Brockville.

Upon December 11, 1915, Bernard Thomas, of Glenorchy, Tasmania, saw a "particularly bright spot on the moon" (*Eng. Mech.*, 103, 10). It was on the north shore of Mare Crisium, and "looked almost like a star." In Dr. Thomas' opinion, it was sunlight reflected from the rim of a small crater. The crater Picard is near the north shore of Mare Crisium, and most of the illuminations near Picard have occurred several months from an opposition of Mars.

In December, 1915, another new formation upon the moon — reported from the Observatory of Paris — something like a black wall from the centre to the ramparts of Aristillus (*Bull. S.A.F.*, 30, 382).

Jan. 12, 1916 — a shock in Cincinnati, Ohio. Buildings were shaken. The quake was from an explosion in the sky. Flashes were seen in the sky (New York *Herald*, Jan. 13, 1916).

Feb. 9, 1916 — opposition of Mars.

In the *English Mechanic* (104, 71), James Ferguson writes that someone had seen, at 11 o'clock, night of July 31, 1916, at Ballinasloe, Ireland, just such a moving thing, or just such a sailing, exploring thing as is now familiar in our records. For fifteen minutes it moved in a northwesterly direction. For three-quarters of an hour it was stationary. Then it moved back to the point where first it had been seen, remaining visible until 4 o'clock in the morning. Whatever this object may have been, it left the sky at about the time that Venus appeared, as a "morning star," in the sky of Ballinasloe, and resembles the occurrence of Sept. 11, 1852, reported by Lord Wrottesley. Inferior conjunction of Venus was upon July 3, 1916. We have noticed that all occurrences that we somewhat reluctantly associate with nearness of Venus associate more with times of greatest brilliance, five weeks before and after inferior conjunction, than with dates of conjunction. Somebody may demonstrate that at these times Venus comes closest to this earth.

Oct. 10, 1916 — a reddish shadow that spread over part of the lunar crater Plato; reported from the Observatory of Florence, Italy (*Sci. Amer.*, n.s., 121, 181).

Nov. 25, 1916 — about twenty-five bright flashes, in rapid succession, in the sky of Cardiff, Wales, according to Arthur Mee (*Eng. Mech.*, 104, 392).

Col. Markwick writes, in the *Jour. B.A.A.* (27, 188), that, at 6:10

P.M., April 5, 1917, he had seen, upon the sun, a solitary spot, different from all sunspots that he had seen in the experience of forty-three years. Col. Markwick had written to Mr. Maunder, of the Greenwich Observatory, and had been told that, in photographs taken of the sun upon this day, one at 11:17 and another at 11:20 A.M., there was no sign of a sunspot.

July 4, 1917 — an eclipse of the moon, and an extraordinary luminous object said to have been a meteor, in France (*Bull. S.A.F.*, 31, 299). About 6:20 P.M., this day, there was an explosion over the town of Colby, Wisconsin, and a stone fell from the sky (*Science,* n.s., 46, 262).

Aug. 29, 1917 — a luminous object that was seen moving upon the moon (*Bull. S.A.F.*, 31, 439).

Feb. 21, 1919 — an intensely black line extending out from the lunar crater Lexell (*Eng. Mech.*, 109, 57).

Upon May 19, 1919, while Harry Hawker was at sea, untraceable messages meaningless in the languages of this earth, were picked up by wireless, according to dispatches to the newspapers. They were interpreted as the letters *K U J* and *V K A J.*

In October 1913, occurred something that may not be so very mysterious because of nearness to the sea. One supposes that if extra-mundane vessels have sometimes come close to this earth, then sailing away, terrestrial aeronauts may have occasionally left this earth, or may have been seized and carried away from this earth. Upon the morning of Oct. 13, 1913, Albert Jewel started to fly his aeroplane from Hempstead Plains, Long Island, to Staten Island. The route that he expected to take was over Jamaica Bay, Brooklyn, Coney Island, and the Narrows. New York *Times,* Oct. 14, 1913 — "That was the last seen or heard of him ... he has been as completely lost as if he evaporated into air." But as to the disappearance of Capt. James there are circumstances that do call for especial attention. New York *Times,* June 2, 1919 — that Capt. Mansell R. James was lost somewhere in the Berkshire Hills, upon his flight from Boston to Atlantic City, or, rather, upon the part of his route between Lee, Mass., and Mitchel Field, Long Island. He had left Lee upon May 29th. Over the Berkshires, or in the Berkshires, he had disappeared. According to later dispatches, searching parties had "scoured" the Berkshires, without finding a trace of him. Upon June 4th, army planes arrived and searched systematically. There was general excitement, in this mystery of Capt. James. Rewards were offered; all subscribers of the Southern New England Telephone Company were enlisted in a quest for news of any kind; boys scouts turned out. Up to this date of writing there has been nothing but a confusion of newspaper dispatches: that two children had seen a plane, about thirteen miles north of Long Island Sound; that two men had seen a plane fall into the Hudson River, near Poughkeepsie; that, in a gully of Mount Riga, near Millerton, N.Y., had been found the remains of a plane; that part of a plane had been washed ashore from Long Island Sound, near Branford. The latest interest in the subject that I know of was in the summer of 1921. A heavy object was known to be at the bottom of the Hudson River, near Poughkeepsie, and was thought to be Capt. James' plane. It was dredged up and found to be a log.

For an extraordinary story of windows, in Newark, N. J., that were perforated by unfindable bullets, see New York *Evening Telegram,* Sept. 19, 1919, and the Newark *Evening News,* Sept. 19, 20, 22, and 23, 1919. The occurrence is a counterpart of Mikkelsen's experience.

The detonations at Reading were heard seven years apart. Here it is not quite seven years later. London *Times,* Sept. 26, 1919 — that upon Sept. 25, a shock had been felt at Reading; that inquiries had led to information of no known explosion near Reading. In the *Times,* Oct. 14, Mr. H.L. Hawkins writes that the shock was "quite definitely an earthquake, but its origin was superficial" and that the shock "was transmitted through the earth more than through the air." In the London *Daily Chronicle,* Sept. 27, Mr. Hawkins, having considered all suggestions that the shock was a subterranean earthquake, had written: "However, as the whole thing terminated in a bump and a big bang, without subsequent shaking of the ground, it points more to an explosion of a natural type up in the air than to a real earthquake." And, in the London *Daily Mail* (Sept. 27), Mr. Hawkins is quoted: that if the detonation were local, he would believe that it was an aerial explosion (meteoric); but, if it were widespread, it would be considered an earthquake. And in the whole series of the Reading phenomena, this violent detonation was most distinctly local to Reading (*Daily Mail,* Sept. 26, 1919).

Reading *Observer*, Sept. 27, 1919 — "The most popular, and most probable, explanation of the occurrence is that there was an explosion somewhere near enough to affect the town ... Officials at Greenwich Observatory were unable to throw any light on the matter, and said their instruments showed no signs of earth-disturbance."

It is said that the sound and shock were violent, and that, in the residential parts of Reading, the streets were crowded with persons discussing the occurrence.

There was a similar shock in Michigan, Nov. 27, 1919. In many cities, persons rushed from their homes, thinking that there had been an earthquake (New York *Times*, Nov. 28). But, in Indiana, Illinois, and Michigan, a "blinding flare" was seen in the sky. Our acceptance is that this occurrence is, upon a small scale, of the type of many catastrophes in Italy and South America, for instance, when just such "blinding glares" have been seen in the sky, data of which have been suppressed by conventional scientists, or data of which have not impressed conventional scientists.

English Mechanic (110, 257) — J.W. Scholes, of Huddersfield, writes that, upon Dec. 8, 1919, he saw, near the lunar crater Littrow, "a very conspicuous and extraordinary black-ink mark." Upon page 282, W.J. West, of Gosport, writes that he had seen the mark upon the 7th of December.

March 22, 1920 — a light in the sky of this earth, and an illumination upon the moon (*Eng. Mech.*, 111, 141). That so close to this earth is the moon that illuminations known as "auroral" often affect both this earth and the moon.

July 20 and 21, and Sept. 13, 1920 — dull rumbling sounds and quakes at Comrie, Perthshire (London *Times*, July 23 and Sept. 14, 1920).

According to a dispatch to the Los Angeles *Times* (July 22, 1920) — clipping sent to me by Mr. L.A. Hopkins, of Chicago — thunder and lightning and heavy rain, at Portland, Oregon, July 21, 1920: objects falling from the sky; glistening, white fragments that looked like "bits of polished china." "The explanation of the local Weather Bureau is that they may have been picked up by whirlwinds and carried to the district where they were found." The objection to this standardised explanation is the homogeneousness of the falling objects. How can one conceive of winds raging over some region covered with the usual great diversity of loose objects and substances, having a liking for little white stones, sorting over maybe a million black ones, green ones, white ones, and red ones, to make the desired selection? One supposes that a storm brought to this earth fragments of a manufactured object, made of something like china, from some other world.

In the *Literary Digest* (70, no. 10, 55), is published a letter from Carl G. Gowman, of Detroit, Michigan, upon the fall from the sky, in southwest China (Yunnan province), Nov. 17, 1917, of a substance that resembled blood. It fell upon three villages close together, and was said to have fallen somewhere else forty miles away. The quantity was great: in one of the villages, the substance "covered the ground completely." Mr. Gowman accepts that this substance did fall from the sky, because it was found upon roofs as well as upon the ground. He rejects the conventional red-dust explanation, because the spots did not dissolve in several subsequent rains. He says that anything like pollen is out of the question, because at the time nothing was in bloom.

Nov. 23, 1920 — a correspondent writes, to the *English Mechanic* (112, 214), that he saw a shaft of light projecting from the moon, or a spot so bright that it appeared to project, from the limb of the moon, in the region of Funerius.

About Jan. 1, 1921 — several irregular, black objects that crossed the sun. To the Rev. William Ellison (*Eng. Mech.,* 112, 276) they looked like pieces of burnt paper.

July 25, 1921 — a loud report, followed by a sharp tremor, and a rumbling sound, at Comrie (London *Times,* July 27, 1921).

July 31, 1921 — a common indication of other lands from which come objects and substances to this earth — but our reluctance to bother with anything so ordinarily marvellous —

Because we have conceived of intenser times and furies of differences of potential between this earth and other worlds: torrents of dinosaurs, in broad volumes that were streaked with lesser animals, pouring from the sky, with a foam of tusks and fangs, enveloped in a bloody vapour that was falsely dramatised by the sun, with rainbow-mockery. Or, in terms of planetary emotions, such an outpouring was the serenade of some other world to this earth. If poetry is imagery, and, if a flow of images be solid poetry, such a recitation was in three-dimensional hyperbole that was probably seen, or overheard, and criticised in Mars, and condemned for its extravagance in Jupiter. Some other world, meeting this earth, ransacking his solid imagination and uttering her living metaphors: singing a flood of mastodons, purring her butterflies, bellowing an ardour of buffaloes. Sailing away — sneaking up close to the planet Venus, murmuring her antelopes, or arching his periphery and spitting horses at her —

Poor, degenerate times — nowadays something comes close to this earth and lisps little commonplaces to her —

July 31, 1921 — a shower of little frogs that fell upon Anton Wagner's farm, near Sterling, Conn. New York *Evening World,* Aug. 1, 1921).

At sunset, Aug. 7, 1921, an unknown luminous object was seen, near the sun, at Mt. Hamilton, by an astronomer, Prof. Campbell, and by one of those who may some day go out and set foot upon regions that are supposed not to be: by an aviator, Capt. Rickenbacker (*Pub. Astro. Soc. Pac.,* 33, 258). In the *English Mechanic* (114, 211), another character in these fluttering vistas of the opening of the coming drama of Extra-geography, Col. Markwick, a conventional astronomer and also a recorder of strange things, lists other observations upon this object, the earliest upon the 6th, by Dr. Emmert, of Detroit. In the *English Mechanic* (114, 240), H.P. Hollis, once upon a time deliciously "exact" and positive, says something, in commenting upon these observations, that looks like a little weakness in Exclusionism, because the old sureness is turning slightly shaky — "that there are more wonderful things to be seen in the sky than we suspect, or that it is easy to be self-deceived."

If is funny to read of an "earthquake," described in technical lingo, and to have a datum that indicates that it was no earthquake at all, in the usual seismologic sense, but a concussion from an explosion in the sky. Aug. 7, 1921 — a severe shock at New Canton, Virginia. See *Bull. Seismo.* (11, 197) — Prof. Stephen Taber's explanation that the shock probably originated in the slate belt of Buckingham County, intensity about *V* on the *R.-F.* scale. But then it is said that, according to the "authorities" of the McCormick Observatory, the concussion was from an explosion in the sky. The time is coming when nothing funny will be seen in this subject, if some day be accepted at least parts of the masses of data that I am now holding back, until I can more fully develop them — that some of the greatest catastrophes that have devastated the face of this earth have been concussions from explosions in the sky, so repeating in a local sky weeks at a time, months sometimes, or intermittently for centuries, that fixed origins above the ravaged areas are indicated.

New York *Tribune,* Sept. 2, 1921:

"J.C.H. MacBeth, London Manager of the Marconi Wireless Telegraph Company, Ltd., told several hundred men, at a luncheon of the Rotary Club, of New York, yesterday, that Signor Marconi believed he had intercepted messages from Mars, during recent atmospheric experiments with wireless on board his yacht *Electra,* in the Mediterranean. Mr. MacBeth said that Signor Marconi had been unable to conceive of any other explanation of the fact that, during his experiments he had picked up magnetic wave lengths of 150,000 meters, whereas the maximum length of wave produced in the world today is 14,000 meters. The regularity of the signals, Mr. Macbeth declared, disposed of any assumption that the waves might have been caused by electrical disturbances. The signals were unintelligible, consisting apparently of a code, the speaker said, and the only signal recognized was one resembling the letter V used in the Marconi code." See datum of May 19, 1919 (page 216, herein).

But, in the summer of 1921, the planet Mars was far from opposition. The magnetic vibrations may have come from some other world. They may have had the origin of the sounds that have been heard at regular intervals —

The San Salvadors of the sky —

And we return to the principle that has been our re-enforcement throughout: that existence is infinite serialisation, and that, except in particulars, it repeats —

That the dot that spread upon the western horizon of Lisbon, March 4, 1493, cannot be the only ship that comes back from the unknown, cargoed with news —

And it may be Sept. this, nineteen hundred and twenty or thirty something, or Feb. that, nineteen hundred and twenty or thirty something else — and, later, see record of it in *Eng. Mech.,* or *Sci. Amer.,* vol. and p. something or another — a speck in the sky of this earth — the return of somebody from a San Salvador of the sky — and the denial by the heavens themselves, which may answer with explosions the vociferations below them, of false calculations upon their remotenesses. If the heavens do not participate with snow, the skyscrapers will precipitate torn up papers and shirts and skirts, too, when the papers give out.

There will be a procession. Somebody will throw little black pebbles to the crowds. Over his procession will fly blue-fringed cupids. Later he will be insulted and abused and finally hounded to his death. But, in that procession, he will lead by the nose an outrageous thing that should not be: about ten feet long, short-winged, waddling on webbed feet. Insult and abuse and death — he will snap his fingers under the nose of the outrageous thing. It will be worth a great deal to lead that by the nose and demonstrate that such things had been seen in the sky, though they had been supposed to be angels. It will be a great moment for somebody. He will come back to New York, and march up Broadway with his angel.

Some now unheard-of De Soto, of this earth, will see for himself the Father of Cloudbursts.

A Balboa of greatness now known only to himself will stand on a ridge in the sky between two auroral seas.

Fountains of Everlasting Challenge.

Argosies in parallel lines and rabbles of individual adventurers. Well enough may it be said that they are seeds in the sky. Of such are the germs of colonies.

CHAPTER 25

That the Geo-system is an incubating organism, of which this earth is the nucleus — but an organism that is so strongly characterised by conditions and features of its own that likening it to any object internal to it is the interpreting of a thing in terms of a constituent — so that we think of an organism that is incompletely, or absurdly inadequately, expressible in terms of the egg-like and the larval and other forms of the immature — a geo-nucleated system that is dependent upon its externality as, in one way or another, is every similar, but lesser and included, thing — stimulated by flows of force that are now said to be meteoric, though many so-called ''meteoric'' streams seem more likely to be electric, that radiate from the umbilical channels of its constellations — vitalised by its sun, which is itself replenished by the comets, which, coming from external reservoirs of force, impart to the sun their freightages, and, unaffected by gravitation, return to an external existence, some of them even touching the sun, but showing no indication of supposed solar attraction.

In a technical sense we give up the doctrine of Evolution. Ours is an expression upon Super-embryonic Development, in one enclosed system. Ours is an expression upon Design underlying and manifesting in all things within this one system, with a Final Designer left out, because we know of no designing force that is not itself the product of remoter design. In terms of our own experience we cannot think of an ultimate designer, any more than we can think of ultimacy in any other respect. But we are discussing a system that, in our conception, is not a final entity; so then no metaphysical expression upon it is required.

I point out that this expression of ours is not meant for aid and comfort to the reactionaries of the type of Col. William Jennings Bryan, for instance; it is not altogether anti-Darwinism: the concept of Development replaces the concept of Evolution, but we accept the process of Selection, not to anything loosely known as Environment, but relatively to underlying Schedule and Design, predetermined and supervised, as it were, but by nothing that we conceive of in anthropomorphic terms.

I define what I mean by dynamic design, in the development of any embryonic thing: a pre-determined, or not accidental, or not irresponsible, passage along a schedule of phases to a climax of unification of many parts. Some of the aspects of this process are the simultaneous varying of parts, with destiny, and not with independence, for their rule, or with future co-ordinations and functions for their goal; and their survival while still incipient, not because they are the fittest relatively to contemporaneous environment, so not because of usefulness or advantage in the present, inasmuch as at first they are not only functionless but also discordant with established relations, but surviving because they are in harmony with the dynamic plan of a whole being: and the presence of forces of suppression, or repression, as well as forces of stimulation and protection, so that parts are held back, or are not permitted to develop before their time.

If we accept that these circumstances of embryonic development are the circumstances of all wider development, within one enclosed system, the doctrine of Darwinian Evolution, as applied generally, will, in our minds, have to be replaced by an expression upon Super-embryonic Development, and Darwinism, unmodified, will become to us one more of the insufficiencies of the past. Darwinism concerns itself with the adaptations of the present, and does heed the part that the past has played, but, in Darwinism, there is no place for the influence of the future upon the present.

Consider any part of an embryonic thing — the heart of an embryo — and at first it is only a loop. It will survive, and it will be nourished in its functionless incipiency; also it will not be permitted to become a fully developed heart before its scheduled time arrives; its circumstances are dominated by what it will be in the future. The eye of an embryo is a better instance.

Consider anything of a sociologic nature that has ever grown: that there never has been an art, science, religion, invention that was not at first out of accord with established environment, visionary, preposterous in the light of later standards, useless in its incipiency, and resisted by established forces so that, seemingly animating it and protectively underlying it, there may have been something that in spite of its unfitness made it survive for future usefulness. Also there are data for the acceptance that all things, in wider being, are held back as well as protected and prepared for, and not permitted to develop before comes scheduled time. Langley's flying machine makes me think of something of the kind — that this machine was premature; that it appeared a little before the era of aviation upon this earth, and that therefore Langley could not fly. But this machine was capable of flying, because, some years later, Curtiss did fly in it. Then one thinks that the Wright Brothers were successful, because they did synchronise with a scheduled time. I have heard that it is questionable that Curtiss made no alterations in Langley's machine. There is no lack of instances. One of the greatest of secrets that have eventually been found out was for ages blabbed by all the pots and kettles in the world — but that the secret of the steam engine could not, to the lowliest of intellects, or to suppositiously highest of intellects, more than adumbratively reveal itself until came the time for its co-ordination with the other phenomena and the requirements of the Industrial Age. And coal that was stored in abundance near the surface of the ground — and the needs of dwellers over coal mines, veins of which were often exposed upon the surface of the ground, for fuel — but that this secret, too, was obvious, too, could not be revealed until the coming of the Industrial Age. Then the building of factories, the inventing of machines, the digging of coal, and the use of steam, all appearing by simultaneous variation, and co-ordinating. Shores of North America — nowadays, with less hero-worship than formerly, historians tell us that, to English and French fishermen, the coast of Newfoundland was well-known, long before the year 1492; nevertheless, to the world in general, it was not, or, according to our acceptances, could not be, known. About the year 1500, a Portuguese fleet was driven by storms to the coast of Brazil, and returned to Europe. Then one thinks that likely enough, before the year 1492, other vessels had been so swept to the coasts of the western hemisphere, and had returned — but that data of westward lands could not emerge from the suppressions of the era — but that the data did survive, or were preserved for future usefulness — that there are "Thou shalt nots" engraved upon something underlying all things, and then effacing, when phases pass away.

We conceive now of all buildings — within one enclosed system — in terms of embryonic building, and of all histories as local aspects of Super-embryonic Development. Cells of an embryo build falsely and futilely, in the sense that what they construct will be only temporary and will be out of adjustment later. If however there are conditions by which successive stages must be traversed before the arrival of maturity, ours is an expression upon the false and the futile, in which case these terms, as derogations, should not be applied. We see that the cells that build have no basis of their own; that for their formations there is nothing of reason and necessity of their own, because they flourish in other formations quite as well. We see that they need nothing of basis, nor of guidance of their own, because basis and guidance are of the essence of the whole. All are responses, or correlates, to a succession of commandments, as it were, or of dominant, directing, supervising spirits of different eras: that they take on appearances that are concordant with the general gastrula era, changing when comes the stimulus to agree with the reptilian era, and again responding harmoniously when comes the time of the mammalian era. It is in accordance with our experience that never has human mind, scientific, religious, philosophic, formulated one basic thought, one finally true law, principle, or major premise from which guidance could be deduced. If any thought were true and final it would include the deduced. We conceive that there has been guidance, just the same, if human beings be conceived of as cellular units in one developing organism; and that human minds no more need foundations of their own than need the super-embryonic cells that build so preposterously, according to standards of later growth, but build as they are guided to build. In this view, human reason is tropism, or response to stimuli, and reasoning is the trial-and-error process of the most primitive unicellular organisms, a susceptibility to underlying mandates, then a groping in perhaps all possible distortions until adjustment with underlying requirements is reached. In this view, then, though there are, for instance, no atoms in the Daltonian sense, if in service of a building science, the false doctrine of the atoms be needed, the mind that responds, perhaps not to stimulus, but to requirement, which seems to be a negative stimulus, and so conceives, is in adjustment and reaches the state known as success. I accept, myself, that there may be Final Truth, and that it may be attainable, but never in a service that is local or special in any one science or nation or world.

It is our expression that temporary isolations characterise embryonic growth and super-embryonic growth quite as distinctly as do expansions and co-ordinations. Local centres of development in an egg — and they are isolated before they sketch out attempting relations. Or in wider being — hemisphere isolated from hemisphere, and nation from nation — then the breaking down of barriers — the appearance of Japan out of obscurity — threads of a military plasm are cast across an ocean by the United States.

Shafts of light that have pierced the obscurity surrounding planets — and something like a star shines in Aristarchus of the moon. Embryonic heavens that have dreamed — and that their mirages will be realised some day. Sounds and an interval; sounds and the same interval; sounds again — that there is one integrating organism and that we have heard its pulse.

CHAPTER 26

Feb. 7, 1922 — an explosion "of startling intensity" in the sky of the northwestern point of the London Triangle (*Nature*, 109, 249).

Repeating phenomena in a local sky — in *Bull. S.A.F.* (36, 201), it is said that, at Orsay (Seine-et-Oise) Feb. 15, 1922, a detonation was heard in the sky, and that nine hours later a similar sound was heard, and that an illumination was seen in the sky. It is said that, ten nights later, at Verneuil, in the adjoining province, Oise, a great, fiery mass was seen falling from the sky.

March 12, 1922 — rocks that had been falling "from the clouds," for three weeks, at Chico, a town in an "earthquake region" in California (New York *Times*, March 12, 1922). Large, smooth rocks that "seemed to come straight from the clouds."

In the San Francisco *Chronicle*, in issues dating from the 12th to the 18th of March — clippings sent to me by Mr. Maynard Shipley, writer and lecturer upon scientific subjects, if there be such subjects — the accounts are of stones that, for four months, had been falling intermittently from the sky, almost always upon the roofs of two adjoining warehouses, in Chico, but, upon one occasion, falling three blocks away: "a downpour of oval-shaped stones;" "a heavy shower of warm rocks." San Francisco *Call*, March 13 — "warm rocks." It is said that crowds gathered, and that upon the 17th of March a "deluge" of rocks fell upon a crowd, injuring one person. The police "combing" all surroundings: the only explanation that they could think of was that somebody was firing stones from a catapult. One person was suspected by them, but, upon the 14th of March, a rock fell when he was known not to be in the neighbourhood.

The circumstances point to one origin of these stones, stationary in the sky, above the town of Chico.

Upon the first of January, 1922, the attention of Marshal J. A. Peck, of Chico, had been called to the phenomena. After investigating more than two months, he said (San Francisco *Examiner*, March 14): "I could find no one through my investigations who could explain the matter. At various times I have heard and seen the stones. I think some one with a machine is to blame."

Prof. C.K. Studley, vice-president of the Teachers' College,

Chico, is quoted in the *Examiner:*

"Some of the rocks are so large that they could not be thrown by any ordinary means. One of the rocks weighs 16 ounces. They are not of meteoric origin, as seems to have been hinted, because two of them show signs of cementation, either natural or artificial, and no meteoric factor was ever connected with a cement plant."

Once upon a time, dogmatists supposed, asserted, angrily declared sometimes, that all stones that fall from the sky must be of "true meteoric material." That time is now of the past. See *Nature* (105, 759) — a description of two dissimilar stones, cemented together, seen to fall from the sky, at Cumberland Falls, Ky., April 9, 1919.

Miriam Allen de Ford has sent me an account of her own observations. About the middle of March, 1922, she was in Chico, and investigated; went to the scene of the falling rocks; discussed the subject with persons in the crowd. "While I was discussing it with some bystanders, I looked up at the cloudless sky, and suddenly saw a rock falling straight down, as if becoming visible when it came near enough. This rock struck the roof with a thud, and bounced off on the track beside the warehouse, and I could not find it." "I learned that the rocks had been falling since July, 1921, though no publicity arose until November."

There have been other phenomena at Chico. In the New York *Times,* Sept. 2, 1878, upon the 20th of August, 1878, according to the Chico *Record,* a great number of small fishes fell from the sky, at Chico, covering the roof of a store, and falling in the streets, upon an area of several acres. Perhaps the most important observation is that they fell from a cloudless sky. Several occurrences are listed as earthquakes, by Dr. Holden, in his Catalog (*Smith. Misc.*, 37, no. 1087: 57, 97, 136, 180, 189); but the detonations that were heard in Oroville, a town near Chico, Jan. 2, 1887, are said, in the *Monthly Weather Review* (15, 24), to have been in the sky. Upon the night of March 5-6, 1885, according to the Chico *Chronicle,* a large object, of very hard material, weighing several tons, fell from the sky, near Chico (*Monthly Weather Review,* 13, 77). In the year 1893, an iron object, said to be meteoritic, was found at Oroville (*Memoirs of the National Academy of Sciences,* 13, 345).

My own idea is either that there is land over the town of Chico, and not far away, inasmuch as objects from it fall with a very narrow distribution, or that far away, and therefore invisible, there may be land from which objects have been carried in a special current to one very small part of this earth's surface. If anyone would like to read an account of stones that fell intermittently for several days, clearly enough as if in a current, or in a field of special force, of some kind, at Livet, near Clavaux, France, December, 1842, see the London *Times* (Jan. 13, 1843). There have been other such occurrences. Absurdly, when they were noticed at all, they were supposed to be psychic phenomena. I conceive that there is no more of the psychic to these occurrences than there is to the arrival of seeds from the West Indies upon the coast of England. Stones that fell upon a house, near the Pantheon, Paris, for three weeks, January, 1849 — see Dr. Wallace's *Miracles and Modern Spiritualism* (284). Several times, in the course of this book, I have tried to be reasonable. I have asked what such repeating phenomena in one local sky do indicate, if they do not indicate fixed origins in the sky. And if such occurrences, supported by many data in other fields, do not indicate the stationariness of this earth, with new lands not far away — tell me what it is all about. The falling stones of Chico — new lands in the sky — or what?

Boston *Transcript,* March 21, 1922 — clipping sent to me by Mr. J. David Stern, Editor and Publisher of the Camden (N.J.) *Daily Courier* —

"Geneva, March 21 — During a heavy snow-storm in the Alps recently thousands of exotic insects resembling spiders, caterpillars and huge ants fell on the slopes and quickly died. Local naturalists are unable to explain the phenomenon, but one theory is that the insects were blown in from a warmer climate."

The fall of unknown insects in a snow storm is not the circumstance that I call most attention to. It is worth noting that I have records of half a dozen similar occurrences in the Alps, usually about the last of January, but the striking circumstance is that insects of different species and of different specific gravities fell together. The conventional explanation is that a wind, far away, raised a great variety of small objects, and segregated them according to specific gravity, so that twigs and grasses fell in one place, dust some other place, pebbles somewhere else, and insects farther along somewhere. This would be very fine segregation. There was no very fine segregation in this occurrence. Something of a seasonal, or migratory, nature, from some other world, localised in the sky, relatively to the Alps, is suggested.

May 4, 1922 — discovery, by F. Burnerd, of three long mounds in the lunar crater Archimedes. See the *English Mechanic* (115: 194, 218, 268, 278). It seems likely that these constructions had been recently built.

St. Thomas, Virgin Islands, May 18, 1922 (*Associated Press*) — particles of matter falling continuously for several days. "The phenomenon is supposed here to be of volcanic origin, but all the volcanoes of the West Indies are reported as quiet."

New York *Tribune*, July 3, 1922, that, for the fourth time in one month, a great volume of water, or a "cloudburst," had poured from one local sky, near Carbondale, Pa.

Oct. 15, 1922 — a large quantity of white substance that fell upon the shores of Lake Michigan, near Chicago. It fell upon the clothes of hundreds of persons, fell upon the campus of Northwestern University, likely enough fell upon the astronomical observatory of the University. It occurred to one of these hundreds, or thousands, or persons to collect some of this substance. He is Mr. L.A. Hopkins, of Chicago. He sent me a sample. I think that it is spider web, because it is viscous: when burned it chars with the crinkled effect of burned hair and feathers, and the odour is similar. But it is strong, tough substance, of a cottony texture, when rolled up. The interesting circumstance to me is that similar substance has fallen frequently upon this earth, in October, but that, in terrestrial terms, seasonal migration of aeronautical spiders can not be thought of, because in the tropics and in Australia, as well as in the United States and in England, such showers have occurred in October. Then something seasonal, but seasonal in an extra-mundane sense, is suggested. See the *Scientific Australian* (22, 1) — that, from October 5 to 29, 1915, an enormous fall of similar substance occurred upon a region of thousands of square miles, in Australia.

Time after time, in data that I have only partly investigated, occur declarations that, during devastations commonly known as "earthquakes," in Chile, the sky has flamed, or that "strange illuminations" in the sky have been seen. In the *Bull. Seismo.* (3, 190), for instance, some of these descriptions have been noted, and have been hushed up with the explanation that they were the reports of unscientific persons.

Latest of the great quakes in Chile — 1,500 dead "recovered" in one of the cities of the Province of Atacama. New York *Tribune*, Nov. 15, 1922 — "Again, today, severe earthquakes shook the Province of Coquimbo and other places and strange illuminations were observed over the sea off La Serena and Copiapo."

Back to Crater Mountain, Arizona, for an impression — but far more impressive are similar data as to these places of Atacama and Copiapo, in Chile. In the year 1845, M. Darlu, of Valparaiso, read, before the French Academy, a paper, in which he asserted that, in the desert of Atacama, which begins at Copiapo, meteorites are strewn upon the ground in such numbers that they are met at every step. If these objects fell all at one time in this earthquake region, we have another instance conceivably of mere coincidence between the aerial and the seismic. If they fell at different times, the indications are of a fixed relationship between this part of Chile and a centre somewhere in the sky of falling objects commonly called "meteorites" and of cataclysms that devastate this part of Chile with concussions commonly called "earthquakes." There is a paper upon this subject in *Science* (n.s., 14, 433). Here the extreme abundance asserted by M. Darlu is questioned: it is said that only thirteen of these objects were known to science. But, according to descriptions, four of them are stones, or stone-irons, differing so that, in the opinion of the writer, and not merely so interpreted by me, these four objects fell at different times. Then the nine others are considered. They are nickel-irons. They, too, are different, one from another. So then it is said that these thirteen objects, all from one place, were, with reasonable certainty, the products of different falls.

Behind concepts that sometimes seem delirious, I offer — a reasonable certainty —

That, existing somewhere beyond this earth, perhaps beyond a revolving shell in which the nearby stars are openings, there are stationary regions, from which, upon many occasions, have emanated "meteors," sometimes exploding catastrophically over Atacama, Chile, for instance. Coasts of South America have reeled, and the heavens have been afire. Reverberations in the sky — the ocean has responded with islands. Between sky and earth of Chile there have been flaming intimacies of destruction and slaughter and woe —

Silence that is conspiracy to hide past ignorance; that is imbecility, or that is the unawareness of the profoundest hypnosis.

Hypnosis —

That the seismologists, too, have functioned in preserving the illusion of this earth's isolation, and by super-embryonic processes have been hypnotised into oblivion of a secret that has been proclaimed with avalanches of fire from the heavens, and that has babbled from brooks of the blood of crushed populations, and that is monumentalised in ruins.

THE END

INDEX

This index had to be trimmed to essentials to fit the available space. The major omisssions were dates, which will be restored if the opportunity arises for a companion volume of combined indexes to all four of Fort's books. Abbreviations used for periodical citations in the text have been included in the sequence with pointers to the full reference.

A

Abingdon, Oxon, England – 206
Academy of Natural Science of Philadelphia – 196
    Proceedings of – 196
Adams, Dr – 9, 15, 17, 24, 63
Advertiser, Dundee – 129
Advertiser and Spirit of the Times, Wolverhampton – 103
aeroplanes, mystery – 214
Africa – 3, 38
Airship, Willows – 208
airships, mystery – 163-5 202-5, 208-12
Airy, Sir George – 9, 33
Al-Sufi – 70
Alaska, U.S. – 4, 186-8
Alaska, Bruce – 186
Albany, NY, U.S. – 203
Albright, Mrs – 201
Alcorn, Robert – 161
Alderburgh, Suffolk, England – 167
Alderney, Channel Islands – 206
Aldershot, Berks., England – 194-5
Algol, star – 25-6, 69
Allah – 175
Allahabad, India – 101
Allegheny Observatory – 43
Alpine Journal – 59
Alps – 83, 230
Amer. Jour. Sci. – see: American Journal of Science
America
    North – 109, 124, 185, 225
    South – 38, 109, 173, 218, 232
American Journal of Science – 9, 20, 48, 71, 83, 84, 98, 105, 111, 197, 198
American Meteorological Journal – 150
American Museum of Natural History, New York City – 177
American Philosophical Society, Proceedings of – 8
Amsterdam, Holland – 30
Amsterdam Island, Spitzbergen – 179
Anderson, Dr Thomas D. – 45
Andrée, Prof – 179
Andromeda, nebula – 75

angels – 112, 153
Ann. Sci. Disc. – see: Annual of Scientific Discovery
Annales de Chimie et de Physique – 85, 87
Annals of Philosophy – 50, 87
Année Scientifique et Industrielle, L' – 106, 153
Annuaire de la Société Météorologique de France – 108
Annual of Scientific Discovery – 85, 87, 105
Annual Record of Science and Industry – 26
Annual Register – 86
Antarctic – 177
Antwerp, Belgium – 166, 178
Apt, France – 83
Arago, Dominique François Jean – 85
Arcana of Science – 101
Arcelin, M. Adrian – 155
Arctic – 187
    Ocean – 132
Argenteuil, France – 190
Aristarchus – 57
Arizona, U.S. – 196-8
Arthur, Prince – 101
Ascension Island – 55
Ashland, OH, U.S.- 154
Aso San, Japan – 88
Associated Press – 231
Asteroid Belt – 8, 9, 10
Astre Cherbourg, L' – 191-3
Astro. – see: Astronomie, L'
Astronomical Journal – 26, 182
Astronomical Register – 26, 27, 48, 89, 106, 108, 109, 119, 120, 123, 124, 136, 137, 150
Astronomical Society of the Pacific, Publications of the – 42, 70, 220
Astronomical Society of Wales – 178-9
Astronomie, L' – 32, 124, 125, 129, 136, 137, 138, 139, 140, 141, 146, 153, 157, 160, 161, 179
Astronomische Nachrichten – 161
Astronomy in a Nutshell, Serviss – 17
Atacama, Chile – 232
Athenaeum – 22
Athens, Greece – 121

Atkins, G.W. – 213
Atlantic Ocean – 189
Atlantic City, NJ, U.S. – 216
Atmosphere, The, Flammarion – 114
attacks, mystery – 213, 214, 217
Auriga, star – 70
auroras – 84, 90, 117, 152
Australia – 106, 231
Austria – 55, 91
Auwers, Prof. – 24, 26-7, 76
Ayling, Mrs – 93
Azores – 161

B

B.A. Rept. – see: British Association for the Advancement of Science, Annual Report
Babinet, Dr – 9
Bacon, Lord Francis – 8
Badlam, Alexander – 186, 187
Bailey, Francis – 86, 90
Balboa, Vasco Nunez de – 222
Ball, Sir Robert – 8, 10, 25, 29, 43
Ballinasloe, Galway, Ireland – 215
Ballyconneely, Connemara, Ireland – 185
Baltic Sea – 139-40
banjite – 141
Banmouth, England (?) – 115
Barber, Mr – 20
Barclay, Andrew – 31, 32, 128
Barga, Italy – 83
Barisal, Bengal, India – 100, 131, 166, 173
Barisal Guns – 100, 131, 166
Barker, Rev. J. Ross – 143
Barnard, Prof – 46, 161
Barnard's Star – 77
Barrett, C. – 136
Barringer – 196-197
Bateman, Rev. J.F. – 132
Bath, Avon, England – 156, 162
Beaufoy, Col. – 50
Beaumont, TX, U.S. – 164
Bedford Canal – 37-8
Bedford Catalogue, The – 33
Beer – 126, 128
Belgian Academy of Science – 102
Belgique Horticole, La – 102
Belgium – 166-7, 169, 173, 210
Bell, Pres. of Nat. Geog. Soc. –

179
Berberich, Prof – 22
Bergamo, Italy – 148
Berkshire Hills, MA, U.S. – 216
Bermuda – 30, 211-2
Bernoulli, John – 64
Bervie, Scotland – 157
Besançon, France – 201
Beswick, Samuel – 106
Betelgeuse (Alpha Orionis),
   star – 4, 164-5
Bélopolsky – 42
Bible – 37
Bilbao, Spain – 156
Bird, Mr – 109
Birmingham, Warks, England –
   4, 6, 103-4, 107, 131, 135, 146,
   148, 173-4
Birmingham, Mr. – 124
Birt, W.R. – 125-7, 136
birth, extraordinary – 169
Blackett, Lieut. R.N. – 183
Blankenberghe, Holland – 169
Bloomington, IN, U.S.- 129
Blount, Lady – 37
Bode's Law – 9, 10
body between Venus and
   Mars, unknown – 184
Bohemia – 91
Bomme – 21
Bond – 44
bones, fossilised – 175, 177
Borden, Robert – 214
Borgo San Donnino, Italy – 84
Boston, MA, U.S. – 202-4, 216
Bozward, Lloyd – 171
Bóne, France – 114
Bradgate, W.K. – 150, 190
Bradley – 41
Brahé, Tycho – 62, 78, 94
Branford, NY(?), U.S. – 217
Brazil – 225
Brenner – 58
Brewster, Sir David – 113, 114,
   117
Brée, Belgium – 166
Bridgewater, MA, U.S. – 202
Bridport, Dorset, England – 156
*Brief Biography and Popular
   Account of the Unparalleled
   Discoveries of T.J.J. See,* Webb
   – 89
Brighton, Sussex, England –
   126, 132
Bristol, Avon, England – 132,
   185-8
   mirage of – 188
Bristol, CT, U.S. – 202
Bristol Channel, England – 208
British Association for the
   Advancement of Science – 4,
   97
   Annual Report – 4, 38, 83,

84, 85, 87, 90, 91, 92, 93, 96,
99, 103, 106, 108, 111, 114,
115, 121, 122, 123, 126, 132,
142, 145, 146, 147
British Astronomical Associa-
   tion – 50, 71
   Journal of – 22, 32, 45, 46,
   50, 58, 71, 136, 137, 201, 213,
   215
   Memoirs of – 17, 60
British Astronomical Society,
   Jupiter Section of – 60
British Columbia, Canada –
   179
British Isles – 170
Brocken spectres – 114, 153,
   185
Brockville, On., Canada – 214
Bronx, The, N.Y., U.S. – 61
Brooklyn. N.Y., U.S. – 158, 216
Brooks, Prof. William R. – 181
Broughty Ferry, Scotland – 129
Brown – 105
Browning – 94
Bruce, Miner – 186-7
Bruguière, M. – 153
Brühl, nr Cologne, Germany –
   130
Brule, WI, U.S. – 165
Brussels, Belgium – 30, 149,
   166-8
Brussels Observatory – 129
Bryan, Col. William Jennings –
   223
Bryant, W.W. – 18, 42
Buckingham – 122-3
Buckingham Co., VA, U.S. –
   220
Buckle, Henry Thomas – 30
Buddha – 121
Büderich, Westphalia, Ger-
   many – 115
Buffalo, NY, U.S. – 211
Bulford Camp, Wilts., England
   – 195
Bull. S.A.F. – see: Société Astro-
   nomique de France, Bulletin
Bull. Seismo. – see: Seismologi-
   cal Society of America, Bul-
   letin
*Bulletin (Universal) des Scien-
   ces, Mathematiques, Astron-
   omique, Physiques et Chimi-
   ques* – 86, 102
Burcleaves, England – 210
Burnerd, F. – 231
Burnham, S.W. – 34, 128
Buschof, Courland (Russia) –
   103
Buss, Albert – 160, 213

C

C.R. – see: Comptes Rendus

Cacciatore – 105
California, U.S. – 131, 182, 228
Call, San Francisco – 228
Camberwell, London, England
   – 119
Cambrian Natural Observer –
   178, 179, 191
Campbell, Prof. – 42, 46, 160,
   220
Canada – 5, 73, 179, 211, 214
Canobbia, M. – 111
Canon Diablo, AZ, U.S. – 198
Cape Town, S. Africa – 86
Capocci – 108
Carbondale, PA, U.S. – 231
Carboniferous Era – 116, 118
Cardiff, Glamorgan, Wales –
   190, 208, 210, 215
Cardiganshire, Wales – 99-100
Caribou, Yukon, Canada – 180
Carlinville, IL, U.S. – 165
Carlisle, Cumbria, England –
   51
Carrington – 105
Cartagena, Colombia – 107
Cassiopeia, const. – 145-6
"Catalogue of Destructive
   Earthquakes", Milne – 99
Catania Observatory – 44
Celestial Objects, Webb – 85,
   87, 94, 105, 183
*Century's Progress in Astrono-
   my, A,* MacPherson – 14
*Century's Progress in Science,
   A,* MacPherson – 58
Ceraski – 67
Ceres, asteroid – 145
Chaigley, Merseyside, England
   – 134
Challis, Prof. – 9
Chambers, George F. – 19, 33-
   34, 54
Chambon, France – 115
Champollion, Jean François –
   127, 189
Chandakopur, India – 101
Chandler – 26
Chant, Prof. – 211-2
Charleston, SC, U.S. – 111
Chase, Prof. Pliny – 8-11
Chasseloup-Laubut, ship – 193
Chatou, France – 190
Chats on Astronomy, Hollis –
   58
Chattanooga, TN, U.S.- 205
Cherbourg, France – 156, 191-
   3, 211
Chesham, Bucks., England –
   143
Chevallier, Prof. – 90
Chicago, IL, U.S. – 71, 163-4,
   176, 187, 218, 231
Chico, CA, U.S. – 228-9

Chile – 231-3
Chiltern Hills, England – 143
China, southwest – 219
Chronicle, San Francisco – 228, 229
Church Stretton, Shropshire, England – 134
Ciel et Terre – 129, 166, 167, 168, 178, 183
Cincinnati, OH, U.S. – 215
cities in sky – 4, 114, 154, 186-8
Clark, Joseph – 195
Clark Jr., Alvan – 26-7, 68, 110
Clarke, James – 113
Clerke, Agnes – 24, 54, 70-71, 124
Cleveland, Grover – 160
Clifford, Herefordshire, England – 170
Clifton, Mr. E. – 37-8
cloud
    dimming stars – 71
    red – 84
Coconino County, AZ, U.S. – 196
Codde, M. – 140
Coggia – 94
Colbert, Prof. – 10, 71
Colby, WI, U.S. – 216
Colchester, Essex, England – 132-135, 173
Cold Harbor, Hanover Co., VA, U.S. – 183
College Bar-sur-Aube, France – 157
Cologne, Germany – 130
Colorado, U.S. – 176
Colton, Prof. – 36
Columbus, Christopher – 38, 150
Comet of 1556, The, Hind – 21
comets – 10, 12, 18-23, 77, 85, 94, 150, 192-3
    Biela's – 22
    Borelly's – 19
    Brooks' First Periodic – 19
    Denning's Second Periodic – 19
    Giacobini's Second Periodical – 19
    Halley's – 16-7
    Swift's – 19
    that did not return – 19-21
    Winnecke's – 205
Commune Signy-le-Petit, France – 155
Complete Course of Meteorology, A, Kaemetz – 102
Comptes Rendus (Hebdomadaires des séances de l'Academie des Sciences) – 29, 30, 69, 83, 85, 87, 94, 102, 103, 105,

106, 111, 120, 133, 141, 146, 151
Comrie, Perthshire, Scotland – 84-6, 96-8, 107, 131, 135, 146, 148, 173, 218-9
Comstock, Prof – 124
concussions, aerial – 84-7, 97-9, 101, 131-5, 142-3, 170-2, 200, 220-1
Coney Island, NY, U.S. – 216
Connecticut, U.S. – 202
Constantinople, Turkey – 106
Converse Co., WY, U.S. – 177
Cook, Dr – 29, 59
Coon Butte, AZ, U.S. – 196
Cooper, Charles – 112
Copernicus, Nicolaus – 39, 40, 78
Copiapo, Chile – 232
Coquimbo, Chile – 232
Cosmos: Les Mondes – 30, 59, 110, 133, 139, 140, 180, 181, 190, 191
Cosmos: Revue Encyclopedic – 106, 115
Coulon, M. Raimond – 179
Countess of Aberdeen, ship – 156
Country Queries and Notes – 184, 185
Courrier des Ardennes – 155
Covington, Richard – 106
Crater Mountain, AZ, U.S. – 196-8, 232
Crediton, Devon, England – 100
Crieff, Tayside, Scotland – 98
Crowe, Catherine – 115
Crowle, nr Worcester, Worcs., England – 134
Crusoe, Robinson – 213
Cuba – 106, 117
Cumberland Falls, KY, U.S. – 229
Curtis, Eli – 112
Curtiss, Glenn Hammond – 203, 225
Cycle of Celestial Objects, A, Smyth – 32, 33, 34

D

D'Abruzzi, Duc – 59, 186, 188
D'Adjuda, M. – 161
Daily Chronicle, London – 134, 217
Daily Courier, Camden (NJ) – 230
Daily Mail
    Hull – 210
    London – 217
Daily News, London – 100, 163
Daily Post, Birmingham – 103, 104, 109

Daily Star, Toronto – 212
Dallas, TX, U.S. – 163
Daniel – 168
    Prophecies of – 64
Darlu, M. – 232
Dartmoor, Devon, England – 100
Dartmouth Harbour, Devon, England – 157
Darwin, Charles – 48
Darwinism – 145, 223-4
Davison, Dr. Charles – 171
Dawes, Dr – 27, 68, 122-3
Day, Dr. Warren E. – 181
De Ballore, Count Montessus – 200
De Cuppis, Pompolio – 105
De Fonblanque, Señor – 107
De Ford, Miriam Allen – 229
De Kerillis, Commander – 193
De Moraes, M. – 161
De Robeck, Madame – 201
De Schryvere, M. – 167
De Solutré, France – 155
De Soto, Hernando – 222
De Speissen, Mr – 160
De Vico, Francesco – 44, 105
Deal, Kent, England – 105
Dean, George W. – 110
Dearborn Observatory – 10
deaths, odd – 183
Delambre, M. – 54-5
Delaware, U.S. – 152
Dennett, Frank – 136
Denning, William Frederick – 30, 50, 73-4, 120, 170, 201, 206-7, 212
Denton, TX, U.S. – 163
Denver, CO, U.S. – 164
Descartes, René – 63-4
Desmoulins, M. – 190
Detroit, MI, U.S. – 219-20
Devon, England – 180
Devonport, Devon, England – 100
Dewsbury, Yorks, England – 160
Dhurmsulla, India – 111
Dipper, The, const. – 42
disappearances – 156, 158, 216-7
Disco, Greenland – 3
Dispatch, Richmond – 152
Dodge City, KS, U.S. – 165
Dolgelly, Gwynedd, Wales – 100
Dolgovoli, Volhynia, Russia – 103
Dominion Observatory – 214
Donegal, Ireland – 161, 163
Doolittle, Dr. Eric – 14
Dorking, Surrey, England – 206
Dourite, France – 181

Dover, Kent, England – 166, 208

Downing, Dr – 18, 32

Dragon, const. – 42

Dulais Valley, Glamorgan, Wales – 209

Dundee, Tayside, Scotland – 129, 157

Dunkeld, Tayside, Scotland – 85

Dunkirk, France – 166

E

Eagle, Brooklyn – 154, 158

Earth
  diameter of – 58
  distance from the sun – 52-7, 78
  motion of – 38-9, 40-2, 47-8, 65-6
  round or flat? – 36, 37, 38
  stationary – 47, 62, 65-6, 76-8, 116, 141, 146, 148-9, 151, 172, 178, 185, 194, 199, 207
  top-shaped – 38, 78

Earth Features and Their Meaning, Hobbs – 38

earthquakes – 83-5, 96, 101, 133, 169-70, 198, 215, 217, 220, 229
  and appearances in the sky – 96
  and falls – 83, 111, 131, 134, 96, 97, 135, 142, 232
  and lights in sky – 83, 98, 116, 131-4, 169-171, 200, 218, 231-2
  and sounds – 83, 96-7, 131-3, 143, 194, 218-9

Earthquakes and Volcanoes, Ponton – 98

earthshine – 92, 137

East Haddam, CT, U.S. – 83-4

East Kent, Ontario, Canada – 155

East Liss, Hants., England – 194

Edin. N. Phil. Jour. – see: Edinburgh New Philosophical Journal

Edina, MO, U.S. – 158

Edinburgh, Lothian, Scotland – 45, 114

Edinburgh Annual Register – 84

Edinburgh New Philosophical Journal – 85, 86, 96, 97, 98

Edinburgh Review – 16

Egypt – 174-5

Eiffel Tower – 205

El Paso, TX, U.S. – 180

Electra, ship – 221

Elements of Astronomy, Young – 43

Elger, Thomas Gwyn – 44, 123, 125-6

Ellis – 50

Ellison, Rev. William – 219

Elstree, Herts., England – 213

Embrun, France – 85

Emmert, Dr – 220

Emmett, Rev. J.B. – 87

Encke – 54, 55

England – 5, 16, 37, 132-4, 151, 160, 162, 167, 169-70, 185, 195, 199, 208-11, 230-1

English Channel – 156-7, 166, 169, 206

English Mechanic and World of Science – 22, 31, 32, 34, 36, 37, 38, 42, 44, 46, 48, 50, 94, 101, 104, 124, 125, 126, 128, 130, 131, 136, 137, 146, 149, 160, 161, 170, 178, 179, 180, 181, 182, 185, 186, 189, 190, 195, 201, 205, 206, 213, 214, 215, 216, 218, 219, 220, 221, 231

Ennis, TX, U.S. – 164

Epsom, Surrey, England – 199, 206

Erkelenz, Prussia – 102

Erman, Dr – 96

Eskimos – 213

Espin, Dr – 46, 71

Estonia – 140

Etwell, Derbyshire, England – 20

Europe – 176, 225

Evanston, IL, U.S. – 163

Evening Express and Evening Mail, Cardiff – 208, 209

Evening News
  Newark – 217
  Portsmouth – 210

Evening Star, Ipswich – 210

Evening Telegram, New York – 217

Evening World, New York – 220

Evolution of Worlds, The, Lowell – 46

Examiner, San Francisco – 228, 229

explosion
  in sky – 145-6, 198, 200, 206-7, 215-8, 220-1, 228-9, 232
  mystery – 158, 161, 163

F

falls – 173
  ashes – 131
  blood – 176, 219
  china fragments – 218
  corpuscles, yellow-brown – 102
  fibres, black – 111
  fishes – 176, 229

  frogs – 176, 220
  from fixed point in the sky – 6
  glue-like – 178
  insects – 230
  luminous – 111
  object, iron – 229
  object, large, very hard material – 229
  object, manufactured – 219
  organic matter – 110, 116
  particles – 231
  powder, black – 96
  repeated – 96, 102, 104, 116, 141, 196, 228-231
  rocks – 228-9
  seeds – 86, 102
  slag or cinders – 98
  soot – 97, 134
  stones – 6, 83-5, 87, 96, 101-4, 116, 134, 141-2, 146, 171, 173-4, 198, 216, 229, 230
  stones, cold, luminous – 111
  substance, black – 134
  substance, pink – 134
  substance, purple-red – 179
  substance, red – 111
  substance, white – 231
  warm water – 102

Farman, Henry – 203

Ferguson, James – 105, 205, 215

Field, The – 37, 134

Figaro, Le – 193

Finsbo, Sweden – 140

fire-balloons – 93-4, 129, 150-1, 157, 162, 190, 211, 214

Fischer – 30

Fison, Alfred Henry – 70

Flagstaff, AZ, U.S. – 189

Flammarion, Nicholas Camille – 26-7, 29-1, 68, 114, 191-2

Fletcher, Lazarus A. – 85, 103

Fletching, Sussex, England – 134

Flight – 210

Florida, U.S. – 74, 172

Fontana – 32

Forbes, Prof – 14

forces, strange – 155, 157, 183

Fordham, Sir George (H.G. Fordham) – 142-3, 169, 194, 206

Formalhaut, star – 181

Fort Klamath, OR, U.S. – 131, 133-4

Fort Worth, TX, U.S. – 163

Forty-One Years in India, Roberts – 115

Foucault, Leon – 54-55

Foucault pendulum-experiment – 48

Foulis Manse, Perthshire, Scot

land – 97
Four Oaks, Staffs., England – 92-3
France – 5, 133, 169, 181, 199, 201, 216
Franklin Institute, Journal of – 8, 110
Freeman – 50
French, Mr. L.B. – 187
French Academy – 9, 30, 64, 232
French revolution – 17
Fritsch – 83
Frome, Somerset, England – 147

G

Gabes, Tunisia – 132
Gaboreau, Mr – 161
Galium spurium – 86
Galle, Dr – 91
Gambart – 51
Gananoque, Ontario, Canada – 214
Gape, Charles – 128
Garfield, President – 153
Garrie, M. A. – 181
Gaudibert – 161
Gazette
  Birmingham – 94, 104
  Westminster -206, 207
Gegenschein – 72-3
Geneva, Switzerland – 102, 105, 161, 230
Genoa, Italy – 98, 108, 111
Geographical Journal – 38, 175
Geographical Society of the Pacific – 180
Geological Society of London, Quarterly Journal of – 100
Germany – 200, 211
Gérard, Prof – 166
Ghelma, France – 114
Gheury, Maurice – 190
Gill, Dr. David – 55, 56
Girdleness, Grampian, Scotland – 157
Glamorganshire, Wales – 208
Glasenapp – 55
Gledhill – 126
Glenorchy, Tasmania – 215
Goldschmidt – 27, 68
Goodacre – 50
Gore, J.E. – 25, 70, 129
Gorton – 51
Gosport, Hants, England – 184, 218
Gothard, M. Eugen – 46
Gothland, Sweden – 140
Göttingen, Germany – 22
Gowman, Carl G. – 219
Gower, Charles – 51, 120
Gowrie, Tayside, Scotland – 97

Granite Range, AZ, U.S. – 198
Gray, William – 137
Great Britain – 103, 173, 209, 211
Green, Joseph – 204
Greenland – 106
Greenwich Observatory – 216, 218
Greg, R.P. – 106
Gregory, Dr – 38
Grellois, M. – 114
Griesau, Silesia – 102
Gruithuisen, Franz von Paula – 85, 87, 90, 124, 126
Guiberteau, ship – 151
Guide to Crieff, Macara – 85
Gulf of Mexico – 109
Gulf Stream – 174
Gunnersbury, London, Eng land – 147
Guthman – 182

H

H.M.S. Coronation, ship – 136
hail, black – 134
Haleakla, Hawaii – 88
Hall, Prof. Asaph – 11
Halley, Edmund – 21
Hallucination and Illusions, Parish – 113
Halm, Dr – 71
Hambledon, nr Godalming, Surrey, England – 206
Hampden, John – 37
Handbook of Astronomy, Chambers – 54
Hansen – 9
Harding – 44
Hardwick, Gloucs., England – 101
Harlton, Cambs., England – 132
Harmer, Mr – 167
Harrison, Prof. Henry – 136
Harwich, Essex, England – 167
Hastings, Sussex, England – 84
Hauser, Kaspar – 154
Havarah Park, nr Ripley, Eng land – 84
Hawker, Harry – 216
Hawkins, Mr. H.L. – 206, 217
Haywood, Prof. John – 137
Heath, Mr – 71
Hegel, Georg Wilhelm Frie drich – 144-5
Heinsberg, Prussia – 102
Hempstead Plains, Long Is land, NY, U.S. – 216
Hennequin, General – 168
Herald, New York – 29, 164, 165, 214, 215
Hereford, Herefordshire, Eng land – 101, 133, 169-70, 172-3

Hereford Earthquake of 1896, The, Davison – 171
Herefordshire, England – 99, 101
Herschel, Sir John – 12, 71
Himes, Prof. – 110
Hind, John Russell – 14, 20-1, 94, 105
Hipparchus – 42
History of Astronomy, A, Clerke – 18, 42, 54
Hobbs, Prof. William Herbert – 38
Hodgson – 51, 90
Hoe, Immigration Inspector – 204
Holbrook, AZ, U.S. – 198
Holden, Dr – 36, 229
Holland – 210
Hollis, H.P. – 58, 220
Holmes, Edwin – 22, 50, 58
Hopkins, Mr. L.A. – 218, 231
Hornsea, Humberside, England – 210
Horrox, Jeremiah – 28-9
horse seen in sky – 152
Hough, Prof. George – 164-5
Houzeau, Jean Charles – 30
Huddersfield, Yorks, England – 218
Hudikswall, Sweden – 140
Hudson River – 217
Huggins, Sir William – 42-3, 46
Hull, Humberside, England – 210-1
Humane Review – 88
Humboldt, Friedrich Heinrich Alexander von – 59, 73
Hungary – 91
Hunstanton, Norfolk, England – 210
Huntington, WV, U.S. – 204
Huntsville, AL, U.S. – 205
Hussey – 160
Huygens, Christian – 53-4

I

Igló (Spisska Nova Ves), Slovakia – 145
Illinois, U.S. – 98, 164-5, 218
Illustration, L' – 191
India – 59, 117
  Northwestern Provinces – 101
Indiana, U.S. – 165, 218
Indianola, MS, U.S. – 152
Ingall, Herbert – 119-20
Ingleby, Dr. C. Mansfield – 103
Intellectual Observer – 68, 120
Intelligencer, St Louis – 99
Introduction to Meteorology, Thomson – 83
Introduction to the Study of

Meteorites, An, Fletcher – 85, 96, 103
Inverness, , Scotland – 85
Iowa, U.S. – 165
Ipswich, Suffolk, England – 85, 210
Irkutsk, Siberia – 85, 87-8, 96, 106, 135, 148
Iron Valley, AZ, U.S. – 197
Italy – 55, 173, 218

J

Jacquot, M. – 153
Jaennicke – 106
Jamaica Bay, NY, U.S. – 216
James, Capt. Mansell R. – 216-7
Japan – 227
Jehovah – 174-5
Jelica, Serbia – 141
Jewel, Albert – 216
Jour. B.A.A. – see: British Astronomical Association, Journal
Jour. R.M.S. – see: Royal Meteorological Society, Journal
Journal des Debats – 192
Juliers, Prussia – 102
Jupiter – 10, 17, 20, 31-2, 49, 50, 61-62, 64, 147-8, 150, 191-2, 220
    moons of – 49-52, 54-5, 60-1, 63, 78

K

Kaemetz, L.F. – 102
Kansas City, KS, U.S. – 163
Kater, Capt. – 86
Kayser – 30
Keeler, Prof. – 43-4, 47, 57
Kenway, Philip T. – 206
Kepler, Johannes – 28-9, 52-3, 60-2, 65-6
Kew Observatory – 206
Kilmarnock, Strathclyde, Scotland – 31-2
Klamath Marsh, OR, U.S. – 131
Klein, Dr – 136, 160
Klinkerfues, Prof. – 22, 46
Knobel, E.B. – 34
Knott – 122
Knowledge – 129, 131, 134, 137, 139, 150, 184
Knyahinya, Hungary – 146
Kropp, Lorenzo – 138
Kuttenburg, Bohemia – 145

L

La Blanche lighthouse, France – 193
La Concha – 30
La Serena, Chile – 232
La Tour, France – 83
Lake Erie, Canada/U.S. – 165
Lake Michigan, MI, U.S. – 231

Lake Orsa, Sweden – 139
Lancashire, England – 133
Lane, Mrs – 195
Langley, Samuel Pierpoint – 225
Lansberg – 29
Laplace, Pierre Simon – 55
Laredo, Spain – 156
Lassen Peak, CA, U.S. – 131
Laurel, DE, U.S. – 153
Lee, MA, U.S. – 216
Leeds Astronomical Society, Journal of – 184
Leo, const. – 42, 73-5
Leonids, meteors – 15, 17-8, 63, 75
Lescarbault, Dr. Edm. – 29-30
Letters on Natural Magic, Brewster – 113
Leverrier, Urbain Jean Joseph – 9, 11, 24, 29-30, 63
Lewes, Sussex, England – 206
Lewiston, MT, U.S. – 154
Lexell – 12
Lick Observatory – 36, 42
light
    aberration of – 41, 47, 72
    velocity of – 49-52, 54-5
lightning – 158, 183
    from clear sky – 183
lights
    in sky – 15, 28, 83-5, 91-4, 105, 107-9, 117, 128-30, 132-3, 137, 146-7, 149-51, 156-7, 160-3, 169-171, 173, 179, 181-2, 184-5, 190-3, 199, 201-3, 204-5, 208-12, 214-6, 218, 228
Lilienthal, Germany – 10
Lille, France – 180
Lilleshall, Shropshire, England – 134
Lindemann – 67
Lindsay, Capt. – 208, 210
Lindesberg, Sweden – 140
Lisbon, Portugal – 30, 221
List of Remarkable Earthquakes in Great Britain and Ireland During the Christian Era, A, Roper – 98, 131, 135
Literary Digest – 219
Littrow – 20
Liverpool, Merseyside, England – 114, 133-4, 150-1, 208, 211
Liverpool Astronomical Society, Journal of – 150
Liverpool Aviation School – 208
Livet, nr Clavaux, France – 230
Llanelly, Gwent, Wales – 179
Llangollen, Clwyd, Wales – 178
Llanthomas, Powys, Wales – 170
Lockyer, Sir Norman – 91, 184

Lofft, Capel – 85
London, England – 5, 90, 101, 106, 133, 142, 157, 162- 3, 167, 190, 206, 210, 221
London Triangle – 133, 142, 169-71, 228
Long Island Sound, NY, U.S. – 217
Loomis – 106
Lost in the Arctic, Mikkelsen – 213
Loughborough, Leics, England – 160
Louisville, KY, U.S. – 61
Louvain, Belgium – 167
Lowe, E.J. – 16
Lowell, Percival – 46-7, 189
Ludvika, Sweden – 139
Luzarches, France – 181
Lyell, Charles – 177
Lynn, MA, U.S. – 204
Lyons, NY, U.S. – 146-7
Lyra, star – 74-5

M

Macara – 85
MacBeth, J.C.H. – 221
Maclean – 51
MacPherson – 14, 58
Madagascar – 106
Mädler, Prof. – 20, 126, 128
Madras, India – 22
Madrid, Spain – 171
Magazine of Science – 19, 20
Magdeburg, Germany – 83
Main – 51
Malmesbury, Wilts., England – 157
Manchester, Lancs., England – 106, 133, 160, 213
Manila Observatory – 205
Mansfield, OH, U.S. – 154
Manual of Astronomy, Young – 40
Marchand, M. – 59
Marconi, Guglielmo – 221
Marienwerder, Germany – 86
Markwick, Col. – 150, 178, 180, 215-16, 220
Marlboro, NJ, U.S. – 204-5
Mars – 10, 31-2, 52-3, 55-6, 61-2, 88, 90-1, 122, 128, 180, 200, 220-1
    atmosphere of – 42-3
    lights on – 120, 160, 189
    lines on – 128
    luminous object from – 91
    messages from – 189, 221
    moons of – 128
    opposition of – 55, 84, 90-1, 128-9, 133, 136-7, 160, 172, 190, 199-201, 215
    viaducts on – 125

Marseilles, France – 4, 94, 123, 140-1, 153, 190
Marshall, TX, U.S. – 164
Martindale, Mr L.E. – 189
Maryland, U.S. – 152
Mascari, Prof. A. – 44
Massachusetts, U.S. – 202
Mattoon, IL, U.S. – 110
Mauna Loa, Hawaii – 59
Maunder, Mr – 216
Maxton, Rev. M. – 97
Mayans – 174
Mc.Bain, Capt. – 156
McCormick Observatory – 220
Mediterranean – 221
Mee, Arthur – 190, 215
Melida, island in Adriatic – 86-8, 100, 173
Mercury – 30, 61-2, 78, 106, 128-9
    superior conjunction of – 129
Merekŭla, Estonia – 140
Met. Mag. – see: Meteorological Magazine
Meteorological Bureau (France) – 192
Meteorological Magazine – 104, 128, 133, 142, 143, 170, 171, 184, 199
Meteors & meteorites – 15-18, 22, 28, 37, 73-4, 84-5, 89, 91, 99, 101, 109, 132-3, 142-3, 146-7, 162, 169, 171-2, 193-4, 196-201, 204, 207, 211-2, 214, 216, 228-9, 232
Meunier, Stanislas – 141-2
Mhow, India – 101
Michael, M. – 178
Michigan, U.S. – 218
Middelkirke, Belgium – 166, 168
Mikkelsen, Enjar – 213, 217
Milford Haven, Dyfed, Wales – 100-1
Millerton, NY, U.S. – 217
Milne, David – 85, 97, 99
Minchin, Prof. George M. – 162
Miracles and Modern Spiritualism, Wallace – 230
mirage – 84, 110, 113-4, 139, 152-4, 185-7, 188
    of Bristol – 185, 187
    of cities & towns – 83, 139-40
    untraceable – 139, 140
missiles, mystery – 155, 157-8, 214, 217
Missionary Ridge, TN, U.S. – 205
Missouri, U.S. – 165
Mitchel Field, Long Island, NY, U.S. – 216

Mohan, India – 115
Mojave Desert, CA, U.S. – 183
Molesworth – 50
Monfreith, Tayside, Scotland – 157
Montana, U.S. – 154
Montevideo, Uruguay – 30
Monthly Magazine – 85
Monthly Notices – see: Royal Astronomical Society
Monthly Weather Review – 117, 139, 152, 172, 181, 183, 98, 229
Montreal, Quebec, Canada – 186
Montrose, Strathmore, Scotland – 156-7
Moon – 4-5, 12, 16, 28, 36, 39, 57-58, 73, 86-7, 89-90, 92, 115, 119, 120-4
    atmosphere of – 42, 124
    bodies crossing – 110, 115
    changing features on – 120, 122-3
    city on – 124-5
    distance of – 57, 59, 78, 88-9, 91-2, 110, 137, 145
    eclipse of – 137, 189, 201, 216
    lights on – 5, 28, 86-90, 119-20, 123, 125-7, 129, 136-8, 160-1, 189, 201, 214-6, 218-9, 227
    object near – 150, 181
    objects on – 136, 161, 215-6, 218, 231
    volcanoes of – 88-9
Moon, features on – 125
    Alps, lunar – 120, 160
    Archimedes – 231
    Aristarchus – 5, 28, 86-7, 90, 120, 123, 137, 160-1, 190, 227
    Aristillus – 215
    Bessel – 136
    Birt – 124
    Carlini – 120
    Cassini – 138
    Copernicus – 5, 161
    Eratosthenes – 124
    Eudoxus – 136-7
    Funerius – 219
    Gassendi – 125, 161
    Group I – 126
    Hercules – 138
    Hyginus – 136
    Hyginus N – 136-7
    Kepler – 137, 160
    Lexell – 216
    Linné – 5, 120, 122-3, 136
    Littrow – 125, 214, 218
    Mare Crisium – 89-90, 119, 215
    Mare Serenitatis – 120

Marius – 137
Messier – 90
Picard – 119-20, 136-7, 201, 215
Plato – 5, 125-7, 160, 215
Plinius – 125, 161
Proclus – 136
Schroeter – 124
Sulpicius Gallus – 123
Mooradabad, India – 101
Mora, M. – 26
Morales – 137
Morehouse, Smith – 158, 161
Morning Post, London – 132, 156, 157, 163
Morristown, NY, U.S. – 214
Moscow, Russia – 67
Moses – 48, 141
motion
    proper – 69, 77
    vorticose – 64
Moulton, Prof. – 74
Mound Builders – 124
Mt. Ararat, Turkey – 36, 38
Mt. Everest, Nepal – 59
Mt. Fairweather, Alaska – 187-8
Mt. Hamilton, U.S. – 220
Mt. Riga, NY, U.S. – 217
Mt. San Gorgonio, CA, U.S. – 183
Mt. St. Elias, Alaska – 59, 186
Mt. Whitney, CA, U.S. – 183
Much Wenlock, Shropshire, England – 134
Muir Glacier, Alaska – 187
Müller – 163
mummy, huge – 177
Murray
    Dr. J.A.H. – 162
    Sir William – 98
Museum of Frankfort – 177
My Life: A Record of Events and Opinions, Wallace – 37
Myths and Marvels of Astronomy, Proctor – 37, 90

N

Naas, Kildare, Ireland – 201
Naples, Italy – 108
Narrows, The, NJ, U.S. – 216
National Academy of Sciences, Memoirs of – 229
National Geographic Magazine – 179
National Geographic Society – 179
National Museum, U.S. – 197
Nature – 4, 18, 44, 45, 46, 71, 87, 100, 106, 110, 130, 131, 132, 134, 136, 137, 139, 140, 147, 160, 161, 166, 167, 170, 171, 200, 201, 206, 214, 228,

229

Nature, La – 132, 141, 149, 155, 181, 188, 201

Nautical Almanac and Astronomical Ephemeris – 30, 50

Neath, Glamorgan, Wales – 208

nebulae – 46, 71, 77
    Andromeda – 71
    that changed position – 71
    that disappeared – 71
    variable – 69

Neison – 58, 136

Neptune – 8-9, 12-3, 15, 58, 63

Nerft, Courland (Russia) – 103

New Canton, VA, U.S. – 220

New England, U.S. – 5, 202-3, 205

New York, NY, U.S. – 5, 58, 106, 109, 152, 203, 211, 221-2

New York State, U.S. – 211

New Zealand – 100

Newark, NJ, U.S. – 217

Newcastle, Tyne & Wear, England – 133

Newcomb, Prof. – 24-5, 29, 34, 55, 57, 59-61, 64, 71, 88, 92, 105, 117, 145

Newfoundland, Canada – 225

Newport, Gwent, Wales – 208

News and Courier, Charleston – 158

Newsome, Mr John J. – 180

Newton
    Prof. – 15-7, 24
    Sir Isaac – 60, 62, 64-6, 92

Nexo, island of Bornholm, Denmark – 139

Niagara Falls, U.S. – 116

Niesten – 129

Night-Side of Nature, The, Crowe – 115

Noah's Ark – 36, 38, 49

Noble, Capt. – 31-2, 50, 58, 128, 150, 190

North Pole – 29, 186

North Sea – 167, 210

Northampton, Northants, England – 109

Northfield, Warks., England – 185

Northwestern University – 164, 231

Norway – 102

Norwood, NY, U.S. – 129

Notes and Queries – 113, 115

Nouri, Archdeacon – 36

Nova Aurigae, star – 45-6

Nova Persei, star – 71

Nymegen, Holland – 163

O

Observations on the Earthquake of Dec. 17, 1896, Yeats – 134

Observations upon the Prophecies of Daniel, and the Apocalypse of St. John, Newton – 64

Observatory – 33, 36, 50, 58, 60, 68, 69, 70, 73, 83, 88, 105, 106, 110, 124, 136, 147, 150, 180, 182, 201, 213

Observatory of Florence – 215
    of Lisbon – 161
    of Meudon – 136
    of Paris – 192, 215

Observer, Reading – 195, 218

Oeuvres Complètes de François Arago – 85

Ogdensburg, NY, U.S. – 214

Ohio, U.S. – 150

Ohrt – 106

Olbers, Dr. – 85-6

Old and New Astronomy, Proctor – 12, 25, 28, 37, 48, 51, 53, 55, 106

Oldham, Mr. H. Yule – 38

Olmsted, Prof. – 15

Omaha, U.S. – 164

Ophiuchus, const. – 70

Orange Co., NY, U.S. – 158

Oregon, U.S. – 131

Orion, const. – 70, 160, 164

Orkney Islands, Scotland – 210

Oroville, CA, U.S. – 229

Orsay, France – 228

Ostend, Belgium – 166, 168-9

Ottumwa, IA, U.S. – 110

Overloop, M. – 168-9

Owen, William – 158

Oxelosund, Sweden – 140

Oxford, Oxon., England – 94, 162

P

Packer, David – 131, 170, 185

Paderborn, Westphalia, Germany – 115

Papplewick, Notts., England – 210

parallax – 41-2, 47, 55, 58, 73-4, 147

Paris, France – 133, 190, 205, 230

Parish – 113

Parkersburg, WV, U.S. – 152

Parkhurst, Prof. – 22

Paroisse, Prof. – 157

Pastorff – 85, 87, 105

Patagonia – 102

Payan, M. – 140

Paysandu, Uruguay – 138

Peach Springs, AZ, U.S. – 197

Pearson – 51

Peck
    Marshal J. A. – 228

Miss Annie – 59

Peking (Beijing), China – 186

Pelseneer, Prof. – 168

Pennsylvania, U.S. – 117

Perseus, const. – 71

Perth, Perthshire, Scotland – 96

Perthshire, Scotland – 28

Petersfield, Susex, England – 195

Petmore, Mrs. Margaret – 169-70

phantom city – 185, 188

phantom soldiers – 4, 84, 110, 113-5, 152-3

Phil. Trans. – see: Royal Society

Philosophical Magazine – 10

Philosophical Society of Washington, Bulletin of – 14, 106

"Phinuit, Dr" – 46

Phipson, Dr – 103-4

Photography – 189

Piazzi, Giuseppe – 10

Pickering, Prof. – 189

Piedmont, Italy – 84

pig, flying – 178-9

Pignerol, Piedmont, Italy – 83

Pike's Peak, CO, U.S. – 38

Pillitsfer, Livonia (Russia) – 103

Piper, Mrs – 45-47

Pittsfield, MA, U.S. – 202

Plaindealer, East Kent, Ontario – 155

planets
    distance of – 52, 77, 147-8
    intra-Mercurial – 8, 30

Plant, Thomas – 104

Plymouth Rock – 3-4, 28, 43

Pogson – 22

Ponton, Mungo – 98

Poor, Prof. – 56

Popular Astronomy (magazine) – 11, 48, 110, 163, 189

Popular Astronomy, Newcomb – 57, 60, 64, 92, 105

Popular History of Astronomy, Clerke – 124

Popular Science Monthly – 155

Popular Science News – 38

Popular Science Review – 22

Portland, Dorset, England – 210

Portland, OR, U.S. – 218

Portsmouth, Hants, England – 194-5, 206, 210-1

Posen, Germany – 86

Poughkeepsie, NY, U.S. – 217

Powell, Walter – 156-7, 180

Prague, Czech Republic – 150

Pratt – 126

Prescott, AZ, U.S. – 181, 198

Prince, C.L. – 108

Principia, Newton – 65

Proctor, Richard – 12, 16, 25-6,

241

28-9, 37, 48, 51-3, 55, 62, 90, 106, 128, 176-7

Procyon, star – 24-5
  companion of – 67

Prussia – 102

Ptolemy, Claudius – 39, 78

Puerto Rico – 150-1

Putzeys, M. – 168

Q

Quigley's Point, Lough Foyle, Ireland – 114

R

Radcliffe Observatory – 94

radiant, meteor – 73-4

Raeymaekers, Dr – 166

rain
  black – 134
  discoloured – 98
  hot – 85
  red – 4

Ramsgate, Kent, England – 162, 166

Rankin, Rev. T. – 90

Ratibor, Upper Silesia, Poland – 91

Reading, Berks, England – 101, 133, 142-3, 184, 194-5, 206-7, 217-8

Reading University – 206

Recent Advances in Astronomy, Fison – 70

Record, Chico – 229

Recreative Science – 20, 21, 105

"Rector" – 46

Reminiscences of an Astronomer, Newcomb – 24, 34, 55

Resolute, ship – 132

Réveillère, Lieut. – 151

Rey, M. – 190

Rheims, France – 203

Rickenbacker, Capt. – 220

Rigel, star – 4, 160

"Rigel" – 205

Ritter – 106

Roberts, Lord, of Kandahar – 115

Robson, J.B. – 180

Rochester, NY, U.S. – 130, 150

Roemer, Ole – 49, 52-4, 61

Rome, Italy – 203

Roper, William – 98, 131

Rosenau, Hungary (Roznava, Slovakia) – 145-6

Rossbrien, Limerick, Ireland – 205

Rowley, Warks., England – 103-4

Rowley ragstone – 103-4

Royal Asiatic Society of Bengal, Proceedings of – 100, 131

Royal Astronomical Society –

22, 31-4, 55, 73, 127
  Memoirs of – 33, 46, 69, 86
  Monthly Notices – 16, 19, 20, 27, 33, 34, 42, 45, 46, 50, 67, 69, 71, 73, 90, 105, 106, 124, 163

Royal Astronomical Society of Canada, Journal of – 211, 212

Royal Geographical Society – 38

Royal Institute of Great Britain, Quarterly Journal of – 85, 86

Royal Meteorological Society, Quarterly Journal of – 134, 188, 199

Royal Society of London – 46
  Philosophical Transactions of – 12, 86

Rugenwalde, Pomerania, Poland – 139

Russell – 106

Russia – 55

Rynik, Upper Silesia, Poland – 91

S

Sadler, Herbert – 32-5

Sage, Dr – 91

Sagittarius, const. – 70

Saigon, Vietnam – 151

Saintes, France – 133

Saladin – 156

Salem, MA, U.S. – 204

San Francisco, CA, U.S. – 36, 164, 179-80, 188
  Bay – 36

San Salvador – 3-4, 28, 43, 106, 150, 174, 221

Sandusky, OH, U.S. – 154

Sandwich Islands (Hawaii) – 117

Santa Rita Mountains, AZ, U.S. – 197

Saratoga, NY, U.S. – 58

Sart, Belgium – 178

Saskatchewan, Canada – 211-2

Saturn – 13, 17, 20, 30-2, 61-2, 138, 149
  black spots of – 44
  luminous object moving near – 149
  rings of – 43-4
  White Spot of – 44

Sawin, Mr. Addison A. – 112

Scarborough, Yorks., England – 162

Schafarik, Prof. – 150

Schaffhausen, nr Beringen, Germany – 155

Schmidt, J.F. Julius – 44, 105-6, 120-2, 136

Scholes, J.W. – 218

Schroeter, Johann Heironymous – 44, 126

Schurr, Henry S. – 166

Schwabe – 44, 105

Schwann, M. – 102

Sci. Amer. – see: Scientific American

Sci. Amer. Supp. – see: Scientific American Supplement

Science – 216, 232

Science Monthly – 130

Science Pour Tous, La – 103

Scientific American – 4, 14, 38, 59, 106, 129, 146, 150, 152, 155, 157, 161, 189, 215, 221
  Supplement – 46, 87, 90, 124, 182

Scientific Australian – 231

Scole, Norfolk, England – 128

Scotland – 113-4, 133, 156

Scott – 105
  Mr. G.B. – 100
  Mr. G.O. – 181

Scriven, Sparkman R. – 111

sea serpent – 176-7

Seattle, WA, U.S. – 186

Secchi, Angelo – 44, 51, 91, 105

See, Prof. – 89

Seismological Society of America, Bulletin – 99, 131, 198, 200, 220, 231

Serbia – 3, 141-2, 146

Serpens, const. – 147

Serviss, Prof. – 17, 58

Shaw, George Bernard – 88, 145

sheep panics – 132, 142-3, 184

Shelbyville, KY, U.S. – 110

Shepard, Prof. – 98, 111

Shipley, Mr. Maynard – 228

ships
  from other worlds – 4
  in sky – 5

Shropshire, England – 134

Siam, Gulf of – 136

Siberia – 108, 175-6

Sidebotham, Joseph – 105

Sidereal Messenger – 10, 71, 136, 137

signals, mystery – 221

Silesia, Poland – 86

Siminton – 51

Sirius, star – 26-27, 41-42, 68
  companion of – 26, 68

Sistersville, WV, U.S. – 165

sky
  appearances in the – 112-4, 117, 152-4
  as shell – 72-3, 76-7
  bodies seen in – 85, 153, 180-2, 202, 212-3
  explosions in – 142, 194, 200
  local – 84, 93-4, 96, 99, 102,

148, 150, 170-1, 182, 185-6, 190-1, 194, 199, 207, 221, 228, 231
objects sucked into – 155, 157
Slipher, Dr – 42
Smith, Mr. W.D. – 131
Smithsonian Miscellaneous Collections – 14, 106, 131
Smyth, William Henry – 32-4, 51
snow, black – 134
Société Astronomique de France, Bulletin – 26, 38, 114, 161, 182, 189, 191, 192, 211, 215, 216, 228
Society for Psychical Research, Proceedings of – 99
Soko-Banja, Serbia – 141
solar system – 56
motion of – 41-2
Solid South, Warrenton (Va) – 152
Somerset, England – 195
sound, velocity of – 51
sounds
"Moodus" – 83
aerial – 5, 28, 83-4, 86-7, 96-101, 112, 131-2, 143, 166- 70, 172-3, 194-5, 198, 206-7, 228
South Africa – 150
South Kensington Museum, London – 85
South Lopham, Norfolk, England – 132
Southampton, Hants., England – 167
spectroscopy – 41-3, 45-48
Spencer, Herbert – 39
spheres, music of the – 61
Spörer – 105
St. Alban's Head, England – 210
St. Cyr, France – 205
St. David, AZ, U.S. – 198
St. Lawrence river – 214
St. Louis, MO, U.S. – 98-9, 106
St. Mary's, OH, U.S. – 189
St. Paul Junction, IA, U.S. – 110
St. Petersburg, Russia – 140
St. Thomas, Virgin Islands – 231
Standard
London – 100, 132, 143, 156, 157, 206, 207, 208
Reading – 194
stars – 41-2, 45-6
1830 Groombridge – 77
changed position of – 69-72
changelessness of – 67, 76
comet-like projection from – 71
companion – 24, 26-7, 67-9,

77
dimmed by cloud – 71
disappeared – 69-71
distance of – 53, 67, 72, 74-6
double – 32-3
fixed in position – 72
motion of – 71
new – 70-1
variable – 24-7
Staten Island, NY, U.S. – 216
Steavenson, W.H. – 213
Steep Island, Chusan Archipelago (Zhoushan Qundao, China) – 214
Sterling, Conn – 220
Stern, J. David – 230
Stockholm, Sweden – 179
Stokesay Vicarage, Shropshire, England – 170
Stoney, Dr. Johnstone – 18
Stonyhurst Magazine – 134
Stonyhurst Observatory – 46, 134
Story of the Comets, Chambers – 19
Story of the Heavens, The, Ball – 8, 10, 25, 43
Struve, Prof. Otto Wilhelm – 24-5, 67, 145
Student and Intellectual Observer, The – 16, 122, 123
Studies in Astronomy, Gore – 25
Studley, Prof. C.K. – 228
Stuyvert, M. – 129
Sullivan, Mrs. Wm. – 180
Sun – 9, 12-3, 20, 23, 29, 39, 41, 47, 53, 57, 65, 73, 78, 90, 105 bodies crossing – 83, 85-6, 105-8, 110, 153, 175, 213, 216, 219
body near – 129, 140, 220
distance of – 141
eclipse of – 8, 110, 140-141, 183-4, 189
Sun, New York – 153, 163, 202, 203, 204
Sun, The, Young – 50
Sunninghill, Berks, England – 206
sunspots – 147, 183, 216
Survey of the Lakes of Cumberland, Westmorland, and Lancashire, Clarke – 113
Sussex, England – 151
Sussex Co., NJ, U.S. – 158
Swaffham, Norfolk, England – 132
Swansea, Glamorgan, Wales – 100
Sweden – 4, 139, 179
Swift
Jonathan – 128

Prof. Lewis – 8, 10-1, 110, 117, 150, 182
Switzerland – 184, 200
Symons, George James – 143, 169
System of the Stars, Clerke – 24, 70, 71

T

Taber
Isaiah West – 187
Prof. Stephen – 220
Talbot, DE, U.S. – 153
Taurus, const. – 10
Telescopic Work for Starlight Evenings, Denning – 30, 50, 120
Tempel – 120, 123
Temple, Capt. – 156
Temps, Le – 192, 193
Tenby, Dyfed, Wales – 101
Tennyson, L. – 131
Tesla, Nikola – 189
Tetbury, Gloucs., England – 147
Texas, U.S. – 164
Thames Valley, England – 143
Theta Centauri, star – 22
Thomas, Bernard – 215
Thomson, David Purdie – 83
Thoreau, Henry David – 115
Thornton, Mr. C.W. – 186
Thury, Prof. – 161
Tice, John H. – 106
Tillinghast, Wallace – 203
Tillington, nr Petworth, Sussex, England – 93
Times
London – 85, 99, 100, 101, 107, 114, 131, 132, 133, 134, 155, 156, 157, 162, 184, 194, 195, 208, 210, 211, 217, 218, 219, 230
Los Angeles – 218
New York – 99, 152, 158, 187, 214, 216, 218, 228, 229
Oxford – 162
Todd, Prof. – 14, 50
Toll, Baron Eduard Vaseliëvich von – 175
Tombstone, AZ, U.S. – 198
Tomlinson – 156
Tonto, AZ, U.S. – 181
Toronto, Ontario, Canada – 186, 211-2
Tottenham, London, England – 84
Totterdown, Glamorgan, Wales – 209
Tours, France – 133
trachodon – 177-8
Traité de Mécanique Céleste, Laplace – 55

Transcript, Boston – 230
Travels in Space, Valentine & Tomlinson – 156
Tremont, France – 147-8
Trewman, Lieut. Col. – 207
triangulation – 55-7, 59-61
Tribune, New York – 186, 203, 204, 205, 214, 221, 231, 232
Trouvelot, Etienne – 136-7, 153
True and Perfect Relation of the Terrible Earthquake, A – 169
Tucson, AZ, U.S. – 197
Tunis, Tunisia – 193
Tupman, Capt. – 22, 147
Turner – 50
Tyler, Capt. W.F., R.N. – 214

U

Uckfield – 108
UFO-like phenomena – 93, 153 (see also: airships, lights)
Ujest, Silesia – 113
United States – 9, 16, 118, 122, 144, 160, 179, 203, 214, 227, 231
  Atlantic coast – 15
United States Commission – 55
University of Liége – 102
Uranus – 9, 13, 58
  discovery of – 12
Urrugne, France – 108

V

Val-de-la-Haye, France – 179
Valentine – 156
Valla, Sweden – 140
Valparaiso, Chile – 232
Van den Broeck, M. – 166-9
Veeder, Dr. M.A. – 146-7
Vega, star – 41-2
Venezuela – 117
Venus – 28-9, 42, 53, 62, 78, 87, 92-3, 95, 109-10, 129-30, 149, 151, 162, 164, 180-1, 190-3, 201, 203, 205, 209, 211, 214-5, 220
  atmosphere of – 42
  bodies near – 87, 92, 109, 205
  distance of – 92
  inferior conjunction – 93-5, 163, 191, 202-3, 211, 214-5
  lights on – 129-30, 161
  lights seen near – 163
  phenomena on – 94
  rotation of – 58, 149
  transit of – 28-9, 54-5

Verneuil, France – 228
Victoria, B.C., Canada – 188
Vidorec, nr Warasdin, Hungary – 153
Vienne dans le Dauphiné, France – 114
Virginia, U.S. – 152
Viziadrug, India – 184
Vogel, Prof. – 25-6, 45, 145
volcanoes – 88, 131, 231
Voltaire (François-Marie Arouet) – 62
Von Cosel, General – 113
Von Zach, Baron – 9
Vroncysylite, Clwyd, Wales – 178

W

Wagner, Anton – 220
Wake, Dr. R.H. – 143
Waldemath – 182
Wales – 170, 191, 193, 208-11
Walker, Rev. M. – 96
Wallace, Dr. Alfred Russell – 37, 230
Walsh, Mr. – 37
Warasdin, Hungary – 153
Ward, Rev. M. – 86
Ware, MA, U.S. – 202
Wartmann, Dr – 102, 105
Warwick, Ontario, Canada – 112
Warwickshire, England – 210
Washburn Observatory – 124
Washington Observatory – 105
Watson, Prof. – 8, 10-1
Weaver, nr Wickenburg, AZ, U.S. – 197
Webb
  Rev. T. – 21, 85, 87, 92, 94, 101, 105, 183
  W.L. – 89
Weekly Express, Chudleigh – 132
Weekly Times and Echo – 186
West, W.J. – 218
West Cumberland, England – 137
West Indies – 230-1
West Mersea, nr Colchester, Essex, England – 133-4
Weston-super-Mare, Avon, England – 132
Where Are You Going, Sunday?, Chambers – 33

White – 50
White River Junction, VT, U.S. – 202
Whitechurch, Bucks., England – 195
Whitmell, Mr – 128
Wilkes – 59
Wilkes-Barre, PA, U.S. – 158
Williams
  A. Stanley – 32-3, 128, 137
  Rev. W.O. – 120
Willimantic, CT, U.S. – 204
Willoughby – 186-7
Willoughby Island, Alaska – 186
Wilmington, DE, U.S. – 152
Wilson – 106
Winlock, Prof. – 110
wireless messages, mystery – 216
Wisconsin, U.S. – 165
With – 94
Wolverhampton, Warks., England – 92, 103, 173-4
Wonderful Phenomena, Curtis – 112
Wonders of Alaska, Badlam – 186
Wood
  James G. – 170
  Mr. W.H. – 109
Worcester, Worcs., England – 101, 133, 169-73, 199
Worcester, MA, U.S. – 203, 204
Worcestershire, England – 134
Wray – 51, 105
Wright Brothers – 225
Wrottesley, Lord – 92-3, 215

Y

Yarnell, AZ, U.S. – 198
Year-Book of Facts in Science and Art, Timbs – 84, 98, 102
Yeats, George P. – 134
Yeovil, Dorset, England – 150
Yorkshire, England – 210-1
Youghal, Co. Cork, Ireland – 83, 108
Young, Prof. – 22, 40, 42-3, 48, 50, 54
Yukon, Canada – 186
Yunnan province, China – 219

Z

Zentmayer, Prof. – 110
Zeta Cassiopeia, star – 71
Zurich, Switzerland – 147-8

244